OKANAGAN COLLEGE
LIBRARY
BRITISH COLUMBIA

OKANAGAN COLLEGE LIBRARY

03473469

P9-ECU-378

LOVE, EMPOWERMENT AND SOCIAL JUSTICE

*Personal Relationships
and Citizen Action*

by Tim Root
with a preface by
Oliver James

OPEN GATE PRESS
LONDON

First published in 2005 by
Open Gate Press, 51 Achilles Road, London NW6 1DZ

Copyright © Tim Root 2005
Preface copyright © Oliver James 2005
All rights, by all media, reserved.

A catalogue reference for this book
is available from the British Library

ISBN 1 871871 62 X

Printed and bound in Great Britain
by Bookforce, Grantham, Lincs.

Contents

Preface

by Oliver James

If only those who rule us were more likely to have read this book than, say, *The Selfish Gene.* Instead of encouraging us to live unfulfilling, empty and destructive lives, it might mean that they start trying to buil society which nurtures a far saner, better balanced existence. Unfortunately, not only is such choice of reading material implausible, there is a high probability that our rulers are largely oblivious of the crucial scientific evidence on which this book is founded. The odds are that most of our leaders would anyway be allergic as people to the importance for democracy of authentic and secure relationships revealed here. The sort of people who are motivated to work long hours, seven days a week – in the case of politicians, actually having the gall to proselytise about the importance of family – are the least likely to put their own intimate relations ahead of the pursuit of glittering prizes.

This book demonstrates the folly of such pursuit, personally and politically. It shows that we are living half-lives in the service of the profits of a few, that the resultant inequalities are causing huge harm to us and to our environment, and that, through strengthening community and family cohesion, grassroots activism could be our salvation. In linking the social and economic with the psychological, the author has achieved an interdisciplinary scholarship which breaks free of the usual chains of academic compartmentalisation.

Here is a sane voice speaking to an insane world. Heed its warnings and act on its injunctions.

Introduction
Fulfilled Citizens, Healthy Society

Margaret Thatcher famously said: 'There is no such thing as society; only individuals and families'. She emphasised individuals' efforts to find fulfilment and provide for their family. Yet she did not realise that the values she promoted, of individual competition, undermine our quest for happiness in all spheres of life. Most of us are on a treadmill, trying to juggle ever more demanding work with commitment to family and friends. As the economy grows, our financial aspirations rise, keeping contentment out of reach. Globalisation threatens to undermine the security of us all, making both well-paid and unskilled workers compete to maintain their incomes. Thatcher wanted us to regard this process as natural; she was trying to undermine our responsibility for our common welfare, including that of our more vulnerable citizens.

In this book I describe how we can find happiness and contentment both in our personal lives, and by building a more friendly society, enabling us to feel valued and secure. Citizen action is vital to achieve this. We are all vulnerable to various risks, including crime, poor health care, pollution, and economic recession. Very few of us can buy immunity from these risks. However governments could do a great deal to avoid or reduce these problems. But politicians do too little to tackle them unless citizens campaign to insist that they do. If campaigns grow strong enough to influence public opinion, they can persuade governments to bring in important reforms. In addition, volunteers in community service help build social cohesiveness and prevent alienation.

In order to gain the motivation to work constructively, activists need confidence in the potential of human co-operation. I will explain how they are most likely to have gained this from understanding parents in childhood, or from emotionally supportive relations or close friends. Research shows that those who receive emotional support are much more likely than others to volunteer or campaign, as described in Chapter Six. Therefore political policies to promote both sensitive parenting and family stability are essential to create the activists needed to promote the health of society. Failure to introduce such policies will worsen crime, weaken communities, and increase stress-related illness. Thus the book will show the importance of the dictum 'the personal is political'.

The Introduction outlines the increasing social division and conflict we face, and gives examples of how certain people have improved their communities by establishing co-operative groups.

Chapter One focuses on the stress we suffer in seeking career success, material wealth, and personal fulfilment, and describes how many of those who are particularly frustrated in these areas turn to crime. Reducing inequality will make status less important, enabling more of us to prioritise quality of life over increasing income.

Chapter Two describes solutions to the serious environmental problems our consumer society has caused. Unless citizens and governments take these measures, the Earth we hold in trust for our children and grandchildren will be gravely damaged, with ever more frequent floods, droughts, and other weather disasters.

Chapter Three shows how parents who feel good about their role respond warmly to their children's needs and thus promote their happiness and maturity. This gives the children the emotional security and self-confidence to make a valuable contribution to society.

Chapter Four describes how many adults have problems in intimate relationships because they lack emotional security.

Learning to trust that they are loveable can give a person the confidence to make a committed relationship.

Chapter Five stresses the importance of crime prevention in arresting social decline. Helping troubled families is the most cost-effective long-term strategy, but tough measures to protect the public are also vital.

Chapter Six explains how ordinary people can gain greater influence over the political process. Once they begin to do so, their recognition of the benefits of co-operation will enhance their ability to build a more peaceful and united society.

The book is the product of a huge volume of research, and reflection on my work with hundreds of troubled families, and on several campaigns in which I have taken part. It builds on an understanding of the roots of individualism in our economic and social system. Since industrialization it has gradually become usual for individuals to become independent of their extended family through finding employment. Many people now move to live in a different area from their relations. As a result people no longer gain the sense of belonging and security many used to experience through their extended family.[1]

This process has affected patterns of childrearing. Because of the competitiveness caused by the endemic insecurity of our economic system, parents encourage their children, once past infancy, to focus chiefly on their own individual learning and success.[2] For most people self-esteem becomes dependent on attaining a desirable lifestyle. The consequent struggle to climb up the career ladder conflicts with the time and patience which are so critical for intimate relationships. Therefore most people experience love either very little, or only in the context of one or two relationships. These are generally seen as being of an entirely different nature to the relationships which are typical of our society, namely those characterised either by indifference, jealousy, or competition.

The demands of everyday life prevent most people from focusing on the needs of those outside their own household. The result is a loss of faith in the feasibility of social co-operation. It leads to a shortage of people prepared to devote time to improving their communities or helping people in need. In the main only a few exceptionally co-operative individuals, and various egotists, are willing to take part in unpaid community service or politics. Unless we reverse this trend, democracy will decline, the environment, and the casualties of economic insecurity, will be neglected, and social disorder will steadily escalate.

Emotional security – the need to feel valued

What was your happiest moment? A young man told me his had been his barmitzvah, when with his family around him he became a full member of the Jewish community. A young woman treasured the memory of her fiance's proposal of marriage. Another said her most wonderful moment was during her graduation ceremony, when her mother beamed at her with pride. At these moments they each felt loved and secure. The key to sustaining this happiness is the confidence that you are valued for your true self, with your unique blend of strengths and weaknesses.

The other most precious times in our lives usually spring from harmony with others, or through absorption in wonder or excitement, in which we are briefly freed from our usual worries. Some such events may appear unexceptional; a mother has a fond memory of her two children running towards her to hug her. A man remembers sitting on his father's lap while his father told a story in which the boy played the main role. But all these occasions express the most valuable aspects of our life and our personality. Those of us who have known moments of great joy or peace, even if we rarely think of them, possess a hope and vision which can raise our spirits when life seems bleak or cruel. These memories, whether of rare or seemingly routine events, can give us a special ability to appreciate life, and hence to enjoy contentment more often. If we know we can see, hear, and touch beauty, and be at one with our world, this peace and joy will come back to us again and again.

But our efforts to find such fulfilment are increasingly thwarted by the competitive nature of society, which satisfies none but a handful at the top, while causing exhaustion, bitterness and crime. Even many of those with secure and relatively well-paid jobs harbour resentment if their pay rise does not match those of 'fat cats' or politicians. I show how these problems stem from the very heart of consumer society, which elevates money at the expense of human relations. Most of us are not confident that we are valued regardless of our achievements. Therefore we work hard to gain the lifestyle and status which seems to show we are valued by society. Hence we downplay our deepest need, to be loved for our individual self.

Work, stress, and more work

Sadly most of us rarely consider the possibility of happiness like that described on page two. Instead we are submerged in routine tasks in order to pay our bills and maintain our lifestyle. Apart from the rich, over the last twenty years most of us have had to work longer hours, while our pay has risen only slightly. In fact for a high proportion of Americans pay has fallen slightly. Two out of five Americans, and similar proportions in other nations, worry that they might be laid off or have their pay cut.[3] Employees are so anxious to please their boss that many scarcely even stop for lunch. One worker in two comes home 'totally exhausted'. Bullying by managers has become common. Absence from work due to stress-related illness costs billions of dollars in sick pay and lost production. Family life suffers, with parents spending less and less time with their children. And at the same time as many full-timers are being worked into the ground, a great many people can find only low-paid, part-time, temporary, or casual work.

All social groups are now prone to redundancy, with thousands of middle managers casualties of 'downsizing'. Enron, WorldCom, and the stock market slide have shown brutally that years of work, pension contributions and savings can vanish overnight. These changes, and the increasingly frequent export of jobs to low-wage countries, have led to many more employees feeling insecure in their jobs. Moreover the fall in unemployment in America and Britain in recent years hides the exclusion of many older people from the statistics.[4]

By replacing labour with technology, companies can sell a greater volume of products at reduced prices, and make higher profits. However, this generates very few new jobs in those industries. Employers find it much cheaper to use robots and computers instead, with just a tiny elite labour force of technical and marketing experts. Even in countries where wages are currently very low, companies are finding it more profitable to build highly automated factories. In advanced nations most displaced workers are employed in low-paid work, such as shops and restaurants. Research from the 1990s shows the impact redundancy has; only a quarter of downsized American workers found a new job without taking a pay cut. Nearly a third were still out of work two years later, while one in four took a pay cut of a quarter or more.

These trends have already increased inequality in all countries, with the poorest fifth of Americans having lost a fifth of their real incomes since the mid-70s. George W. Bush has given a massive tax cut mostly to the very rich. Over a sixth of Britons are now on less than half average income, compared to one in fourteen in 1977. Most welfare-to-work programmes have been too modest to do more than help a minority of the unemployed into insecure, low-paid work.[5] In Chapter Five I will discuss measures to boost employment, and thus reduce the inequality which various experts, including Alan Greenspan, Head of the US Federal Reserve, consider 'a major threat' to society.

So what do we have to show for all our work? Though incomes have grown a lot over the past forty years, surveys show that people are no happier. High proportions of Americans say their income is too small to provide what they need; this applies even to two fifths of those earning between $75,000 and $100,000 a year. The amount Americans say they would need to fulfil their dreams doubled between 1987 and 1994. As individuals become wealthier, this amount increases, ensuring continued frustration.[6] Studies of individuals' comparisons with those of different income levels show that it is the gap between a person's income and that of the richest fifth in their region that most detracts from happiness. This suggests that many people compare themselves with the wealthy. So if inequality continues to rise, will we condemn ourselves to stay on the treadmill?

Stress, crime and illness

As well as the growing stresses of work, everyday life is becoming less friendly and relaxed. Crime has increased enormously since the 1950s, and is one of Americans' and Europeans' greatest concerns. Throughout the West nearly a quarter of adults feel unsafe when out alone after dark. Even in school our children are not safe. Each year on average the appalling number of thirty American children die in school violence. Nearly half of American high school students believe one of their classmates is capable of murder. The French government has assessed that more than four hundred schools have a serious violence problem. In Britain as many as a quarter of a million people are victims of racial attack each year. Road rage now causes a majority of American traffic accidents. The potential for even more violence is huge, with a substantial number of young men often carrying a weapon.

Fear has contributed to people being more distant towards their neighbours. In large cities only about a tenth of people feel that there is 'a sense of community' in their neighbourhood. Many people are so driven by their desires that common courtesy is declining. Incredibly it is at Christmas, supposedly the season of goodwill, that London Underground staff are most likely to be attacked, by impatient shoppers.

In addition, the more individualistic nature of our society is increasingly making us ill. Insufficient friendship and emotional support decreases stress tolerance, and hence increases the rate of physical illness and psychological problems. This is comparable in strength to the effect of smoking on physical illness. While working-class people tend to have poorer health, research has found that the illness-inducing effect of a lack of social support is greater than that of class. This is a matter of life and death; men in their 50s who lack good social support are at least three times more likely to die prematurely. For men being married, and for women having a close friendship, have been shown in long-term studies to have the strongest influence on remaining alive. Improving our social relations so that people feel valued is the key to enhancing both quality and length of life.[7]

Those who enjoy the support of an emotionally intimate relationship suffer from stress much less than others. The most important influence enabling adults to create loving relationships is being brought up in a warm and respectful family. Nevertheless many people whose family lacked these qualities have had experiences in adult life enabling them to find love and understanding. Satisfying family life requires a balance of loving commitment, and personal fulfilment. In Chapter Four I describe how we can achieve this despite the sex roles which tend to limit men and women's understanding of each other.

Improving family life

The greed and insecurity which dominates society has obscured a vital fact: satisfaction with family life has been found to exert the most influence on one's overall satisfaction with life.[8] This shows that the most important factor in the quest for happiness is the ability to create co-operative and trusting relationships. Those of us who have had an emotionally supportive relationship have learned that we are loveable and deserve respect. Knowing our loved ones value us, we feel confident of their support in times of trouble. This eases our worries and frees us to appreciate life's delights more deeply. Recognising the potential value of human friendship, asserting our wishes, and treating other people fairly, enables us to stimulate positive responses from them.

Cohesive families foster the belief in togetherness which society urgently needs in order to co-operate in halting social breakdown. A large study of exceptionally happy families found that each had a shared belief in helping humanity or practising their faith. Their members also had a strong commitment to each other, enabling them to resolve disagreements. These families consciously put caring for each other first, over career advancement or making more money, realising that this choice brings much greater fulfilment.

Lorraine is a hard-up single mother who has gained a belief in togetherness which saved her from the brink of suicide. Her story, in contrast to that of a well-off businessman named Colin, shows how emotional warmth can foster a positive outlook and love of life much more than money. Lorraine's involvement in Newpin, a remarkable mutual support network for stressed parents, has given her the qualities more fortunate people acquire from a loving family. Through being valued by the members of Newpin, she has become able both to form supportive relationships, and help others. Three years ago she had severe post-natal depression, and found every aspect of life harsh and futile. Attending Newpin gradually transformed her:

> Society's so dog eat dog, and people losing their humanity, it's being boiled out of them, and I feel Newpin puts back the goodness that society's boiled out, so it's like you really do want to, feel warm to your fellow human beings, rather than vindictive and spiteful and untrustworthy and hostile; I wish everybody could have a taste of Newpin.

On the other hand Colin, who is married and lives in a peaceful suburb, says he tends to worry a lot, although he feels he really has nothing to worry about. When asked how much anyone was concerned about him, Colin said:

> I don't know really, I think people tend to get so wrapped up in their own small circle, . . . I think people have problems enough, and they don't worry about the bloke next door.

Colin would like to spend more time with his children, but said that as taking them out entails spending about £40 he needs to work long hours in order to earn enough. It seems that he rarely enjoys the company of his wife and children in less costly ways. The key to his outlook may be that his wife seems to give him little emotional support. He lacks the sense of humour and capacity to make warm friendships which Lorraine has gained from Newpin. In Chapter Six I describe other people who have joined self-help groups to solve their problems, and thus found fulfilment and zest for life.

Like Lorraine, other people who have received enough emotional support have gained the ability to join with others to improve society. Blake gained considerable self-respect from an exceptional school, and from his father, and now has a supportive wife. He does voluntary work helping run a charity for children. Laurence was encouraged and inspired in his youth by the priest at his church, and then married a very loving wife. She helped him to devote a lot of energy to voluntary political work fighting poverty.

Community decline

If personal relationships can be sustained on a long-term basis, the togetherness which makes people feel valued builds trust and commitment. Therefore they are able to co-operate with each other. In these circumstances people are more likely to help others, confident that others would help them if they were in need in the future. This commitment is shown by research which found that the longer a person has lived in an area, the more likely they are to perform voluntary service there, until they become too old.

However, people's attachment to their community is declining, especially among the under 40s. The importance of this trend is shown by a British survey in which the decrease in involvement in community life was rated the second most important reason for the rise in crime. Nowadays people are less likely to join with others to tackle community problems, and more likely to seek individual solutions in the private sector. Spending on private education, health and pensions has increased steadily since 1988. But as incomes stagnate, people will realise that only the rich can afford to rely solely on the private market for these services. The vast majority of us need good public services, so that all have dignity, and none need feel bitter and excluded.

Promoting social cohesion

Our contribution to society through tax expresses the vital fact that we depend both on each other, and on the social stability which can be preserved only through government action. If wealthy nations such as America ignore this, for instance by leaving 11 million children with no health insurance, they should not be surprised when many of their citizens grow up either unproductive or criminal. In order to secure political support for essential public services it is important that politicians cease competing for votes by promising tax cuts, and thus promoting the indifference towards others which is becoming widespread. In fact, if governments meet citizens' important needs effectively, most people will support the taxes required. In recent years surveys have shown consistently that a clear majority of Americans favour increased spending on health, over tax cuts. [9] In March 2004 Americans were asked which issues they worried about a great deal. Nearly two-thirds named the affordability of healthcare, which was top of the list by a long way. By contrast, when asked in 2003 to name the most important problem facing the country, only 3% said it was tax, which trailed far behind other issues including health and education.[10]

Half of Americans said in 2004 that their personal taxes were too high. Yet nearly two-thirds said that the amount they had to pay was fair, suggesting that they distinguish between their personal wish, and what is right for the country. However polls in 2002 and 2000 found that Americans thought nearly half of federal tax money was wasted. Britons show a similar ambivalence towards government. A Commission studying attitudes to taxation reported 'a deep sense of disconnection from the taxes people pay', arising chiefly from doubts that government uses the money well. However the research clearly showed that people were willing to pay more tax if they were confident it would improve priority public services.[11] This is in line with many polls in recent years consistently showing that more than two thirds of Britons are willing to pay more tax to improve health and education. Throughout the European Union about two-thirds of citizens share this view.

A major reason why public services are inadequate is that governments do too little to reduce the fluctuations of the economic cycle. Due to constant technological progress, a strong annual growth rate of two and a half per cent is needed merely to maintain existing employment levels. Yet most governments fail to train enough displaced workers with the high-level skills needed for the modern economy. Employers offer higher pay to workers with scarce skills, causing inflationary pressure.

Therefore interest rates have to rise, unemployment follows, and tax revenue falls. Governments should raise more tax while the economy is growing. By doing so they could afford to boost employment with public investment when the growth rate slows, and thus speed economic recovery.[12]

Most people believe the gap between rich and poor is too great. Over half of Americans considered the 2003 tax cut unfair in its distribution between the rich, middle class, and the poor, while only a third thought it fair. However governments are doing much too little to reduce social divisions. Minimum wage laws and tax credits for poor families are valuable, but only scratch the surface of social disadvantage. In Chapter One I outline how inequality makes a major contribution to levels of illness and crime. To reduce these effects, governments need to invest sufficiently in deprived children, who otherwise underachieve in education, and are more likely to have a range of problems throughout life. Wasting the talent of the young as much as we do at present hurts all adults. We all depend on a highly trained labour force, and many of us will become victims of the school dropouts who turn to crime.

The tax rises needed to boost education and child health are not excessive. Sweden has higher taxes and better public services than most nations, yet its economy has been thriving in recent years. Most Scandinavians accept their somewhat higher levels of taxation in order to obtain security and decency for all.

Active citizens improve government

We desperately need more people like Lorraine, Blake, and Laurence to help build a more co-operative society. To do so we must reclaim politics from the spin-doctors and corporate backers, and move it above the sterile battle for the floating voter. The desire for secure communities should be harnessed in order to moderate individualism and restore social cohesion.

Citizen action can have a strong influence, both on government, and the quality of life. An inspiring example comes from San Antonio, Texas, where the independent community group COPS transformed the lives of the city's poor Hispanic and Black majority. Through the commitment of its many activists, who encouraged thousands to vote in local elections, COPS became 'the dominant element' in city politics, persuading the council to invest millions on vital improvements.[13] Italy provides an well-known example of the value of what has become known as social capital, namely networks of social relationships, which promote trust and co-operation. It played a vital part in creating the vast difference between the prosperous North, and the mostly inefficient and corrupt South. The northern and central areas, which for over a century have had strong voluntary organisations and political participation, now have much more efficient regional government than the southern regions. The ability of their people to co-operate for the benefit of the community enabled them to develop much more rapidly than the South, whose cynical outlook is reflected in proverbs such as 'He who behaves honestly comes to a miserable end'.

Italian surveys over many years show that the proportion of citizens who are active in voluntary organisations and interested in political issues has a very strong impact on the efficiency of the regional government, and the overall quality of life. This factor accounts almost completely for the tendency of more prosperous regions to have better government. Research comparing the American states found the same result, though to a slightly lesser degree, It is clearly the long tradition of citizens' self-organisation that creates a climate in which regional politicians become responsive to popular concerns.[14]

Disaffected youth

In most countries, local government has been weakened in recent years, and political power is becoming more remote from the people. Electoral turnouts are falling. Increasingly politicians are held in contempt or considered ineffectual. This attitude is particularly prevalent among the young. Of the under-25s, less than a quarter voted in America's 1996 presidential election, and less than two-fifths in the British election of 2005. Nearly half of British under-30s never talk about politics.

Young people's alienation goes far beyond politics; over half of British under-25s 'feel disconnected' from society and from their own neighbourhood. They are showing increasing rates of a wide range of psychological problems.[15] Alarmingly, a quarter of men aged 18 to 24 believe that violence is acceptable 'to get something you want'. Under 25s commit well over half of all crime.

In addition, a gulf may be opening up between the young and the rest of society in attitudes towards drugs. A high proportion of teenagers have tried illegal drugs. Mainstream warnings about drugs lack credibility; as an eighteen-year-old put it,

> when a teacher tells you drugs can kill you, and your best mate tells you that you'll have the time of your life, who are you going to believe? [16]

If the current laws are not to entrench the detachment from society of many young people, we should decide objectively and democratically which drugs should be illegal.

Fostering social responsibility among young people is crucial not only to cut crime, but also to sustain the health of our democracy. In Chapter Three I describe how it is in our interests as a society to tackle the roots of young peoples' problems by helping parents and their children enjoy better relationships. In government terms the resources needed to do this are modest. But to ensure that promoting high-quality parenting will be a government priority, we need to create a consensus for a more just society which values educating the young more than raising middle-class consumption. Such a society would give each citizen the chance to develop their potential to the full and earn a fair income. This will also involve instilling in children a sense of responsibility for the common welfare. This may sound idealistic, but evidence shows that certain schools have created a strong spirit of togetherness and co-operation while also enhancing individual learning.[17]

Citizen power

Scepticism about the ability of ordinary people to improve society is understandable. Individuals' efforts may seem tiny when set against the power of big business and government. Some people believe that forces which are now beyond the control of individuals determine the nature of our society. It is true that the economic history of many years has shaped both our social structure and the political ideologies through which we perceive the world. These have a strong impact on political decisions, but human beings can also bring about change. Differences between similar countries in levels of inequality, and of state provision for people in need, show that public opinion and the strength of political organisations are also influential. [18]

Ordinary people can have a political influence if they band together to make their voice heard. The massive opposition to the Vietnam War eventually led the American government to end it. The Nuclear Freeze campaign influenced politicians to make arms limitation agreements with the Soviet Union. American student organisations pressured Nike to improve the conditions of its workers in the developing world. Another option is joining a political party, provided it has a real prospect of winning enough votes to make a significant impact. Extensive evidence shows that the amount of canvassing by local Party members strongly influences the size of their candidate's vote. [19] Even a relatively small campaigning group can affect political decisions provided its members work together, and public opinion supports their aims. [20] The two thousand members of the Los Angeles Bus Riders Union, among the poorest people in the USA, won a remarkable court victory ordering improvements in the bus service. They convinced the court that the local Transportation Authority had discriminated by giving much less subsidy to the buses than to the trains, used mostly by white middle-class passengers.

Many people consider politics corrupt, and therefore prefer to give any spare time or money they have to charities which help people in need. These charities do excellent work, but small changes in political policy can achieve much more. For example, imagine that in response to campaigns and public opinion the

British government increased its overseas aid budget by just one fifteenth. The extra money it would spend on combating malnutrition and disease in poor countries would easily exceed the combined income from public donations of the three leading British aid charities. We have seen an even greater achievement by the campaign Jubilee 2000. Its global coalition, and petition signed by a remarkable 17 million people, persuaded politicians to write off much of the debt of the poorest countries. Although the politicians' commitment is inadequate, and falls far short of their rhetoric, this should not obscure the fact that Jubilee 2000 attained an excellent result for a great many poor people.[21]

However activists will only improve our society if they pursue achievable aims. Despite its faults, the capitalist system has shown its resilience for over two centuries. It recovers from recessions, which governments have learnt how to mitigate. It has provided increases in wealth which would have been unimaginable to earlier generations. Only a tiny minority would favour radical change to it. Capitalism has engendered an individualist mentality which in turn sustains it. Society will only become more harmonious by gradually nurturing a more collaborative culture.

Organisations working for a better society vitally need members whose personal emotional security gives them dedication and tolerance. These crucial qualities can give the group sufficient cohesion and commitment to attain its goals. As I have described, our need to feel valued and secure is frustrated by job pressures, inequality, crime, and family breakdown. In this book I consider how to enrich marital and family relationships, which as well as providing emotional security, will also give us the confidence in human co-operation we need to build a less divided society. The first obstacle I will address is the modern curse of stress.

Chapter 1
Stress, Inequality, and Crime

The huge cost of stress

In developed countries psychological conditions now cause nearly a quarter of the total impact of all illness, substantially more than either heart disease, or cancer. This figure is based on their duration, and the harm they inflict on sufferers. In both the USA, and the United Kingdom, each year over a quarter of the population see a doctor with symptoms of psychological illness.[1] Doctors sometimes fail to diagnose these conditions, and the sufferer may be unaware of the psychological cause. The wide range of symptoms are mostly due to depression and anxiety.

Each year one American in every ten suffers major depression.[2]

At any time, between one in seven and one in five adults are suffering a significant degree of depression. Some will not survive; depressed people or those with a distressed personality have a much higher heart attack rate. As I will show below, this illness is probably to a large extent an indirect outcome of our over-emphasis on money and social position. Therefore it is ironic that each year it costs Britain the vast sum of £32 billion. If we could cut stress, much of this money could be spent instead on improving health and education, or preventing crime and pollution. Admitting one is suffering from anxiety or depression is still often seen as a sign of weakness, despite the fact that two-thirds of adults report recently having suffered moderate or high stress. People would like to rectify this: a European survey found that most people think adopting 'a simpler and more natural lifestyle' would be a good thing.

1

Pulled in three directions: work, family, self

Why do so many of us have such difficulty finding a relaxed lifestyle? We are inconsistent on certain key issues. The European survey found that a high proportion believe there should be 'more emphasis on family life', while only slightly fewer think there should be 'more emphasis on the development of the individual'. These two aims are bound to clash, given that individual development is normally viewed as involving interests such as career advancement, which are separate from the family. Work leaves little energy for family life, with American fulltime workers averaging 46 hours per week. While many American workers are dissatisfied with the stress their job causes, a great many Britons say they 'take a great deal of pride in their work'.[3] When asked if they would continue in employment if they had a reasonable income without needing to work, most Britons said they would. Employers' pressure is not the only reason many of us work long hours; many people, particularly men, invest much of their need for self-esteem in the work role.

However a male identity dependent on being a full time breadwinner is becoming harder to sustain. Only about a third of the adult population have secure full time jobs, compared with more than half in 1975. Most of the growth in jobs in the next few years is expected to be in occupations usually filled by women. Many men have considerable anxiety about the possible loss of their work role, going far beyond its financial implications. Long-term unemployment is considerably greater among young men than young women. A growing number of men are working part time. Most would probably prefer to work full time, but do not have the choice.

Women are becoming increasingly committed to employment. However while men are devoting more time to family life, mothers still undertake the majority of childcare and housework. Though many men wish they could spend more time at home, the more children they have, the longer hours they work. Most women are often exhausted, with employed American women working over 80 hours a week, at work, and at home. Surveys have found that a major reason for men's limited involvement in family life is that over half feel their 'real' personality comes out chiefly at work. Remarkably, most men regard 'job satisfaction' as being of greater importance than their partner is to them.[4]

Viewing themselves as a good provider for their family is the chief way many men feel valued. They also appear more confident of being able to meet the expectations of work than of being able to provide the emotional support which is a much more important aspect of personal relationships. For some men work can actually be less stressful than the emotional demands of family life:

> I know what I'm supposed to be doing when I'm at work. I seem to know less and less what I'm supposed to be doing outside of work. I seem to be less and less capable of being a friend or a father or a husband . . . so I get more and more scared of trying, I just go back to the office where I know what I'm supposed to do.[5]

As well as being very involved in their work identity, most men have a stronger attraction to their hobbies than to spending time with their family. When asked which of their spare time activities was most important to them, far more men mentioned sports, DIY, or other hobbies, than spending time with their wife or children. Male involvement in hobbies sometimes appears to be an indirect way of trying to cope with or compensate for discontent about themselves or some other aspect of their lives. An engineer spends a lot of time training his dog. When he comes home his dog gives him a much warmer welcome than his wife and children do, causing him to remark that 'you can't get love from a human being in that way'.

Such men may come to regret not having found fulfilment in their family. The less men involve themselves in family life, the more likely their wives are to seek a divorce. A survey of employed married women found that the extent to which their husband was an affectionate and supportive confidante was by far the strongest influence on the women's marital happiness.[6] Two other studies found that the husband's failure to do much housework, or his 'neglect of home or children', were the most important reasons for women wanting a divorce. In each study these factors were far more influential than the level of the husband's income.[7]

Rising incomes, rising debts

One of the major features of a job which contributes to the level of a man's self-respect is the pay. West Europeans surveyed considered 'good pay' the most important characteristic of a job. Nearly three-quarters rated it important, while 'not too much pressure' was joint bottom of the list. Only two out of five West European workers were satisfied with their pay. However surveys suggest many people have conflicting feelings about money. About two-thirds of Europeans polled agree there should be 'less emphasis on money and material possessions'.[8] A narrow majority of Swedes say that they would prefer shorter working hours to higher pay. The average American worker would give up one twentieth of their pay to work shorter hours. But overall the desire for more money seems stronger than that for more time.

Public opinion on personal wealth and income distribution can be summarised as follows: most people favour a modest reduction in income differences between rich and poor, but at the same time they want average incomes to rise, and an above-average income for themselves. Therefore most people borrow in order to obtain the things they want. While average incomes have risen, savings have fallen, and the amount of debt (excluding mortgages) as a proportion of income has increased rapidly.[9] Most American workers feel they are not saving enough for retirement. Yet financial need is not the main reason for having large debts; households with a high level of debt tend if anything to have higher incomes, and fewer children.[10]

Researchers have concluded that the main hope and desire of a great many people is to become rich. An American study similarly found that although people say that wealth does not bring happiness, in fact they still want enough money to achieve 'the good life'.[11] Each week Britons spend £90 million on National Lottery tickets. This amount has nearly doubled since 1994. While a high proportion of people believe certain aspects of consumption should be curbed in order to protect the environment, less than a third are 'willing or fairly willing' to accept a cut in their standard of living for this reason.

The desire for affluence does not apply only to the less fortunate. Three-quarters of American students aspire to wealth, whereas between 1967 and 1970 only around two-fifths did so. This change is mirrored by a steep decline in the percentage of students considering it very important to 'develop a meaningful philosophy of life'.[12]

Some people doubt the relevance of responses to surveys such as these. But research has found that in most cases there is a strong relationship between people's expressed attitudes and their actual behaviour.[13] For instance, people who said they felt that too much emphasis is given to material possessions were more likely to give up their time to do regular voluntary work.

Self-esteem and social approval

People's desire for certain expensive items often derives more from the social meaning of possessing them than from any enjoyment in actually using them. Researchers who involved people from a wide range of backgrounds in group discussions about consumption found that a common topic was 'the pressure to consume'.[14] A mature student I interviewed felt that now he was thirty he ought to smarten up his home, partly because his friends 'have such nice flats'. People under such pressure feel that the extent to which others value them depends on how they present themselves and what they own. Buying certain gifts, luxuries, or home improvements, because of a wish to enhance others' view of oneself, is very common. This wish is so strong that the purchase is rarely the outcome of careful reflection. People's aspirations for their home are usually influenced by what they feel is expected for someone of their age and status. Once one new item has been bought, other items which seemed fine before no longer appear up to standard; hence people can find themselves being seduced into greater debt than they had originally intended.[15]

5

Most people compare their pay with that of others with whom they identify. Studies have found that these comparisons have a much stronger impact than the actual amount of someone's income on their level of satisfaction with it.[16] The desire to enhance one's image often overrides the aim of maximizing one's income. Although a company car forms a fairly small part of managers' pay, many haggle more over details of their car than over more financially significant benefits such as share options and pensions. The aim for fulfilment through possessions is rarely successful; research has found that 'as one's debts increase, pleasure in consumption is outweighed by problems and worries' due to the debts.

People rarely recognise the effect of consumption pressure on themselves. A researcher found that most young people considered that everyone but themselves was a 'victim of consumer culture'. For many presenting a fashionable image is an overriding priority, despite the expense, and a key factor in seeking peer-group acceptance. Studies have shown that those who are most clothes-conscious are less personally fulfilled than others, more insecure, more anxious to conform in other respects, and more likely to be compulsive buyers.[17] Such people lack the confidence that others will value them because of their individual character, and instead buy socially valued goods or experiences in order temporarily to feel acceptable. This insecurity can lead to crime; young delinquents spend large sums of stolen money on clothes for these reasons.

Neither possessions, nor the success they represent, ultimately satisfy the underlying need, which is for the appreciation and respect of others. This wish is a constant theme in interviews with people about their work, and is expressed by those at all levels of the social scale. A dentist feels resentful because, unlike an artist, his work cannot be hung on a wall and admired. A taxi driver is upset if he feels that someone shows insufficient respect towards him because of his occupation. His self-esteem is determined by his perception of his status in others' eyes. This is typical in our society. Such emotions are not confined to men. Many 'housewives' do not feel valued because they are not in paid work.

Women and self-esteem

In her fascinating book *Our Treacherous Hearts*, Rosalind Coward comments that there are few women who do not, consciously or sub-consciously, long for their mother's approval. This unresolved yearning makes it difficult for many women to decide whether to seek self-esteem through devotion to their family, or to give priority to career advancement. Their decisions are strongly influenced, consciously or subconsciously, by the way they have interpreted their mother's views about women and employment. Such women try to avoid making choices of which they feel their mother would disapprove, which imply criticism of the way their mother brought up her family, or which fail to do justice to their mother's 'sacrifices' for them. Therefore some are reluctant to continue in employment after having children, if their own mother did not. Others feel they would not fulfil their mother's hopes if they did not develop their career potential.[18] Their views about their mother may also underlie the fear that if most of their hopes are focused on the children, their own life will prove to be empty or disappointing as the children grow up.

A further source of deep anxiety, particularly for women, is their appearance. One study found that physical attractiveness was the factor which had the strongest influence on females' level of self-esteem. However self-evaluations of appearance are often distorted in line with one's level of self-esteem; teenage girls whose self-esteem is low are more likely than other girls to worry about their weight, whether they are actually overweight or not. An American survey found that women said they would rather lose 10–15 lb than achieve any other wish. Researchers have concluded that concern with appearance is a source of 'discontent and unhappiness'.[19] This anxiety is now causing misery even among five- to seven-year-olds, more than a quarter of whom want to be thinner, even though very few are overweight. Media stereotypes bear much of the blame.

The sources of happiness

Having the money to buy a prized possession, or securing the approval of others through an achievement such as losing weight, has only a brief effect on our feelings of well-being. Once a particular possession becomes the norm at a particular social level, desire becomes focused on something else. This shows why so many surveys have found that in industrial nations the amount of one's income, or other aspects of social status such as education and occupation, have only a slight influence on personal happiness.[20] A thorough analysis of most of the relevant research found that a person's level of satisfaction with family relationships, especially marriage, has the strongest impact on their overall happiness. Another study investigated the influence on adult happiness of a range of factors. A happy childhood had the strongest effect.[21]

Happiness is also closely linked to self-esteem. In Chapter Three I describe how emotional security in infancy leads to better social relations and fosters happiness on a long-term basis. Among adults emotional security promotes both happiness, and satisfaction with marriage, and is also related to high self-esteem (see Chapter Four).[22] The ability to form emotionally secure relationships clearly plays an important part in freeing people from a fruitless search for self-esteem through the achievement of what they perceive as a socially desirable image.

Although emotional insecurity tends to persist, it can be overcome. Research shows that if people reflect on the unhappiness in their childhood, and understand the stress their parents suffered, they can gain the confidence and determination to create happy and intimate adult relationships. If we can find the key to a happy family life, we are likely to gain much greater fulfilment than by devoting most of our energy to work or the quest for wealth.

In a relationship with sufficient trust and mutual respect one can be tolerant and understanding towards one's partner, secure in the knowledge that the partner values and likes one enough to do likewise. Those who have secure intimate relationships have been found to be more conciliatory and emotionally resilient, less anxious, and to experience more positive emotion than other people.[23] In Chapter Four I will describe the common problems which prevent so many people from enjoying secure relationships of this kind, and how to overcome them.

Seeking consolation

When partners are discontented with their relationship, this can cause difficult emotions. Therefore most such people avoid this by reducing their emotional involvement with each other. As a result many turn to substitute sources of satisfaction:

> I bought a diamond ring for myself. It made me feel worthwhile, loved, secure. My husband doesn't believe in giving diamond rings, so I had to accept the fact I had to buy one for myself if I wanted to get all those good feelings. . . . I did something expensive for me and I did it because I truly feel that I'm worth it.[24]

Clearly making oneself feel valued, or making life seem worthwhile, by buying oneself a diamond ring, or even more ordinary treats, adds to one's expenses. This in part explains why those who lack a sense of purpose in their life have been found to be less satisfied with their income, compared to others with the same income. The lower a person's degree of satisfaction with life, the more additional possessions and leisure experiences they wish to buy.[25] A woman who says that she has a 'fear of intimacy' reacted to her unrequited love for a man with what she called 'obsessive shopping':

> I guess I was trying to fill up my life. Those possessions don't make you any happier, but I love clothes to the point that it's an obsession. . . . Probably again because you feel your life's out of control, you'll go and spend money because that's the one control you do have . . . I want to be loved, but I don't know how to love.[26]

Obtaining the money to buy these possessions or experiences

makes a person temporarily feel both more in control of their life, and relatively satisfied. This briefly reduces the effect of previous disappointments which made life and other people seem frustrating. One woman had repressed her childhood memories of being beaten by her father and disregarded by her mother. Before she realised this she used to spend a lot of money; later she saw that this had been a substitute for inner deprivation. While presenting oneself with a diamond ring is clearly rare, trying to soothe discontent with some kind of treat is very common, as those of us who respond to boredom or setbacks by eating too much can recognise.

Emotional and financial insecurity

Why do norms about what is desirable and fitting for someone of a particular social status have such a strong influence? The answer lies in the way our status-driven society distorts our biological need to maintain the goodwill of those to whom we are close. The behaviour of every human being is influenced by the fact that at any time we may become dependent on others in order to ensure our survival. This is why evolution has equipped us with the ability to make close relationships with others who will care for us when we are in need. In the environment in which humans evolved, even something as simple as a sprained ankle could have led to the death of someone who had no family to care for them.

As most people nowadays live at a distance from most of their relatives, they do not feel the sense of security of previous generations who could turn to many members of their extended family in times of need. Nearly half of marriages now end in divorce. An increasing number of adults of all ages live alone. Only a minority of adults see their parents, brothers, or sisters frequently. Half of divorced fathers lose contact with their children within ten years of the separation. While of course one can develop close friendships on the basis of an affinity one may not share with relatives, it is rare for friendships to have the depth of commitment and permanence of family relationships.

So because family relationships appear too unreliable to guarantee financial and emotional security, many people have developed a strong subconscious need for the respect or admiration of others outside their family. This leads them to conform to social norms regarding consumption and possessions, in the hope that anyone whose friendship or aid they may seek will consider them worthy of such help. Conforming may also reduce anxieties about their relations letting them down if they need help in future. By contrast in most pre-industrial societies practically everyone had the same standard of living, patterns of consumption continued for generations according to custom, and individual attempts to become better off were both rare and discouraged.[27] Few such societies imposed pressure on people to raise their status in order to feel accepted.

Couples who share

In an industrialised society the need of most adults for a sense of emotional and financial security depends heavily on the behaviour of their partner, if they have one. If a couple derive enough emotional strength from their relationship to take joint decisions about money which each considers fair, this will enhance their feeling of financial security. Such partner support is vital; while state benefits are available for those on low incomes, they are seen as an inadequate safety net. Because of the unequal distribution of wealth in our society many of those reliant on benefits feel stigmatised or depressed at being unable to afford much of what is considered the norm. They are also anxious that if any of their possessions are stolen or wear out, they will lack the money to replace them. In this situation the partner can potentially play a crucial role in providing friendship and support.

The extent to which people feel a sense of financial insecurity depends also on the amount of their savings, their confidence about job security, their ability to avoid debt, and the level of deprivation they would feel if their income fell. The more they have invested their hopes or self-esteem in achieving a certain lifestyle, the more they would feel its actual or threatened loss to be a severe blow.

When a family suffers a financial setback, its members need to decide together how to adjust to their reduced income. The situation may give rise not only to disputes about financial priorities, but also to quarrels about past decisions. People's reaction to having less money than they want or had expected can put a severe strain on their marriage or on their relationships with other household members, unless these are particularly supportive. Nowadays few people perceive their job as being really secure. In view, therefore, of the fragility of current family relationships, and the widespread desire to achieve a high standard of living by acquiring socially desired possessions, feelings of both emotional and financial insecurity are very common among both employed and unemployed people.

Desires, inequality, discontent, and illness

Unless politicians reverse it, the trend of recent years towards greater income inequality is likely to increase; this has been recognised right across the political spectrum. It is chiefly inequality, rather than low income itself, which generates discontent, consumption desires, and consequent feelings of financial anxiety. Research has found that those of low social status desire more possessions than those of higher status.[28] This is probably because they have a greater need to try and bolster their ego through acquiring the trappings of 'success'. As the incomes of the wealthy have been increasing so much faster than other incomes since the 1980s, the discontent arising from this comparison has grown.

While happiness within any individual industrial country increases slightly from the bottom to the top of the income scale, this seems to be due largely to people comparing their situation with that of others. As incomes rise throughout society over the years, average levels of happiness do not increase.[29] Moreover, the average happiness of one industrial nation compared to others bears no relation to their differences in average income. However, most evidence shows that the greater the inequality *within* a nation, the more unhappy its citizens tend to be.[30]

As inequality erodes happiness, it is not surprising to find that it also harms health. Research findings on inequality and health are complex, and have some inconsistency. However, I will summarise a large volume of evidence to explain how inequality has this effect.

Absolute poverty causes illness in the developing countries of Africa, Asia, and South America. However in advanced nations, on which this discussion is focused, it is inequality rather than poverty itself which is a major cause of illness and death.[31] Differences between developed nations in income per head are not significantly related to differences in life expectancy between those nations. But within any one country, life expectancy and health, increases *at each level* ascending the income scale, showing that poverty is not the relevant factor.[32] Both the rates of sickness absence, and mortality, of British civil servants, were found to be greater in each successive pay grade going down the hierarchy. Social class differences in illness have increased with inequality in recent decades despite the fact that the incomes of all social strata have risen. As Japan's inequality fell from 1970 to 1990, its life expectancy rose much more than in Britain, where inequality, and the social class differences in death rates, both rose.

The inequality–illness link has been found to be partly due to differences in levels of education within the population. This is because inequality has its harmful effects largely through the medium of social status, which is more directly measured by education.

Research shows that the scale of the inequality–illness link is too great to be caused by differences between social strata in either health-relevant lifestyle (smoking, diet, etc.), or access to medical care, whose influence is less.[33]

A victim of inequality speaks

While carrying out my research I encountered a man who bore prominent psychological scars of inequality. He had also had a serious physical illness a few years earlier. He clearly feels that no one values him, either personally or economically. He is a mature student on a low income. He says 'Those bastards in the boardrooms getting £60 per hour . . . make me really angry'. He had once aspired to be 'a yuppie', with a 'black BMW and pretty woman'. Now, although he would like 'a nice soulmate', his self-confidence is such that he feels no woman would be 'interested in a 41-year-old balding bachelor'. He makes no complaint about the physical condition of his flat, which he says he loves because 'it's my home'. But then he describes it as 'crap', because he feels it puts him 'in close proximity with . . . thieves, low life, drug abusers . . . and other assorted "housing estate" tenants'. He feels other people would take advantage of him if they had the chance. He rarely obtains enjoyment from life. He has certain hopes, but says he has no chance of achieving any of them. As he lacks social support, and feels devalued by being poor in a society of whose inequality he is keenly aware, he is one of many at great risk of becoming ill.

Grade, degradation, and illness

The links between inequality, happiness, and health are underlined by the fact that positive social relationships are not only the chief determinant of happiness, but are also very important in promoting health. Inequality harms health chiefly by the way that social status differences or racial discrimination taint relationships. This tendency to illness is linked to certain measures of body chemistry which have been shown both in humans and monkeys to increase all the way up the social hierarchy. Studies found that when a monkey was moved to a different group in which it could assume a dominant role, its body chemistry became more health-inducing, showing that it was the subordinate situation which induced illness, not the nature of the monkey.[34]

An important factor contributing to these findings is that in less equal countries fewer people feel in control of their life. This is linked to difficulty in achieving their social goals, and consequent loss of social status. Evidence shows that people's negative feelings about their social status, and the associated lack of control over their life, are linked to illness and premature death. These feelings have a much stronger effect on health than income does.[35] The health of British civil servants, who all had safe jobs with pay ranging from moderate to high, was studied over 25 years. When the effect of a civil servant's employment grade on their illness record was compared with that of their total household income, grade had a much greater effect. In addition, those who felt they had little control over their working situation were more likely to become ill, even when compared to others of the same social class and with the same risk factors for heart disease. Another study showed that the health of a group of workers declined after forthcoming redundancies were announced, but well before any of them were actually laid off.

It is common for those held to be lower in the social hierarchy to be treated with varying degrees of disrespect. This can be lethal; comparison of American states shows that the prevalence of disrespectful attitudes towards black people is closely linked to the mortality rates both of black *and of white people*. This relationship persists after the effect of average incomes in each state have been taken into account.[36] Canadian hospital cleaners described how many people consider them to be 'hospital trash', a status which some actually seemed to have internalized. In America many customers treat fast food restaurant workers with indifference and rudeness. Britons who had had to become tenants after being unable to keep up payments on the home they had been buying felt ashamed; they said they had become second-class citizens.

Lower social status causes, in varying measures, feelings of inferiority, and anger.[37] The need to suppress this anger raises blood pressure, and, like feelings of inferiority, contributes strongly to the risk of depression. Research shows that people are more likely to suppress anger towards people higher in the social hierarchy, and inflict it on those who are lower.[38] Greater inequality increases the above phenomena. This is partly because less equal societies have weaker protection for workers in terms of employment and trade union rights, thus inhibiting their ability to stand up against bad treatment. The other major reason is that they are less able to afford a lifestyle considered decent in that society. It is no accident that unequal America uses the disrespectful term 'loser' to describe a poor person with no prospects. America's inequality is a major reason why it ranks only 24th in the world in life expectancy.

People's comparisons of their income and social status with that of others play a vital role in transmitting the effects of inequality. When most of the population were manual workers, inequality was lower. This is probably why class differences in wealth were felt less keenly. A man brought up in a working-class family in the 1960s said:

> in Cardiff, I don't think it occurred to people to think what they were in a class sense . . . We didn't have a very high material-content background, but then we didn't know many people who did. . . . we regarded ourselves as everyone else's equal . . . it didn't cause any great interest that there were others who lived in say the wealthier parts of Cardiff who were definitely higher up the social scale than we were.[39]

People compare their income to that of others with similar qualifications or doing similar work. For instance, a sample of white-collar workers were found to be less satisfied with their pay than were manual workers on the same income. The former compared themselves with the majority of white-collar workers, who were more highly paid.[40] Similarly, among unemployed people, those with higher levels of education suffer greater mental distress, presumably because they feel particularly unfortunate relative to employed people with comparable qualifications. It seems likely that such dissatisfaction is a key pathway through which inequality renders its ill effects. By contrast, research shows that happy thoughts, and laughter, protect against illness by boosting the immune system.

One expression of dissatisfaction which has been shown to be linked to illness is hostility. Research shows that people with high levels of hostile feelings are more likely to develop various serious illnesses. Hostile feelings are damaging even if they do not lead to overt aggression. Hostile people use more alcohol and tobacco than other people, but they still suffer a higher level of illness beyond that caused by their greater use of these drugs. They receive less social support than others, and this is another reason why they suffer more illness. Working-class men are more likely than other people to have high levels of hostile feelings.[41] This is probably due to their dissatisfaction at their relatively low status and income, and may thus account in part for the greater rates of illness towards the bottom of the pay ladder. There is every reason to believe that hostility is linked to inequality. The perception of hostility certainly is linked: throughout the USA the proportion of people in a state who believe that 'most people would try to take advantage of you if they got the chance' is very closely related both to the degree of inequality, and to mortality rates, in their state.[42]

Social support and peaceful communities promote health

A study of the United States shows that one of the main reasons states with more inequality have higher mortality is the lower levels of trust and social connectedness in those states. Illness is more prevalent among individuals whose level of social support is low. This causes dissatisfaction and weakens the immune system, as does inequality. Conversely, those who feel content with their social status, and who feel valued by friends, have more to live for, and their health is better as a result.

People in the lower social classes tend to have less social support from relations and friends. Inequality heightens this effect because less equal nations have greater residential segregation of rich and poor. Neighbourhoods with a greater concentration of poor people have weaker social relations and psychological functioning, and more crime. Research comparing the impact on health of personal income, and neighbourhood characteristics, shows that poor neighbourhoods cause illness beyond that which is due to their individual inhabitants' low incomes.[43] People who lived in neighbourhoods with many poor people were more likely to die sooner than those whose income and health were the same at the start of the study, but lived in less deprived neighbourhoods.

There are additional factors operating in poor neighbourhoods which account for these negative outcomes. Infants have lower birth weights, and smoking, domestic violence, and other illness-inducing behaviours are more prevalent than would be accounted for by families' income levels. One such factor is cold or harsh parenting, which contributes both to children being more likely to suffer from depression as adults, and to the emotional insecurity associated with various types of mental ill-health.

Studies of people whom local authorities enabled to move from poor to non-deprived neighbourhoods showed that they appreciated most the absence of crime, and the peace, cleanliness, and space. Research also shows that being close to trees and other vegetation promotes well-being, and recovery from stress. On a deprived estate, residents who had a view with grass and a few trees showed better concentration than those in neighbouring blocks whose view was only of buildings. It was this concentration that largely accounted for their somewhat greater ability to tackle their personal problems.[44]

The more unequal a society, the more its poorer neighbourhoods will be neglected by government, and considered unpleasant to live in. The feelings of powerlessness they evoke also cause illness. Yet devoting limited funds to providing some green space, and to the crime prevention measures I will outline in Chapter Five, can significantly enhance residents' quality of life, and thus improve their health.

Measuring the inequality effect

A few recent studies have cast some doubt on the illness–inequality link, but their interpretation is open to dispute. These studies tried to distinguish the effect on mortality of the variations in inequality between regions of a country, from that of individuals' income. However as individual income, via its link to social status, is strongly related to mortality within any nation, removing its effect from the inter-region comparison of mortality rates led to a gross under-estimate of the influence of inequality. This is because the explanatory power of thousands of individual income measurements overlaps with the degree of inequality with which this income is distributed.

Other studies have suggested that the apparent effects on health of inequality between regions of the USA are actually due to variations in racial composition, and the associated tensions in relations between the races. Evidence on this point is mixed. The critical factor is probably the inequality. It causes blacks to receive poorer education, and thus perpetuates their concentration in relatively poor areas, due to the less attractive jobs and housing there. Moreover inequality between the races is a major factor perpetuating racial tensions. Research shows that the more inequality white Americans perceive between themselves and blacks, the more they regard blacks as lazy. This attitude is linked to the view that efforts to alleviate racial inequality are pointless. The more that whites regard blacks as responsible for their own disadvantage, the more tense relations between the two races become. This shows how inequality detracts from the community harmony which would promote health.[45]

The relation between inequality and illness needs further study to show the effect of inequality on individuals later in their lives. One study found that inequality was related to international differences in mortality rates among the under fourteens, but not among older people.[46] Another study comparing the states of the USA found that a state's inequality was linked to higher mortality among people under 45, but not among older people. It may be that older people are less susceptible to the effects of inequality, having grown up at a time when a much larger section of society was working class, social mobility was more limited, and therefore most people paid less attention to their social status in relation to others. Young and middle-aged people *will* probably be susceptible as they age. In addition, as international differences in inequality have become more marked since the 1970s, they are likely to cause greater international differences in levels of illness across the age range in future decades.

Social support, self-esteem, and health

Poor health has also been shown to be linked to low self-esteem, which in turn is strongly related to holding a negative view of human nature.[47] Those whose self-esteem is low have probably received less kindness than most, and hence feel relatively negative about people. What is the connection that causes both inequality and low self-esteem to be related to illness? As those with low self-esteem are likely to have a relatively poor view of human nature, they will expect less support and sympathy, either from family members or the state. As they have relatively low expectations of other people, they behave less positively towards them, seek less support, and consequently receive less help. This may relate to inequality as follows: the lower an individual's income compared to those around them, the more they feel actually or potentially dependent on the assistance of others to maintain the standard of living to which they aspire. As those with low self-esteem receive less social support, they are more likely to become ill.

Another standard for comparison with those who appear more fortunate is social class. Self-esteem has been found to be related to social class moderately among adults, slightly among adolescents, and hardly at all among children. Income is only slightly related to self-esteem.[48] The reason the middle class tend to have higher self-esteem is due much more to their better education than their higher average income.

The difference between adults and children in the influence of social class on self-esteem probably arises because adults' social class has a much greater influence on their lives, including on their awareness of their status. In contrast children do not need to earn a living or decide where they can afford to live, and are less aware of the scale and meaning of social status differences. As children encounter social inequality much less directly, it is not surprising that it also affects their health less. Their relationships with their parents have a stronger impact.

A survey of 1000 Scottish 15-year-olds found that social class influences neither their physical nor mental health. However teenagers who had more conflict with their parents had poorer health, did less well at school, and were more likely to smoke and use illegal drugs. Youngsters who at age 15 smoked or used illegal drugs were more likely to be unemployed at age 18. From then on, such young people will be more likely to suffer the adverse effects of social inequality and become ill. It seems that they will develop a particular vulnerability to these effects for two reasons: as they have lacked emotional security in their family, they have been unable to do well enough at school to get a job; in addition, they will lack the social support which boosts self-esteem and morale in the face of life's ups and downs. In Chapter Three I describe how these persisting emotional problems begin in childhood.

The beauty we miss

I have described how social inequality stimulates both widespread discontent, and the desire to relieve it by buying socially prized possessions or experiences. Doing this narrows our focus to what is valued in financial terms, but in fact we are continually surrounded by freely available and potentially fascinating sights, sounds, and smells. Aldous Huxley has pointed out that in mediaeval times pilgrims were filled with wonder at the sight of stained-glass windows, and were willing to make donations from their limited incomes for their maintenance. Nowadays we can all see various kinds of brilliant light and colour close at hand, for instance city lights at night, or flowers in neighbours' gardens. Even certain images on television can be very impressive if we cease taking them for granted. But most of us have lost the ability to marvel at such sights.

We can regain this appreciation of the beauty of light and colour if we can give it our full attention, without being distracted by worries or the demands of our goals and commitments. Our inattention is not due chiefly to the pace of modern life; as long ago as 1843 John Ruskin remarked that while nature is continually producing 'glory after glory', very few people noticed these sights, such as the striking cloud formation he saw as being like white mountains. After a friend pointed out a copper beech tree, the author Adewale Maja-Pearce was surprised to find that he had never really noticed either trees, or other aspects of his environment:

I was like a person with defective vision who saw only the hazy outlines of the surrounding world . . . I have only recently begun to understand that my partial vision was a comment on the fragility of my own sense of identity.

Maja-Pearce was unable to focus on his surroundings as his emotions had been trapped by anxieties about whether he belonged in Nigeria, his father's homeland, or Britain, his mother's homeland.[49] Other more common emotional problems can also limit our appreciation of the huge range of sensations our five senses can offer. The singer Joni Mitchell had once been moved by the beauty of the clouds, which she had visualised as 'ice-cream castles in the air'. But later disappointments in love made her disillusioned with life, and she could see clouds only in a negative light.

Our individual personality, and the emotions it generates, have a profound effect on our appreciation of all aspects of life. For most people, even how healthy they feel has been shown to be related more to their personality than to physical measurements of body function.[50] The effects on emotion of extroversion and neuroticism have been compared. When individuals were given the same stimulus, extroverts experienced more positive and less negative emotion than introverts. Those assessed as being neurotic felt more negative and less positive emotion than those who were not.

The painter Constable had an unusually positive appreciation of life. When his companion described an engraving as being ugly, Constable explained that for him light, shade, and perspective could make any object beautiful. Constable's fondness for the world around him seems to have been related to the joy he brought to his relations with people.[51]

Some may say that happiness or appreciation of beauty depend on one's situation, for example that if one was fortunate enough to earn one's living as a painter, as Constable did, one would be likely to be happy. But this did not apply to certain other professional artists, such as Mark Rothko and Willem De Kooning, both of whom suffered considerable emotional turmoil despite being highly respected and very well paid. Research shows some people tend to experience events more positively than others, have higher self-esteem, and are more able to put

knowledge about how to reform offenders is limited, as described in Chapter Five. Therefore it is vital that we understand how to prevent young people becoming offenders in the first place. Explaining crime is not excusing it. While most people who suffer social disadvantage do not commit crime, it plays an important role in the making of most criminals, in conjunction with other important factors, especially poor parenting. Given that spending on law and order has grown fourfold since 1982, it would be foolish not to improve education and other services which would reduce crime.

Inequality leads certain people into crime because it provokes discontent. The growing dissatisfaction of youth in recent years is partly due to the increased proportion of children whose families have low incomes. During their formative years these young people learned that their families could not afford many things which most people own and consider important. Youngsters who feel they have little prospect of acquiring these items become bored with the available means of amusement, which seem second-rate. Many who live in high-crime areas, which are nearly always poor areas, believe that most people throughout society have a strong desire to obtain as much money as possible, and that theft and fraud are common in all walks of life. Highly publicised cases of executives committing fraud, or awarding themselves huge pay rises, seem to confirm this view.

Neglected education, neglected society

As I will outline in Chapter Five, educational underachievement is a major reason why young people get involved in crime. The rise in inequality of recent decades has increased the gap in educational attainments due to social class.[54] This shows how inequality will perpetuate itself unless governments reduce it. It will also harm the economy. Underachievement due to disaffected youngsters dropping out of under-resourced schools costs the American economy a massive $50 billion each year at least.[55] A recent American Secretary for Education said children's results in science and maths are poor and must be raised 'dramatically'.

Nearly half of American children in poor areas leave school functionally illiterate.

Governments who criticise the performance of schools in poor areas ignore the fact that the better results of schools in suburban areas are partly due to many middle-class parents paying for private tutors for their children. These governments fail to accept the overwhelming evidence that by far the greatest influence on a school's results is the social class background of its students.[56] The average exam results of children of professional/managerial parents are about two-thirds better than those of the children of manual workers. One study found that the proportion of poor students, and the truancy rate (which is linked to poverty) account for 90 per cent of the difference in schools' exam results. Many schools have huge handicaps; two-fifths of American city children attend schools with a very high proportion of disadvantaged students. Teachers can surmount the difficulty of a small number of disinterested children, but once their number reaches a 'critical mass' it becomes impossible to compensate for their low morale or disruptiveness.

Recognition of this problem must not provide an excuse for teachers to have low expectations of children from poor backgrounds. The success of Sweden in cutting the social class difference in education shows that genetic factors play only a fairly small role in it. Increasing the economic security of working class people was the biggest factor.[57] Giving schools in disadvantaged areas extra resources also improves their results. And studies show that if housing policy changed so that poor families were not concentrated in certain districts, their children would do better in school.[58]

It seems that many governments are neglecting children's education. A survey in the United States and the largest West European countries showed that about three-quarters of people feel that state schools have serious problems. As long as governments do not give teachers the recognition they deserve, and fail to inject enough resources to meet children's actual educational needs, teacher morale will decline. Three-quarters of British teachers say they are absent from work increasingly often due to stress-related illness. In many countries there is a serious shortage of applicants to train as teachers, whose starting pay is not attractive in the United States.[59] At the same time more teachers than ever are leaving the profession, with a remarkable three times more retiring early due to illness than those who retire at the normal age.

Inequality and economic failure

Recent international studies show that countries with less income inequality have higher growth rates and more investment. Greater equality leads to faster growth more than vice versa.[60] Until recently America and Britain ignored this, and let poverty grow much more rapidly than in other wealthy nations. Economic growth in both countries was slow until the mid-90s. We have been given a misleadingly positive view of America's growth rate in the late 1990s. Much of America's growth was due to its population rise. Output per head is currently rising faster in Western Europe. Moreover America's statistics on national income, and productivity, have been raised artificially by technical adjustments. In fact America's productivity grew much less in the 1990s than in the 1960s.[61]

While inequality in America seems to have declined slightly in the late 1990s, this was probably no more than a brief result of the economic boom. President Bush's huge tax cuts benefited mostly the rich, and have contributed to a rise in inequality.

Corporations and their political backers would like us to believe that only low taxes will deliver economic growth. But the international evidence shows that there is no consistent link between tax levels and growth. The effect of tax on growth depends on how wisely the tax revenue is invested, including how much the government creates an environment in which companies compete and innovate.[62] Limited tax increases to improve training and education, and raise poor people's purchasing power, would boost economic growth.

Because of the marked inequality in America and Britain, neither country has achieved the co-operation between employers and trade unions which has fostered prosperity in some European countries. When workers' representatives have been given some influence over company policy, they have realised that their welfare depends upon the viability of the company, and have taken a constructive approach. In Sweden the trade unions have regularly accepted lower pay rises for most workers in exchange for better increases for the lower-paid. This has promoted the development of the most efficient companies, which employ relatively few lower-paid workers. Due to the trade unions' policy, their wage costs did not rise excessively.[63]

In the 1980s Dutch trade unions and employers reached a deal which involved cutting working hours in exchange for pay restraint. Since then the Dutch economy has grown comparatively quickly, unemployment is low, and industrial relations good.

The other major aspect of such countries' success has been the stability enjoyed by industry within a financial system which promotes long-term investment. This has been achieved by tax incentives and state support for certain financial institutions. Appropriate regulation of the banks, of the type which is usual in nearly all advanced countries, would discourage their tendency towards excessive and inflationary lending when the economy is expanding. Had Britain followed such policies, the banks would not have lost so much to bad debts during the recession of the early 1990s, and would not have needed to restrict credit so severely thereafter, harming the economy in the process.

As a result of the stability produced by the financial policies of most West European countries, their banks have not been under excessive pressure to make high profits. Instead they have had the overriding incentive to secure their long-term prosperity by promoting the success of the companies to whom they lend. These companies are less dependent on share capital, and therefore are released from the search for a quick profit to satisfy fickle shareholders and avoid takeover.[64]

By contrast, on the American and British stock markets the average length of time shares are held has fallen substantially in the last 15 years. This produces a short-term mindset in company directors which is not conducive to sustained economic growth. Many manipulated unsustainable rises in their company's share price in order to enrich themselves. This often involved company takeovers, rather than building up a sound business. Many takeovers were misconceived and led ultimately to bankruptcy. As a result, after the Enron, WorldCom, and other scandals, loss of confidence in American companies has led to a sharp fall in investment.[65]

Creating social harmony

As we have seen, inequality is a recipe for discontent throughout the social hierarchy. Our lives would instead be much more fulfilled if we could create a sense of increased unity and thus improve social relationships. Schools can make a vital contribution to this aim by building an understanding atmosphere in which children learn to co-operate and enjoy each other's company. We must ensure that the large sums we invest in education are not devoted solely to a narrow curriculum focused excessively on the interests of business. Schools produce not only the workers, but also the citizens and consumers of tomorrow. They will fail if they turn out citizens who lack the commitment and insight to build a responsible and caring society, however efficient they may be as workers. They will also fail if they turn out consumers who buy more and more polluting products and escapist leisure. Education must concern itself with children's desires and values, as well as their abilities. Schools should give children experiences to show them that great fulfilment often comes through being completely absorbed in an activity, free from anxiety about others' evaluations of one's ability or status. Recent policies give a different message; under-funded American schools have been seduced into accepting electronic goods in return for making their pupils watch 'Channel One' commercials. Research showed these made them far more likely than children at neighbouring schools to endorse statements praising material possessions, to which school was unfavourably compared.

If children feel that education's chief purpose is to amass qualifications, equipping them to earn money so they can buy pleasure, they will become unfulfilled adults. They will undervalue the immense satisfaction to be gained through intimate relationships, or through activities which foster expression of their deepest emotions. Schools should enable children to experience the beauty and excitement of music, art, and drama, the teaching of which is in decline. Greater emphasis on these subjects would give children a priceless lifelong gift by showing them how to find pleasure in their five senses and their imagination. It is only in modern society that the arts have become restricted largely to passive consumption, mostly by the middle class. In pre-industrial societies everyone took part in artistic rituals.

Probably the most important source of satisfaction we should help children to value is friendship. Unfortunately many children's school experience undermines their confidence in human relations. Bullying appears to be widespread. One quarter of London females aged 15 to 19 said they had been sexually harassed, mostly at school. It is vital to tackle this problem, not only to relieve children's misery, but also because school bullies are more likely to become persistent criminals.

Until recently most schools regarded bullying as inevitable. But now a few are harnessing children's maturity and enthusiasm by training them to act as mediators or counsellors, and reduce conflict between pupils. Evaluation of a number of such initiatives in North America found that schools which had trained children to mediate in disputes enjoyed remarkable reductions of 60 to 80 per cent in the frequency of conflicts requiring teacher intervention. Video assessment showed that the child mediators were successfully applying the methods they had been taught. An English school's service using trained child counsellors to support victims of bullying proved so popular that pupils chose to donate money they had raised through school activities towards its expenses. These child counsellors 'proved to be utterly responsible and reliable', and are now playing an important role in managing the service.[66]

Such schemes could yield huge long-term benefits for society by showing children how to reduce antisocial behaviour by co-operating with others. They could also cut the rate of psychological illness; the president of the International Association for Suicide Prevention pointed out that youngsters are more likely to seek help from someone of their own age such as a child counsellor. Well-established programmes of Personal and Social Education have also been shown to help pupils apply themselves to their other lessons.[67] The British government plans to modify its National Curriculum to give teachers the time and resources to develop this neglected subject.

I have described how secure intimate relationships are the major source of happiness. But in our unequal society work pressures, financial instability, and the pursuit of status and wealth, cause stress, illness, and family breakdown. Emotional insecurity has led to the pursuit of consumption in line with social norms, but it provides little lasting fulfilment. Unless we can repair our relationships so that friendship becomes more attractive than consumption, the greenhouse gases the latter produces will leave our children and grandchildren a damaged planet. In the next chapter I discuss how we can reduce the harm our lifestyle has caused to the environment.

Chapter 2
Urgent – Repair our Planet!

Pollution and wealth

Although crime, health, and unemployment are the public's main political concerns in most Western countries, governments have failed to take sufficiently radical steps on these issues. Politicians remain stuck in the view that what most people desire is a higher income, and that this can best be achieved by keeping taxes as low as possible. Incomes have increased considerably over the past forty years. A fixation on increasing them further takes no account of two vital facts. Firstly, as shown above, income levels have less effect on personal and social well-being than does the quality of family life, and the degree of inequality within a society. Secondly, it has been the West's insatiable desire to improve 'living standards' that has caused the severe environmental dangers we now face.

The most serious of these threats is global warming. Scientists consider it to be largely responsible for the alarming increase in natural disasters, which caused a three- to six-fold rise in damage compared to the 1980s. Extreme weather caused the deaths of no less than 3 million people in the second half of the 1990s, including more than one hundred in the West European storms of 1999.[1] The United Nations estimates that global warming is already causing additional disaster costs of an incredible $300 billion at least each year.[2] Since 1992 these disasters have included heatwaves, floods and gales in North-west Europe, North America, Japan, China, India, Hawaii, and Pakistan, with 56 million people made homeless in China in 1998. Global warming is responsible for the spread of deserts, with an area of

Africa over a quarter the size of the USA suffering soil erosion. It has also caused increased insect damage to crops, and more frequent droughts, with American farming severely affected. There can now be no doubt that global warming is a reality, with the ten hottest years on record all having been since the late 1980s. Carbon dioxide (CO_2) and the other 'greenhouse' gases are clearly the culprits: there is now more CO_2 in the atmosphere than at any time in the past 400,000 years. Its level has risen by a third since the start of the Industrial Revolution.[3] Practically all scientists agree that unless we drastically reduce emissions of these gases, average temperatures will rise by between four and six degrees centigrade in the next hundred years. This is a meteoric rate of warming, over fifty times quicker than that which has taken place since the last Ice Age. It is clearly *not* a natural phenomenon.

These findings of the Intergovernmental Panel on Climate Change (IPCC) have been endorsed by the US National Academy of Science, and the National Scientific and Technical Council. Unless we take radical action now, global warming is likely to cause desperate problems for our children and grandchildren. Rainfall will decline in many areas. In 2025 an estimated 5 billion people will live in countries in which water is scarce. Scientists calculate that this century sea level will rise by between 400 and 800 centimetres, flooding several large densely populated areas, and making many millions homeless.

The response of world leaders to this huge risk is woefully inadequate. The IPCC has calculated that it may be necessary to reduce greenhouse gas emissions by 60 per cent to 80 per cent. However the Kyoto agreement, with its many loopholes, provides only for an average reduction among developed countries of 5.2 per cent by 2012. Far from reducing, the United States' emissions have risen by no less than a fifth since 1990.[4]

As I write, in 2005, there is no prospect of the United States taking even the limited Kyoto measures. America emits twice as much CO_2 per person as Germany and Britain, discharging a quarter of the world's total, despite having only one-twentieth of world population. In opting out of Kyoto, George W. Bush is ignoring not only a unanimous vote of the Senate Foreign

Relations Committee, but also America's citizens. In July 2001 only a third of them approved of his decision.[5]

Three-quarters of Americans consider global warming a serious problem. Over half believe priority should be given to protecting the environment over economic growth, while only a third favour economic growth.

Cooling the earth

It is urgent that we conserve energy and use non-polluting fuels in order to cut CO_2 substantially. This requires a relatively small investment by governments. It could be achieved with just a tiny short-lived cut in living standards, as the former head of the British employers' federation (CBI) describes. For instance, Denmark is set to obtain half of its energy from wind power by 2030, and other countries could do so if their governments invested in it. Solar power is rapidly developing, and could generate at least two-thirds of current electricity usage with no pollution whatsoever. In some countries we individuals can help by switching to a supplier of electricity generated by these methods.[6] Nations which fail to support these green technologies will lose out in a global market worth about $300 billion. New buildings should copy designs pioneered in Germany to use one-tenth of the energy of conventional buildings. Governments should back the large amounts being invested to develop the use of hydrogen, a potentially abundant and clean fuel. And farmers will soon be able to slow global warming by feeding their cattle and sheep a special ingredient to reduce their emissions of methane, a potent greenhouse gas.

In particular governments need to strengthen the Kyoto agreement and reach a radical agreement with China and other industrialising countries. If China starts to use as much energy per head as the United States, world CO_2 emissions will increase by a disastrous threefold.[7] The West will have to reduce its emissions, and provide the latest technology to developing countries, in order to ensure that they do not follow our polluting example. It would be a foolish false economy for us not to do so.

An improved Kyoto would end the absurd international agreement by which aviation fuel is not taxed. Planes produce much more CO_2 per passenger mile than any other form of transport. The European Union should tax fossil fuels to encourage energy conservation, and invest in clean fuel development. Legal experts suggest that the EU should then take a case to the World Trade Organisation or the International Court of Justice, seeking to penalise other countries which fail to price fuels in line with the pollution they cause. This would probably entail imposing tariffs against their imports. Polls show that people will accept increased fuel taxes if they are confident the money will be used to cut pollution.[8] Taxes of this kind have already been successful, for instance in the United States to reduce the use of ozone depleting chemicals.

The emphasis in the Kyoto treaty on rich countries gaining permits to continue polluting by paying poor countries to maintain forests as so-called carbon 'sinks' is likely to prove a serious mistake. It ignores the fact that CO_2 levels have risen so much despite the existence of forests. While forests currently absorb a lot of CO_2, their ability to do so depends on them continuing to grow. Global warming will cut rainfall in many areas. This will kill many trees, which instead of absorbing CO_2 will then release it into the atmosphere as they rot.[9]

There is no alternative to conserving fuel and switching to renewable energy, to prevent the CO_2 getting into the atmosphere in the first place. Doing otherwise would be a betrayal of future generations.

Western governments should urgently give developing countries substantial help to preserve their forests, and plant suitable trees in arid areas to prevent the spread of deserts. As well as keeping CO_2 out of the atmosphere, healthy forests help to prevent flooding. In many poor countries at present, forests are being cleared for agriculture and for fuel, thus worsening droughts and leading to soil erosion.

Besides helping to cut CO_2 levels somewhat, tropical forests should also be preserved because they contain thousands of unstudied plants, many of which are likely to be of great value. One in four of the medicines we use, including the contraceptive pill, are derived from tropical forest plants. These medicines sell for over $30 billion annually. Experts calculate that the drugs waiting to be discovered from forest plants could be worth a staggering $147 billion. Scientists estimate that given the worldwide rate of destruction of the natural environment, three animal or plant species are made extinct every hour. Will we humans be able to maintain our self-respect if our species continues to decimate so many of the plants and animals whose world we share? Given the huge losses we stand to suffer, and the richness we gain from our love of nature, it is vital that we assert ourselves to protect the few remaining unspoilt parts of the world.

As the United States has refused to ratify even the minimal Kyoto measures, how can politicians be persuaded to take the radical steps required? Campaigns such as 'Stop Esso' could potentially have a significant impact. Exxon Mobil (known in Europe as Esso) is not only the world's largest oil company, but was also one of George W. Bush's biggest backers in his presidential campaign. Unlike other large oil companies, it is investing 'virtually nothing' in developing non-polluting fuels. It pays for propaganda to try and undermine the evidence of the causes of global warming. Polling showed that the campaign in Britain succeeded in getting one driver in twenty to boycott Esso within its first fourteen months, at which point half of the remainder polled said they would begin to do so. A boycott on this scale is easily large enough to cut the company's profits substantially, telling both it and Bush that unless they take global warming seriously they stand to lose considerable support.[10] At the same time motorists are reminded that reducing their mileage will help save the planet for the next generation. 'Stop Esso' is already well-established in Germany, Britain, Norway, Canada, the United States and New Zealand. Such campaigns help make complacent politicians more receptive to the need to cut global warming. In Chapter Six I discuss other ways in which ordinary people can exercise more political power to achieve a sustainable and harmonious society.

The responsibility of global warming for causing climatic disasters is becoming known to ever-increasing numbers of people throughout the world. As the major country spurning the Kyoto process, America's government and citizens will be blamed. For instance, many Bangladeshi Muslims may be attracted to Islamist terrorism as more and more of their low-lying country is lost to the sea. Vicious reprisals are likely to target innocent Americans as well as the guilty government and business leaders.

Certain charities are taking action to avert environmental problems. Some are having great success in promoting contraception to help people in poor countries. World population is expected to grow by 50 per cent in the next half century. Even if resources were shared more equally, this increase would still pose a severe threat to the environment. The more population growth can be slowed, the less likely tropical forests are to be destroyed by people desperate to grow food. If we fail to help poor countries develop, and also moderate their population growth, the wealthy nations will face increasing numbers of illegal immigrants fleeing from poverty aggravated by drought, soil erosion, or flooding. Some Western citizens will resent the minimal resources devoted to these immigrants, and perpetrate violence towards them. A few environmental refugees will turn to violence to try and improve their situation. This is a recipe for serious conflict.

Pollution causes illness

Investing money in cutting pollution will also preserve our health. Global warming is aiding the spread of pests and bacteria which cause disease, our resistance to which is being weakened by overuse of antibiotics by farmers and doctors. Research has estimated that up to 20,000 Americans may die each year due to residues of agricultural pesticides in food or water. Intensive chemical agriculture also causes soil erosion. Excessive use of agricultural chemicals should either be banned, or discouraged by imposing taxes on them in order to make good the harm they cause. This would give farmers an incentive to grow organic food, which would then become cheaper.

Research shows that air pollution, much of it brought about by vehicles, causes 6 per cent of all deaths. In the first half of 2001, 25 major American cities had air which breached federal quality standards. Pregnant women living near main roads are at increased risk of having babies with heart defects.[11]

The higher rates of leukaemia among children living on the edge of towns may be due to their exposure to pollution during the longer car journeys they make. Drivers sitting comfortably in their cars seeing cyclists wearing masks should be aware that car pollution is worse *inside the car*, especially in traffic jams. Because of car pollution, the disease we know as hay fever is now more common in the city than in the country!

Despite new roads opening, many journey times have actually doubled in the past decade, while trends suggest congestion itself will double over the next 14 years. Already American congestion costs a massive $74 billion annually.[12] Therefore it is vital to improve public transport and give motorists much greater incentives to use it.

Cocooned in the car?

Cars bear considerable guilt for global warming, emitting *25 times* more CO_2 per passenger mile than trains. Reliable, safe and inexpensive public transport, funded partly by increases in petrol tax, would discourage excessive car use. Disabled people and country dwellers would need to be compensated for the increased price of petrol, as public transport is less convenient for them.

Large petrol tax rises will be needed to entice drivers out of their traffic jams. The time that the average American driver is delayed by congestion has nearly tripled since 1982, to 45 hours each year. Yet the number of Americans who drive to work has increased greatly, and their average journey length has grown by over a third since 1983.[13] In 1999 less than a quarter of Britons said that doubling the price of petrol would reduce their car use. In 1999 and 2001 only a third said that improved public transport would encourage them to drive less. Britons' attachment to their cars persists despite their understanding of the toxic gas they emit; more than half, including no doubt a high proportion of drivers, agree that car exhaust fumes are a 'very serious cause of air pollution'.

Politicians should remember their duty to future generations, and explain why it is right to cut car use. In the medium and long term the price of petrol *does* influence the amount people drive, as the much greater mileage of Americans compared to Europeans shows.[14] Increases in petrol tax stimulate car manufacturers to improve fuel efficiency and thus cut emissions. They have had little incentive to do so in America, as petrol has remained relatively cheap. As a result the average American new car is no more fuel-efficient now than in the mid-1980s, with Sports Utility Vehicles (SUVs) doing only 13 miles per gallon. Petrol tax rises can be partly offset by cuts in other taxes, to protect those on low incomes, while the remaining revenue should be invested in improving public transport. It is absurd that America's SUVs enjoy tax subsidies, due to being wrongly classed as commercial vehicles. And yet, contrary to popular belief, their drivers are more likely to die in an accident than drivers of ordinary cars are. While many people are fond of their SUV, it is important that they understand the harm they will cause our children and grandchildren by accelerating global warming.[15]

In 1995 the then British Transport Minister Steven Norris sympathised with drivers who prefer their car, saying

> You have your own company, your own temperature control, your own music, and don't have to put up with dreadful human beings sitting alongside you.

A month later Mr Norris said that he had received many letters from motorists agreeing with him. Many Americans have a similar view; nearly half agree that 'driving is my time to think and enjoy being alone'. In addition the possession of their own car is an ego boost for many people, mostly men. Some identify with the power of the car, as if it was their shield on the unruly roads. Such drivers often admire their own car in a way that they do not admire many other potentially admirable things around them. This may be largely because they experience owning it as a mark of achievement. Those who command public respect should set an example in helping us love our environment more than our cars. Measures to encourage car sharing, such as exist in Los Angeles, should be extended.

The belief of many drivers that there are 'dreadful human beings' on public transport may be due partly to snobbery. But nearly a third of people avoid public transport because they fear being attacked. Many women who can afford to drive do so partly because they feel unsafe on public transport and on the street. Thuggish behaviour on trains and stations is much more likely when there are no staff present. Given the substantial costs, in benefits and lost taxes, of maintaining unemployed people, it would make sense to employ more people to ensure order on public transport, and provide a reassuring presence for those who might otherwise travel by car.

Other fairly modest measures could make public transport more popular. In the Canadian city of Calgary there is a telephone number corresponding to each bus stop. One can ring the number for one's local stop and be told by a computerised system exactly when the next bus is due to arrive there. The system uses sensors on each bus stop which note the time when the bus passes. The traveller can thus arrive at the bus stop just before the bus. This gives public transport the convenience drivers want, without the stress of having to find a parking place.

It will be the younger generation who will suffer most from global warming. They will need the ability to co-operate if they are to surmount the problems it will pose. In the next chapter I explain how we can nurture the generosity and resilience they will need to repair the environment, and build a fairer society. I also describe how family life can be made less stressful, and more fulfilling.

Chapter 3
Confident Parents, Secure Children

It is preferable to avoid phrases such as she/he. Therefore when gender is not a relevant factor, and I am referring to a child and parent as an example of a certain point, I will designate the child to have one sex, and the parent the other.

Parents and children: stress or fun?

Once when I was about eight, my father and I were playing catch. We enjoyed throwing the ball to each other really hard. He drew back his arm like lightning, then hurled the ball with a groan of great power. I expected a supersonic throw, only to collapse in laughter as the ball floated gently towards me. He grinned at his trick, making me laugh even more.

Some of us have enjoyed warmth and affection like this with our parents. All of us have been deeply influenced by certain crucial incidents with them, whether for better or worse. The quality of these events gradually shapes one's outlook, creating expectations that life and people will be either more, or less, kind, stressful, empty, or cruel. In this chapter I will show how children of all ages and their parents can have a more relaxed and enjoyable time together, thus giving the children a positive approach to life.

Nowadays few parents live near relations who are able to help them with their children on a regular basis. Therefore it is understandable that many find their constant responsibility for child care causes stress and irritation. Over half of parents say they sometimes lose their temper and 'go over the top' with their child. I have done so, and know how upsetting it is. This chapter contains ideas which will interest parents, and those who are concerned about how adults are affected by their childhood. I offer these ideas in the belief that most of all the individual parent needs understanding, especially from her- or himself. Theories which encourage a parent to strive for perfection cause pointless stress. Parents enjoy a better relationship with their child when they give due consideration to their own needs as well as those of the child.

One of the best accounts of a happy family includes comments by the children, once they had become young adults, reflecting on their upbringing. One stressed that because her parents had respected her and her siblings, they had 'found it easy' to respect the rights of their parents. She and her sisters are very fond of each other. This contrasts sharply with the cool or superficial relationships of most adult siblings. Having each been loved by parents who gave them maximum choice in all aspects of life, they grew up with exceptionally good relationships with each other. As they learned to expect love and fairness from their parents, they had no reason to fear that the arrival of a sibling would dilute their parents' love for them. Having received frequent kindness, they became generous themselves, lacking the selfishness of those who begrudge caring for others as few people have cared for them. They thus acquired the inclination to love others. When aged two, one of the girls climbed on to the bed where her newborn sister lay. Without anyone telling her 'to be gentle or careful':

> For twenty minutes she sat there visibly overflowing with love, saying most tenderly 'nice baby', and bending down to kiss and stroke Jonquil with a tenderness which had to be seen to be believed.

Such loving sibling relationships spring from the self-respect and love of life these children were given by their parents. The latter believed that children naturally behave decently and considerately provided parents trust them, and restrict them only as is necessary to ensure their welfare and that of others. The mother and father evidently supported each other closely in bringing up the children. The way they treated each other showed the children that a loving relationship is precious and enriching.[1]

The relationship between parent and child can potentially bring great joy to each. If in the critical early years our parents are generally loving, and balance our needs fairly with theirs, we will probably be happy and generous, both as child and adult. But if their love is too inconsistent, we are likely to be anxious. If they are emotionally distant, our adult relationships will probably lack real intimacy and trust. Recent research has shown that how we remember and evaluate our childhood relationship with our parents influences how positively we relate as adults to our children, spouse, and parents. (See pp. 74–5 below) Receiving too little parental warmth in childhood tends not only to erode the ability to find true intimacy as an adult, but also can permanently raise vulnerability to stress, as outlined below. However, understanding our parents' shortcomings can give us the hope and self-confidence to make relationships which meet our deep needs for intimate acceptance. We can change the effects of childhood on our personality, as I describe below.

Some people say that they have not been influenced by their parents. One such woman had cultivated a sophisticated and witty personality, but eventually could not escape feelings of loneliness and emptiness. She realised that while she had hidden her true self in response to her mother's cold behaviour, she did actually need an intimate and accepting friend. She was then able to outgrow her self-sufficient facade and establish an open, sharing relationship.

In this chapter I will outline how society, through organisations in which any of us can take part, can help at relatively little expense to improve parent–child relationships, and thus promote social harmony and justice.

Children are our future

The quality of childhood is vital to the future of society. We all need children to grow up with sufficient creativity and responsibility to keep our communities and economy healthy. Now that birth rates have fallen and the population of Western countries is set to decline, tax revenue from a falling number of workers will need to support a rising number of pensioners. This potential labour shortage underlines the need to improve our children's education, so that as many as possible gain the skills society needs. Half of secondary school children lack motivation, and between a tenth and a sixth are seriously disruptive. Nearly a fifth of children aged 5 to 15 suffer long-standing illness. Around a third of teenagers suffer moderate to severe depression.

Young people also need to grow up to be honest and democratically active in order that our government and civil service are not in corrupt hands. As we get older, we will become increasingly conscious of our need for reliable young people to work as nurses and doctors to care for us when we become ill, and police officers to maintain order fairly. Unless children's families give them self-confidence and enthusiasm, they are likely to grow up resentful, apathetic, or criminal. I will describe how reducing parents' stresses would improve the younger generation's contribution to society.

There is extensive evidence that the quality of children's relationships with their parents and other close relatives has a large impact on whether or not they grow up to be responsible adults. The importance of children's early years has been recognised for centuries; for instance in the famous claim of the Jesuits that if they had charge of a boy for his first seven years, they could shape his adult personality. While the Jesuits operated a systematic programme to implant their values, parental influence is great even in disorganised families. This is because children's survival depends on their ability to form strong attachments to their parents.

Crucial evidence is now accumulating that if parents and carers do not respond with sufficient care and affection to a baby's physical and emotional needs in the vital first few months, this permanently harms brain development. It increases the production of stress hormones, and renders the brain less able both to alleviate stress, and to experience pleasure. Illnesses including depression and post-traumatic stress disorder have shown how our emotions cause illness, whose chemical effects on the brain can be measured. Studies which tracked children from babyhood to age five have now underlined that their brain chemical levels are the effects, rather than the causes, of emotion. Moreover research has shown that the way individual parents treat their children, whether appropriate or inappropriate, tends to persist over long periods of time.[2]

Therefore society has a vital interest in ensuring that parents have the necessary support and commitment to help their children learn that a fulfilling life can best be achieved through friendly co-operation and loving relationships. As parents are their first role models, children generally copy whichever parental behaviour seems the best way of coping with life. If they feel disappointed or under-valued by their parents, they may adopt other, less suitable, role models. Unfortunately parents' morale is often low nowadays. Studies consistently find that on average parents are more dissatisfied than childless couples with their marriage. As many as a fifth of parents say they obtain no pleasure at all from time spent with their children.[3]

Childhood, however, can enrich the life of anyone who is open to its magic. One mother said she had had 'hundreds' of special moments with her young daughter, most of which were 'precious beyond words', including hearing her laugh, and seeing her and her father asleep together. If we can step beyond a world-weary absorption with our bills, waistlines, or career prospects, and share the wonder of the young child, we can re-enter a sensual world of awesome sights and joyful sounds. My neighbours' car bears the sticker 'Had I known grandchildren were so much fun, I'd have had them first!' Whether as grandparent, aunt, uncle, or cousin, we have the chance to share the fun of hide-and-seek, or feel the warmth of a small sleepy head on our lap. Parents can also gain these joys if they can free themselves from the excess anxiety they suffer today.

Valuing parenthood

A father complained that his teenage children avoided his company, recalling that when they had been keen to play with him in earlier years he had been too busy. Like many other such fathers he has probably realised his loss rather too late. He may never be able to share the deep gratitude of parents who treasure a close relationship with their adult children. Such a relationship is the culmination of parental warmth and commitment. We can see its beginning in infancy:

> One day her bright, interested face suddenly lights . . . She smiles and in that magic moment you feel warmed, and rewarded in full measure, for all the work and worry, stress and exhaustion of her first weeks . . . you will love that smiling face more than you have ever loved anything before.[4]

From a happy start like this, the securely loved child will develop a deep affection for her parent, which can arouse the parent's playfulness. I remember feeling privileged that my son liked to share our game of jumping down into my arms from a wall. His trust, and enjoyment of my company, gave me many treasured moments.

What interferes with parents developing such a close relationship with their children? As with so many other aspects of life, our expectations shape our experience. Probably the most influential expectation of parenthood in our culture is that of Dr Spock whose *Baby and Child Care* has been read by over 40 million people:

> child rearing is a long, hard job . . . At best, there's lots of hard work and deprivation . . . [including] preparing the proper diet, washing clothes, . . . stopping fights and drying tears.

Another best-selling book for parents has a similar view, saying that while motherhood has its pleasures, it is repetitive, tedious, wearing, and extremely demanding. [5] Clearly parenting does involve considerable effort, and a radical change in lifestyle. It is much more onerous in modern society, now that the extended family gives parents much less assistance and company in caring for their children than in previous years. Parents should be encouraged to respect their own needs, and try to strike a balance in attending both to their own, and to their children's needs. But parenthood need not be tedious deprivation. If we are confident we can enjoy our children at least some of the time, we can find fulfilment as parents. Deborah Jackson tells how her happiness in the company of her baby enabled her 'to enjoy ordinary, everyday jobs for the first time'.[6]

Like any commitment, parenthood has some aspects which in themselves are uninteresting. However, viewing washing clothes and preparing food as *work* merely ensures we will find those tasks boring. Every lifestyle has its drawbacks. But if we can arrange our commitments to allow some regular time for pursuits we enjoy, this can enable us to accept those aspects of our life we would not have chosen. Being able to look forward to regular pleasures enables us to tolerate chores and frustrations.

This attitude helps us to focus not on the fact that it takes hours to do mundane tasks, but on the fact that we do them to promote our children's well-being, both now and in the future. Having confidence that one's children will grow up to be worthwhile people also helps parents to find meaning in these tasks. In addition, having a loving confidante is vital in helping a parent feel a valuable person in their own right, and therefore feel supported and motivated in the parent role.

Reflecting on parenthood and childhood

In order to achieve a happy life for all the family parents need most of all to reflect on their own attitudes towards parenting. How much we regard the tasks of parenting as tiresome or frustrating depends a great deal on the pattern of parent–child relationships we have grown up with and come to regard as typical. This pattern varies considerably throughout the world. Children and their parents have much more positive and enjoyable experiences in some societies than others. Ronald Rohner analysed reports of parent–child relationships in 101 diverse societies worldwide. He found that the more parents treat their children with warmth and affection, the more generous and emotionally stable are the adults, and the less hostile and attention seeking the children, in that particular society.[7] There are several descriptions and surveys of certain pre-industrial societies in which babies are carried practically all the time, fed whenever they wish, and, because their needs are met so promptly, very rarely cry.[8]

Many Western parents would fear such treatment would cause children to grow up spoilt and demanding, unable to tolerate frustration. On the contrary, children in such societies are sociable and co-operative, and show very little of the aggression to other children we in the West consider natural. It is striking that these particular societies are free from the jealousy and friction between siblings which is so common in industrial society. Both in childhood and adulthood, people in these societies have learned that children's friendly and reasonable nature stimulates caring and enjoyment in adults. Consequently when they become parents they have positive expectations of the role and are able to respond generously and happily to their children. These societies' experience is relevant to us; they are not isolated exceptions. Fears of spoiling children are absent in nearly all pre-industrial societies.

Parenting behaviour is influenced not only by social attitudes, but also by the expectations the parent learned from their own childhood. Even when parents have decided not to repeat certain of their own parents' unwise actions, they often find themselves unintentionally treating their children in the same way, especially when under stress.[9]

Careful reflection on the feelings the role of parent evokes is necessary to avoid this. A parent usually needs an emotionally supportive relationship to gain the confidence to think deeply about this issue. By reflecting on how they felt during the most memorable incidents of their childhood, parents can judge which aspects of their parents' behaviour made them feel secure and confident. In this way they can gain insight into their own children's perspective on the everyday issues which affect children surprisingly deeply.

While parental behaviour has a crucial impact on children, parents do not deserve the guilt they often direct towards themselves. Guilt tends merely to sap confidence, arouse anxiety or anger, and impair the ability to seek help from others. Parents deserve goodwill and understanding, and it is in society's interests they are given it.

Some parents who are aware that parental influence is strong aim to be extremely considerate towards their child. If they attempt to meet all their child's wants while neglecting their own desires, eventually this will cause too much stress. Some parents have learned how to avoid problems by refusing certain inappropriate requests, but doing so in a sympathetic way which shows the child that they understand how he feels. This helps to prevent the child feeling rejected, and by reminding him of the parent's concern enables him to learn to tolerate a degree of frustration.

Some people underestimate parents' influence on their children, and suggest that children's genetic inheritance determines both the way their parents treat them, and the type of adults they grow up to be. Later I discuss the evidence, which suggests that the impact of parenting on the child is considerable, and derives from the parent's emotional history. Studies of twins show that attachment security often varies from one twin to the other, indicating that genes are far from being the only factor, and parental treatment does have an important effect. Many children adopted in infancy have been studied, with a view to comparing the impact on their development of their genetic inheritance with that of their adoptive upbringing. However recent evidence mentioned above shows that distress in the early months of life is likely to cause long-term harm to the brain's ability to withstand stress. This suggests that the adoption studies have underestimated the effect on babies of parental treatment in the crucial period before adoption, including that in the womb, such as alcohol or drug use.[10]

If we reflect briefly on the much greater capability of an adult compared to a baby, we can see why babies are ill-equipped to withstand parents' influence. Some have suggested that babies have abilities enabling them to bring forth good care from their parents. They can cry in a way which makes their parents attend to their needs because they find the crying irritating and therefore wish to stop it. Babies can smile in a way which stimulates parents' fondness. It is likely that evolution selected these abilities because they aid infant survival by increasing the likelihood of good parenting. But they are not enough to overcome the negative view of babies which often causes parental care in industrial society to be somewhat reluctant, and variable in quality. There are many ways in which parents can distance themselves physically or emotionally from the baby's care-seeking behaviour. They may agree with the belief that too much or too prompt attention spoils the baby. They can distract themselves from the baby's crying by going into another room, watching television, getting someone else to mind the baby, or having a drink. In contrast babies cannot distract themselves from their needs for parental care. They cannot tell the time and judge from previous experience how long it will be before the parent will feel ready to meet their needs. Unlike the adult, they cannot travel to seek help from other people, and anyway have no language with which to ask for it.

Can babies be spoilt?

Many parents are delighted when their baby is born, and look forward to finding fulfilment in their caring role. However once they come face to face with the reality of baby care, they nearly all find the experience much less agreeable than they expected. Their hidden fears about the baby resurface to trouble them.[11] They worry that unless they regulate the baby's demands it will never settle into a routine.

The common fear that parents may find a baby's crying intolerable is revealed by a congratulations card for new parents showing a baby whose head lacks eyes but consists almost entirely of a huge open mouth. The baby's screaming is creating visible vibrations, and its decibel level is being measured by an anxious man from the Noise Abatement Society. A Royal Mail ad echoed the usual assumption that babies cry too much, showing earplugs being sent to some new parents along with a congratulations card. Even seeing a crying baby on video has been shown to make parents feel irritated and raise their blood pressure. Speaking to parents both personally and professionally over many years, I have encountered on numerous occasions the belief that children's ordinary behaviour is often not a sign of need, but a demand which will escalate if 'indulged', in keeping with the dictum 'Give 'em an inch, and they'll take a yard'. Dr Spock reinforces this common fear of children's insatiable 'demands'. The fear of the effect of 'over-indulging' children is shown by a postcard depicting two parents being deafened by sound coming from a 'playroom'. The caption reads

Insanity is hereditary – you get it from your children'.

When parents find that a crying baby is neither hungry, nor needs her nappy changing, but ceases crying when picked up, this is taken as a sign not that the child needs human contact, but that she is well on the way to becoming spoilt. But in fact babies can state their needs only by crying. One writer reminds us how dependent babies are by asking us to imagine how we would feel if we were paralysed and unable to speak due to a stroke. We would soon become desperate. But we tend not to realise how close a baby is to despair if left to cry for a while, as we rarely compare the baby's frustrations with our own. If our activities do not go according to plan, we can speak to our friends, get our feelings off our chest, and discuss what to do. We can work out what the future holds. Babies do not have these options. Lacking any systematic memories with which to interpret the lack of parental response, they can only persist in crying.

Evolution has equipped babies with a fear of solitude, and with the instinct to cry for parental contact, because in the environment in which humans evolved solitude could lead to being eaten by a leopard. Hence a solitary baby may cry desperately as for all she knows, she may be crying for her very life. It is important to spare her this distress, which if repeated regularly must make the world seem a frightening place and lead to an anxious outlook.

As parents wish their children's development towards greater independence to be accelerated, babies' desires are often felt to be excessive, and child rearing considered a 'tedious' job. One example of this is that many parents devote considerable effort to 'toilet training' children when they are slightly too young. Because children feel pressured or confused by their parents' instructions about an issue whose importance they cannot yet understand, they tend to become either resistant or anxious about it. The transition from nappies to using the toilet is achieved painlessly both in societies which have greater confidence in children maturing at their own pace, and in families I have interviewed which trust their infants to exercise autonomy responsibly. But in a great many families in industrial society the process causes a lot of stress.

The desire to speed the child's progress away from dependence on its parents leads to certain aspects of parental caring being seen not as warm and pleasurable, but as restricting the parent's freedom. For instance a mother who was anxious that her 2-month-old daughter should sleep longer thought that stopping breast feeding would achieve this. She said to the baby 'this is *my* body, just have your bottle, OK.' Her expectation was that the baby would make excessive demands on her, either by keeping her awake or by wanting to be breastfed. Like so many parents in our society, she lacked confidence in the baby's normal gradual progress towards maturity, one aspect of which is waking at night less often. Therefore she was over-anxious to speed up the process. Hence she seemed to experience the link between herself and her baby, represented by breastfeeding, as draining. She was unable to be truly welcoming towards her baby, and therefore did not experience the 'tremendous satisfaction' so many mothers have gained from breastfeeding.

As babies' instincts require them to be confident of their parents' commitment not to leave them alone, a baby whose experience has led her subconsciously to feel this commitment may be lacking wakes regularly to check her parents are still present. This is an example of the many vicious circles in parenting:

1. The mother considers the baby likely to be too demanding.
2. Therefore she tries to limit the baby's demands.
3. Because of the mother's limitation strategy the baby doubts her commitment.
4. The baby becomes anxious and therefore makes more demands to seek reassurance.

It is clear that child-rearing in modern industrial society departs radically from the pattern which was typical of human life until relatively recently. From a sample of 37 societies worldwide, in only 2 were babies weaned from the breast or bottle as early as American babies.[12] Mothers who breast feed for longer than most feel pressured to stop. As we lack confidence in our children's natural capacity to mature in their own time, we worry about whether they are reaching their milestones by the average age. This anxiety is heightened by mothers' common fear that if their child is behind other children in his development, other people will consider this due to their maternal shortcomings. Anxiety that one's child may not be progressing at the appropriate pace appears to be absent in cultures such as those described above which respond to expressed infant need unreservedly. When asked if they ever worried about how soon their babies would learn to walk, a group of women in the sub-Himalayan province of Ladakh were most amused, saying that of course babies learn to walk when they are ready.

Civilising children?

A study of Texan parents helps us to understand the origin of our parenting problems. The researcher found that the more a parent held a negative view of human nature, the more they emphasised a desire to accelerate the development of the child, restrict its autonomy, and retain parental authority.[13] From this perspective a child needs to be trained; otherwise he will be disobedient, demanding, and immature.

Such a view is evident in our society in many ways. Even children as young as twelve months are smacked by nearly two-thirds of mothers when their actions are considered 'naughty'.[14] We speak of certain babies being fed 'on demand' (i.e., not according to a time schedule), rather than on request, as if a baby's cry for food was inherently impolite. The age during which older toddlers assert their desire for autonomy is commonly known as the 'terrible twos.' A TV special on parenting began with a sketch of a judge sentencing a couple to '18 years of parenthood'. The influence of this image of children is also shown by the way we expect adolescents to be moody and troublesome. Pre-industrial societies rarely see adolescents in this way.

The year during which the child is two acquired the adjective 'terrible' because children are generally considered to be very disobedient at that age. Two careful studies observing the behaviour of children aged 2 with their parents found that parents exercise control over the child's actions on average about every two minutes (in one study), or every six to eight minutes (in the other). The child's actions parents most commonly stopped (or aimed to stop) were playing with or potentially damaging objects, and also talking, annoying the parent, interfering with the parent's activity, and potentially dangerous behaviour.[15] In these studies, and another of several different cultures throughout the world, the more parents tried to control their child, the less often the child obeyed.[16]

It is striking that parents in our society subject themselves to the continual hassle of frequent confrontations with their children. If we think about how frustrating it would feel to be told to curtail one's actions at least every eight minutes, we can see why more frequent control attempts lead to less obedience. It is hardly surprising that children of two have temper tantrums when their actions are interrupted so often.

I have observed toddlers playing in a wide range of different homes and repeatedly been surprised that parents seem to require children who are just beginning to explore their surroundings to exercise incredible restraint. They are surrounded by all manner of novel, and therefore potentially fascinating objects, most of which they are not allowed to touch. Very few parents appear to have thought about the situation from the child's point of view and realised that it is a lot less frustrating both for child and parent if the parents alter the home somewhat so that most of the objects the child is not allowed to touch are out of reach. As the child would not encounter these objects they would not distract her, and she would have plenty of other things to explore.

Instead parents feel that they have the right to organise and enjoy their home in the way they wish. They also believe that children should learn that they are not to touch others' possessions. But they impose this view on toddlers when they are too young either to understand the nature of property and the fragility of common objects, or to tolerate the frustration caused by such frequent demands for restraint. As adults, we would not place ourselves in a situation where we had to refrain from doing something we wished so often. Because we are accustomed to freedom of movement, we overlook the fact that the toddler cannot say 'Well, if you don't want me to touch your things, I'll go out', or 'I'll go to my room'.

Part of the reason that very few parents consider this issue is that the 'need' to check small children's actions so frequently is taken for granted due to the negative view of human nature through which the child is seen. Deep down most parents believe it is not in the young child's nature to be considerate to others.

Can children be trusted?

Parents can avoid the stress of having to supervise and restrain their toddlers constantly. Experience shows that children who have been subject to a minimum degree of restriction obey immediately on the occasions when their parents find it necessary to issue an instruction.[17] If young children are trusted by being given freedom of movement, they are able to use their judgement to avoid hazards, as shown by the daughter of a mother I interviewed. This girl had been allowed to climb the stairs as soon as she could crawl and had never fallen. She is one of a number of children I have known whose families gave them considerable autonomy, while teaching them not to do anything dangerous or anti-social.

These children's carefulness should not surprise us. Our species evolved close to predatory animals, and therefore infants are genetically equipped with the drive to stay near enough to their parents to avoid danger. Observations of infants aged about 15 to 30 months in parks found that in general, 'in spite of the opportunities for wandering', most kept a regular eye on their mother and did not go too far from her. The difference between the acceptable behaviour of most toddlers in parks, and parents considering it necessary to check them so regularly at home, is that in parks there are few hazards, and little the toddler can damage. However in the adult-structured home environment it is much harder for the toddler to stick for long to parental requirements.

Another example of infants' caution was provided by an experiment which showed that babies could not be persuaded to crawl onto a sheet of very thick glass spanning what appeared to be a sheer drop. Tiny children placed in the shallow end of a walk-in swimming pool take care not to venture out of their depth.[18] In those pre-industrial societies which give small children greater freedom, they very soon learn to be cautious towards hazards such as fire. But if children are frustrated by being regularly reprimanded at home, and kept on a very short rein elsewhere, they may become so rebellious that their instinctive caution is overridden by recklessness.

Restricted children become troublesome

Nevertheless we can sympathise with the view of children as being egocentric and needing close supervision, because like so many aspects of life, it tends to become a self-fulfilling prophecy. Early parental restriction does not lead to peace as children get older. At least half of the parents of children aged 9 to 10 and 13 to 14 say they discipline them either every day, or two to three times weekly. As young children are checked so much more frequently, their irritation makes them emotionally volatile. They seek attention from their parents as their ability to amuse themselves is stunted by their independent activities having been interrupted so often.

Young children usually have a strong desire to copy adult behaviour. If we can exercise a little planning and patience, we can give them the chance to find useful tasks such as sweeping and washing up enjoyable. Such children learn that any activity which gives one the opportunity to use one's physical skill can be pleasing. But if children learn that parents frequently stop them from doing what they choose to do, they are likely to view the tasks their parents want them to do as distasteful work.

Childhood freedom lost

Nowadays children lead much more regulated lives than they did in the early seventies, when two-thirds of English 7- to 11-year-olds were allowed to go out in the daytime without an adult. The chief reasons parents give for the much greater restrictions they place on their children today are traffic danger, the perceived risk of the child being molested, and the child being considered 'unreliable'. Yet research found that West German children were allowed out much more, but child pedestrians suffer fewer road accident deaths there. Contrary to parents' belief, the numbers of children being abducted, murdered, sexually abused, or hurt in car accidents, have fallen in recent years.[19] Parents are suffering undue levels of anxiety; in fact children are much more likely to be molested or killed by family members and friends than by strangers.

These restrictions seem not to teach children to exercise due caution when they are deemed independent. Road accident deaths are four times higher in the 15 to 19 age group than among the under-15s.

The increased need parents feel to restrict their children imposes an added workload on mothers. Once a norm has been established that children below a certain age do not go either to school or elsewhere alone, few parents can disregard it. They would be anxious about the risk, and worry subconsciously that others would consider them negligent. Hence children and parents are in each other's pockets excessively. This causes friction; over half of children object to these restrictions.

Youngsters need the chance to show sufficient responsibility to be given more freedom. Most child abductors exploit the ignorance or naivete, rather than the physical weakness, of the child. Attacks on children in public places are extremely rare. Bodies such as the police, schools, and youth organisations could help parents tremendously by running short courses for children aged ten upwards to teach them how to avoid potential hazards on the street. Children could achieve 'safety in numbers' by learning how to support each other and get help in the unlikely event of encountering a troublesome person. Paedophiles prefer a solitary child, so a pair of children are at even less risk. Children could be taught to warn each other if one was being careless of road safety. The prize of greater independence would give children a strong incentive to succeed on such courses.

Why are children demanding?

Certain parents find their children's demands excessive, but feel obliged to strive for the ideal of 'child-centred' parenthood. One such parent found it a relief to get away from her children by going to work. When she was at home, she felt she ought to be doing an activity with them all the time. She considered her children to be hard work, but felt guilty for thinking this. Because she was influenced by the Western view that children need considerable adult stimulation, she felt her children could drain her, and therefore gave them her attention with some reluctance. Unfortunately such children sense their parent's ambivalence. In order to reassure themselves of the extent of parental commitment, they often 'demand' attention, or substitutes for it such as gifts, thus increasing the parent's negative feelings about the child. If the parent does not meet the child's demand, the child may react to its weaker position by sulking or having a tantrum. Such tantrums reinforce the view of children as difficult and irrational.

One common way in which children either demand their parents' time, or frustrate their desire for peace, is defiant behaviour at bedtime. A survey of British parents found that nearly half had children who at least once in the previous week would not go to bed as instructed. Nearly a quarter of parents had this problem two or three times weekly. One in six Dutch children aged nine to fourteen has a sleep problem.[20]

I knew a child brought up by parents who did not share the common anxiety about getting children to sleep. The way he would play quietly, and then fall asleep effortlessly, often attracted visitors' comments. Throughout his childhood he was left to decide for himself when he needed to sleep, and was always awake in good time and full of energy the next morning.

Bedtime may be a particularly acute source of conflict due to our anxiety that children should as soon as possible outgrow certain 'demanding' or 'childish' behaviours, e.g. waking at night, and wanting to come into the parents' bed. It is probably stressful for small children to be alone at night. Their instinct to want their parents close to them is more acute at night when unseen dangers could be present. Consequently a fear of the dark may be better understood as a fear of solitude in the dark. A small baby crying urgently for its parent does not know that the parent will respond in due course. This anxiety naturally interferes with sleep, as it is unwise to sleep if danger may be nearby. In practically all pre-industrial cultures very young children have slept with their mothers, and older children with their siblings. Sudden Infant Death Syndrome, the medical term for 'cot death', is almost unknown in these cultures.

Given our society's departure from this standard practice, it is not surprising that poor sleep and reliance on sleeping tablets is so common among adults. What a contrast with one of the 'child-trusting' societies mentioned above, in which a group of hunters on safari were so confident of relaxing sleep that sometimes one would wake his companions in the night to tell them a joke. Having laughed, within a few seconds the whole group would fall asleep again.

The extent of a child's desire for parental attention may be determined by how freely that attention is given. As with the law of supply and demand, scarce or reluctantly given resources are sought more keenly. One couple who gave their children ample affection and autonomy usually spent most of the evening in a separate room from their children, once they were beyond infancy. The children did not disturb their parents' relaxation by demanding attention in the evenings, but felt free to join them when they had a particular wish to. Such a relationship is based on each generation having confidence that both parents and children are sensible, and that children's needs are reasonable and can be met without stress.

The amount of time parents spend actively caring for or playing with their children has nearly doubled in recent years, while the amount spent simply being with them in the same place has nearly halved. The increase in actual parent–child interaction has not led to a rise in family harmony. This may be partly because parents are more likely to be tired when with their children, given that many work long hours. When the child is with the parent again, after several hours apart, his heightened feelings may induce the parent to provide 'quality time' to quell any resentment at her absence. These strains magnify parents' tendency to feel their children's wants are insatiable. Hence they either play with them with a lack of enthusiasm which merely increases the children's desire for attention, try to train them to suppress their desires, or give them something else to 'keep them quiet'. Television is commonly used as a 'baby-sitter'. But it is no substitute for the parental interest which children come to crave if it seems scarce. Three out of five children feel that they do not see enough of their parents.[21] About one child in six is at home without an adult after school.

Parents' negative view of children, and children's consequent demandingness, undermine both parental warmth, and children's confidence in their parents. As a result more than a quarter of children aged 6 to 17 say they have no one in whom they feel able to confide.[22]

Does praise promote good behaviour?

Some parents believe they have solved the problem of children's excessive desire for attention. They feel it is obvious that if children are rewarded for good behaviour and reprimanded for bad behaviour, they will learn to fit in with others amicably. A common strategy is to praise the child when she behaves as the parents wish. Most parents focus far more on training young children to be obedient than on teaching the nature of considerate behaviour. They feel they must influence the child to obey them and refrain from wrong behaviour by using the sanction of parental disapproval: 'You're a very naughty boy', and the reward of approval: 'There's a good girl'. This remark reinforces the dependence of the child, as the parent has the power to reject him by deeming him 'naughty'. Thus the child learns that the way to be accepted is to do as the parent wishes, rather than learning directly to behave in a way which respects both other people's and his own needs.

When the child fails to behave as the parents wish and is either not praised, or is rebuked, his self-esteem is harmed. One parent eventually realised that regularly praising her daughter made the girl tense, feeling she had to behave excellently or the praise would cease. Such a child is almost bound at some level to resent the power her parents have over her through her dependence on their approval.

Parents may feel that they praise their child's good behaviour as part of their overall attempt to teach concern for others. But a child who has become dependent on parental approval to preserve her self-esteem may misbehave, but take care to hide her actions from her parents. She may deliberately get a younger sibling into trouble, subconsciously hoping to appear good in comparison. Some children who have become dependent on parental praise may be driven by anxiety to misbehave, subconsciously seeking reassurance that their parents will accept them even when they do not deserve praise. Other children become insincere, or selfishly devious.

Children respond much better when parents simply thank them, or mention briefly why they appreciated a helpful action, much as they would with another adult. By not making an overall evaluation of the child parents do not set themselves up as judges of his worth. They thus free him from anxiety about his merit in their eyes. Hence he is able to move his concern away from himself and reflect on the effect of his actions on others.[23]

Children need trust and understanding

Certain parents have learned from attending support groups how to stimulate more co-operative behaviour from their children. The key factor in this process is gaining confidence that children can be reasonable. However our culture is so steeped in the belief that young children tend to be irrational that parents easily become irritated when the child will not comply with what the parent considers a perfectly reasonable request. The reasons for this irritation usually go back to the parent's own childhood. When parents are faced with a distressed or demanding child, they are influenced by memories, often subconscious, of being unable to gain the sympathy or understanding of their own parents. The feelings of impotence from such occasions are evoked by being in a similar situation. Because these repressed emotions make parents feel very uncomfortable, they wish to eliminate the conflict with their child as soon as possible. Doing so prevents these distressing memories from becoming more than fleetingly conscious. Moreover the parent has learned the usual pattern of dismissive or irritated parental behaviour for such situations and almost automatically behaves much as her own parent did towards her.

Parents who have attended such support groups have been able to see how their irritation towards their child derives from similar encounters in their own childhood. Having gained a more understanding and positive view of children they have learned how to listen to their child when he is distressed and 'reflect' his emotions back to him by repeating the essence of what he has said or done. This comforts a distressed child as he can see that his parent understands what he is feeling and is willing to try and help. This enables the child to withstand disappointments, and avoids them leading to bad behaviour. A little boy became frustrated when he could not trace letters as neatly as he wished. His mother said that in similar situations, before she had attended the support group, she would have told him 'to snap out of it'. But once she started to acknowledge the reasons for his distress on these occasions, he was able to cease throwing things around in anger.[24]

Mothers' burdens

Parents' reluctance to indulge their children's 'demands' is understandable when we remember that the vast majority of their care falls upon the mother. The average American employed woman works more than 80 hours per week, both outside and inside the home. Most fathers are full time workers, working long hours. While many fathers devote quite a lot of time to child care and housework soon after their baby is born, their involvement soon declines. Research shows that nearly all employed mothers experience problems in combining their roles, and nearly half feel they have too little time for themselves.

Even if they all have very busy lives, mothers' personalities vary considerably, influencing how they feel about their situation.

For two weeks 49 mothers reported their mood five times daily, when prompted by a pager at random times. Both those mothers who had a stronger sense of self-acceptance, and those who felt more competent and satisfied as a mother, were most often happily involved in what they were doing.

Another factor which influences levels of happiness and energy is emotional support from others. Mothers of 1-year-olds who were visited monthly by a trained supportive 'community mother' were less likely to feel tired regularly than other similar mothers. One mother I interviewed had gone through a long period during which she lacked energy and was very isolated, but some time after joining a support group she became much more active, despite having had a second child by that time. While mothers' tiredness derives partly from the work they do, the evidence overall suggests that the extent of tiredness is influenced by a range of stress factors, particularly social and emotional isolation. This can also cause severe distress; children are more likely to be assaulted at times when only one parent is present.

In view of the distress caused by isolation, it is not surprising that the children of families which have the least social contact have the highest rate of school problems and delinquency. The lack of adult company which so many mothers experience is another feature of our society's child-rearing arrangements which is unusual when compared to pre-industrial cultures. Out of a world sample of nearly two hundred such societies, in only four did the mother provide all or practically all the care for her infant, as is so often the case in modern industrial society.[25] In the lifespan of the human race, industrial society arranged into nuclear families is a very recent innovation. Centuries of evolution have shaped us to live in groups containing among others several mothers and their children. Observers of such societies describe how there are always people around keen to hold a friend or relation's baby.

In comparison most Western mothers have very little help with their children. One survey found that among non-employed mothers of children aged under twelve, only one in seven 'arrange regularly for a relative, friend or neighbour' to look after them. The scarcity of decent affordable housing often results in young couples needing to move some distance away from their relations. Consequently many parents lack local social support. A study of 50 married women, each with two or more children, reveals the prevalence of mothers' dissatisfaction. The researcher discussed with the women whether they enjoyed looking after their children in practice, and assessed whether they experienced a strong sense of meaning and purpose in doing so. If a woman had positive feelings on each of these criteria she was considered to be 'fulfilled' in her mothering role. On this basis less than two-fifths of the women were 'fulfilled'. Half were either ambivalent or 'alienated' in their mothering role. Another study found that only two-fifths of mothers had 'good' (rather than 'medium' or 'poor') feelings for their baby at five months. This evidence predicts a poor future for mother–child relationships. Babies of five months sleep a lot.[26] Most parents feel that they need much less attention then than when they become mobile. Therefore we would expect the proportion of mothers having 'good' feelings for their toddlers to be even less than the two-fifths who have 'good' feelings for their baby.

Father involvement is good for children

Rohner's worldwide survey of the effects of parental acceptance or rejection (see p. 47) found that mothers were warmer and more affectionate to their children in societies in which at least one other adult in the household was at home during the day. Children are treated with greater fondness and acceptance in societies in which fathers spend more time with them. An extensive survey of children in five diverse societies found that in each society children were more attention-seeking in nuclear than in extended families.[27] It seems likely this was due to attention from more than one adult being less frequent in nuclear families, as in our society. The difficulty of many parents in giving their children enough warmth and interest causes problems for us all. British children whose fathers took less interest in them at age 7 were more likely to have gained a criminal record by age 20. There is a higher rate of violent crime in societies in which fathers have little involvement with young children.[28]

A high proportion of children in Western society lack meaningful contact with their father. One quarter of children will experience the divorce of their parents before the age of 16, most of these before they are 10. Couples often end their marriage with great hostility or distress. Hence many fathers find that contact with their children and former wife leads to friction or brings back painful memories they prefer to avoid. This is a major reason why around half of divorced fathers lose contact with their children within 10 years of the separation.

Children from low-income families who lived with both their parents at least until leaving school had more successful lives at age 23 than similarly disadvantaged children from lone-parent families.[29] Why should children from two-parent families be more successful? Much writing on this point has largely failed to address the basic fact that single parents cannot have the energy of two people. I do not wish to criticise single parents: the vast majority are dedicated to their children. But it is important to recognise the stresses they face. Men in full-time employment spend 98 minutes per average day on domestic work. Having to get by without this labour is a strain for the single mother. If she decides not to go out to work so that she has more time for the children, or cannot earn enough to cover the cost of childcare, she has the added pressure of trying to manage on state benefits. This in itself involves additional work, for instance in repairing or making things which most employed parents would replace or buy. Not only does the single mother have all this physical work, she is also likely to feel burdened by having total responsibility for the family, particularly at difficult times.

Moreover single mothers have less support from their children's grandparents, who on average see their grandchildren less after a separation or divorce. Single mothers may also need to deal with conflict over how much contact the children and their father have with each other. Children often cause single mothers stress by agitating for the same possessions and treats as the children of dual-earner families. In view of these problems it is not surprising that more than twice as many single parents smoke as married parents of the same social class background, and that single parents tend to have poorer health.[30]

Therefore it would be remarkable if single mothers were able to give their children parenting as responsive and sensitive as that given by contented and united married couples. But those who make critical comments about single parents will not help unhappily married people to improve their marriages and avoid divorce. As with any anxiety-provoking issue, it is the offer of understanding assistance which best enables unhappy couples to tackle their problems constructively.

Transcending sex roles

A unique study of families, in which both parents had chosen to play a committed parenting role, found that their children were strongly attached to each parent, but had no anxiety about being looked after by other carers for certain periods. Such children's emotional security is deeper and more stable because it does not depend only or chiefly on one relationship. If all a child's emotional dependence rests on his relationship with his mother, he is almost bound to be disappointed regularly, for instance when his mother is tired or preoccupied with other concerns. But if he has learned that either parent can comfort him when he feels distressed, his confidence in being able to make a secure intimate relationship as an adult will be much greater.

Girls in these joint parenting families, compared to those in typical families, did not have envious or stereotyped ideas about what it would be like to be a boy. The boys, unlike boys in other families, had no negativity about girls when asked to imagine what life would be like as a girl. Many of these children, unusually for preadolescents, had strong friendships with children of the opposite sex. They probably held these attitudes because they had experienced the parent role being regarded by both their parents as no less important than the employment role. As they saw the parent of each sex having access to both roles, they had no need to regard themselves as belonging either to a dominant or a subordinate gender. Such children are less likely to suffer through denying some aspect of their personality in order to conform to restrictive roles.

Boys in families in which each parent undertakes a substantial share of the parental care are less prone to the pressure to define themselves as male by renouncing the desire for affection. They will be no less masculine; boys whose primary parent was their father were found to have a secure and confident male identity. Concern that a boy needs to be tough in order to hold his own in a competitive world is misplaced. This stereotype is largely to blame for males aged 15 to 24 having an accidental death rate four times higher than females of the same age.[31]

Giving parents time

A crucial issue which we need to clarify is who actually *wants* to spend time looking after children. The traditional sexual division of labour gives the mother practically all the worries of parenthood while isolating her in a situation in which other interesting opportunities are limited. Social contact for full-time mothers is even less available now that so many mothers work. Traditionally the father has most of the worries about 'providing' for the family. His ability to know his children well and enjoy their company is undermined by long hours of work, and the fact that the children often relate more closely to their mother.

If men and women could choose their work and parenting hours free from narrow sex roles, they would be more able to pursue them wholeheartedly, without the feelings of lost opportunities and excessive burdens. But due to social pressures many mothers feel that others would hold them in somewhat low regard if they were a full-time mother. As the traditional mother role is in decline, while men remain committed to full-time employment, we need policies to promote wholehearted parenting.

If full-time work becomes the norm for both mothers and fathers, this would probably not be in line with most parents' true wishes. Research shows that over the past two decades women have increased their working hours not through choice, but largely because they feel they need the money.[32] More than half of women say they 'define themselves by being a parent', while only one in seven say their career is very important to them.[33] Only about one in seven British women under 60 explicitly prefers the housewife role. However nearly all the remainder are not career-minded, and in recognition of the difficulty of combining both roles, opt to adapt themselves to a role focused primarily on their family.[34] Among women workers, part-timers have the highest levels of job satisfaction. Many women, even among those with high-status jobs, become disillusioned with employment, and consider caring for their children more 'real' and satisfying. Only one employed man out of four believes that his work commitments have *not* harmed his family life. Surveys show that most men see their own fathers as negative role models, wish to be more involved fathers themselves, and value time with their children very highly.

While women devote more than twice as much time to childcare as men, men's childcare time has increased substantially since 1975. Efforts to safeguard employment by cutting working hours, as described in Chapter One, and tax cuts for lower-paid workers, could reduce men's average working hours. Most countries now give part-timers the same employment rights as full-timers. These changes would all help couples to negotiate more equally and freely about how much parenting and employment each partner should undertake.

Not all views of women's equality require them to give employment priority over parenting. Although Dutch women's rate of employment is lower than that of similar countries, this did not stop them progressing towards equality before women in most other advanced nations.

There is little evidence that mothers' attitudes would be different if subsidised childcare were available. Research found that fewer than one in twenty British non-employed mothers of under-10s felt they were prevented from working by a lack of childcare.[35] Various studies show that after they have had a child, women largely follow the hopes they had beforehand, often conceived several years earlier, regarding whether or not they return to employment, and if so, whether full- or part-time. Their prior plans had much greater influence than their social class or their income.[36] Other British and Dutch studies also show that part-time work appears to be the favoured option among a large proportion of mothers.

Deciding whether to go out to work is difficult for many mothers as the question of the effects on children evokes such strong feelings. Research findings on the effects of out-of-home care on children are complex and inconsistent. This issue will not be clarified in an atmosphere of blame. Instead we should work for policies which give parents choices, but also recognise the needs of children, on which point accuracy and objectivity are required. The child's age, the quality of the day care, and the time spent in it all influence the effect on the child. Children's need for their father should also be considered. Research both from America and Britain shows that time spent with fathers helps improve children's education, as does time spent with mothers.

Children's welfare requires that we give as much attention to the factors which discourage parents who would like to care for their children at home, as to the quality of the care provided both by parents and paid carers. We also need to heed the view that full-time motherhood is boring. This isolation of so many parents could be reduced by establishing more social groups and community centres for families. Such centres would be a lifeline for many parents, and would help decrease the incidence of post-natal depression. First-time parents would have the chance to learn from the experience of parents of older children. Once established, such centres need not be expensive to run. Most of the labour would be supplied by the parents themselves. The centres would play a vital role in helping parents enjoy their role.

The ability to be a wholehearted parent could be fostered by increased government encouragement for maternity and paternity leave. The early months of a baby's life are a precious and influential period for the whole family. As described above, a birth often stimulates considerable anxiety about the baby, and tension or distance between the parents. Many more mothers would overcome these stresses and find fulfilment in caring for their baby if they knew they could look forward to several months off work in which to establish a strong relationship with the baby and an effective pattern of caring for him.

Governments should note that mothers of young children who had been employed 80 per cent of the time since giving birth were twice as likely to divorce as mothers who had not been in employment.[37] Better maternity pay could also reduce the much higher rate of premature birth among pregnant women working more than forty hours weekly. If women could expect an adequate period of reasonably paid maternity leave, fewer would work long hours during pregnancy.

Paternity leave is vital

As we have seen, caring for a new baby, especially a firstborn, without help, can be very stressful. The more this is so, the more parents begin to doubt that they can have a harmonious relationship with their baby. These feelings can lead to the baby increasingly being seen as encroaching on the parent's autonomy. State funded paternity leave could help a mother settle into motherhood by freeing the father to support and help her during the crucial early weeks. At this time maternal anxiety is often high. Mothers tend to be very tired, partly because they have not yet become accustomed to the baby waking at night. Many fathers tend to resent their partner's preoccupation with the new baby. This tension between the couple can increase the mother's anxiety and weaken her relationship with the baby. If fathers were off work the couple would have more time and energy for each other, and thus would be more able to experience caring for their new baby as a joint pleasure.

Few fathers take paternity leave in those countries where it is paid at a low rate. By contrast, three-quarters of Swedish fathers take the reasonably paid paternity leave available there. Those who had done so had a positive view of the experience. Four-fifths said they had 'liked caring for the child'. The same proportion said they would take paternity leave after the birth of any future child.[38] Men would be able to create a closer, more caring role towards their child if they could from the start perceive the baby positively, rather than as a noisy competitor for their partner's attention. Paid paternity leave would help in this regard. It is no accident that Swedish men, who have had the chance to take paid paternity leave longest, are more involved in the care of their children than men in other industrial countries. Paternity leave may yield other benefits: close involvement with their children has enabled men to become more patient and sensitive to the needs of other people in general.

The popularity of paternity leave shows that maximising their income is not parents' overriding priority. When Swedish mothers were asked about the likelihood of their taking parental leave for any future birth, the reduction in family income did not influence their decision. For Swedish men it had only a small impact, which was greatly outweighed by the degree to which the man had enjoyed caring for the baby during his paternity leave.

The younger generation appear to approve of fathers becoming more involved with child care. Of six hundred London children aged 13 to 16, two-thirds thought fathers should be able to take paid paternity leave. When asked if they were satisfied with the amount of time each parent had to talk with them, only three-fifths were satisfied in relation to their father.[39] By funding paid paternity leave society would be telling all fathers, especially those who would not contemplate taking annual holiday after the birth, that caring for their baby and its mother is a more important role for them at that time than any other.

The emotional upheaval of parenthood

Sheila Kitzinger has described how many first time mothers find their changed way of life a considerable shock, and often lack the support from more experienced mothers which most women in pre-industrial societies enjoy. Ann Oakley describes the 'trauma' of coming home to be mostly alone with a first baby. It is not merely having to adjust to caring for a baby's physical needs which is stressful: writers describe the 'storm of emotions a new baby evokes', which many mothers and fathers experience.[40] Women have powerful but dormant emotions of neediness and competitiveness, arising from their childhood relationship with their own mother. These are revived, and can confuse their feelings for the baby.

As many women find it hard to accept these negative emotions in themselves, they are unable to surmount them by expressing them in an insightful way. Such emotions are very hard to face as they derive from insecurities which arose in childhood but were not resolved. Their strength lies in their origin in the intensity of infant impotence. The infant has had too little time since birth to be able to build up systematic memories, and therefore when distressed is unable to foresee the ending of its distress and console itself thereby. If a small child felt she might lose her parents' care, for whatever reason, her complete inability to cope without them would cause panic. Anyone who remembers losing their parents briefly, for instance in a crowded place, will know what fear this causes. The emotions which are commonly awoken after becoming a mother are an unwelcome reminder of this childhood dependence, evoked by feeling responsible for the totally dependent baby.

Women whose parents could not respond sensitively enough to their needs when they were babies usually have a deep belief, conscious or subconscious, that babies cannot be satisfied. Alice Miller describes a woman who had felt that her first two babies were 'exploiting' her with their 'excessive demands', but felt guilty for thinking this. Years later she thought about how upset she used to feel as a girl when her mother went out, leaving her to look after her younger siblings. Though they cried, she never did:

> Who would have wanted a crying child? I could only win my mother's love if I was competent, understanding, and controlled, if I never . . . showed her how much I missed her.

Before she had her third child she realised that going out often, leaving her first two children, had been her subconscious attempt to avoid being reminded of her own childhood distress by her children's cries. Having resolved these feelings she was able to 'enjoy her unity' with her new baby.[41]

The belief that babies are very demanding sometimes arouses hostility to the baby. These are the words of a woman who felt she had never received loving care as a child:

> When my daughter used to cry and have tantrums I would think, Cry! Life is tough and unhappy, so cry like I did![42]

A woman who nearly lost her temper and injured her crying baby remembered at the crucial moment how annoyed she had been when her newborn sister had 'shown up out of nowhere, crying and crying'. It appears she had felt neglected in favour of her baby sister, although she had not previously recalled this. As she had not resolved these distressing feelings from childhood, her repressed anger had been reawakened by her own baby's cries. Another woman felt her parents had not wanted her enough when she was a girl, and that her mother had hoped she would be a boy. Becoming pregnant re-awoke both her need for emotional support, and her memory of lacking it during childhood. She felt extremely alienated by her husband and his relations wanting her to give birth to a boy, while appearing indifferent to her feelings. After she did have a boy, her husband seemed to value the baby more than her. She was devastated, and felt hatred towards the baby.[43]

A common way in which children suppress needs for a greater degree of adult acceptance and attention is to feel embarrassed or guilty about having such needs. This leads to a devaluing or unconscious avoidance of emotional intimacy in adulthood, and a reluctance or inability to attend sensitively to babies' needs for care and affection. Thus a woman whose mother had been unable to love her in childhood, due to chronic depression, became involved with an uncaring man, and when faced with her own baby's needs became severely depressed. A woman who had a similar outlook said, 'I feel I couldn't cope with a girl [baby] because I felt so horrible myself as a child'. Another mother often felt very angry towards her baby as she interpreted his waking up after she had put him down as a criticism of her for poor mothering. The guilt and confusion these feelings cause is heightened by the fact that many mothers feel under pressure to conform to an ideal image of motherhood. As a result they 'are constantly berating themselves for falling short'.[44]

This guilt appears to be linked to an increased risk of postnatal depression.

Secure child becomes sensitive parent

How parents have dealt with the strong feelings arising in their own childhood has a great influence on the nature of the emotions they experience after their own child's birth. A team of psychologists have developed the 'Adult Attachment Interview', which is used to assess an adult's state of mind about parent–child, and other intimate relationships. Studies using this interview have found that a parent who values close relationships, and is able to recall and discuss their childhood objectively, without distortion, idealisation, and without continuing excessive dependence on their parents, is far more likely than other parents to have children who have a secure emotional attachment to her or him. Such parents are said to have a secure state of mind with respect to attachment. They have been found to be more supportive and sensitive to their young children than parents assessed as insecure in the Adult Attachment Interview. Many such parents recalled sensitive and warm treatment by their own parents during their childhood.[45]

Later I will outline in more detail the responsive parental behaviour which fosters the growth of a secure emotional attachment in a child, and how it promotes contentedness and responsible behaviour.

About a quarter of people who have been given the Adult Attachment Interview tend to downplay the importance of relationships in childhood, remember little of emotional significance from their childhood, and/or sum up their parents as having been very good. But their remarks reveal incidents showing their parents' insensitivity towards them, which they fail to recognise or acknowledge. As they appear to have had to repress any sensitivity they may once have felt to instances of indifferent or rejecting behaviour from their parents, they have not conceived the possibility of avoiding such behaviour in their own parenting. Their children usually do not have a secure attachment to them.[46]

Other parents who remember and realise that their parents were unable to meet their emotional needs sufficiently in childhood resolve to be more responsive towards their own children. But despite these good intentions, many such parents often find themselves repeating their own parents' mistakes.

A large three-generation study found that in each generation children's emotional difficulties were related to unresponsive treatment by parents who were discontented in their marriage. Nearly a third of parents who had been abused or neglected as children ill-treated their own children. An extremely valuable study of mothers of 3-year-olds found both that conflict in their marriage, and recollection of rejecting behaviour by their own parents in childhood, were related to mothers expressing negative feelings towards their child. However mothers who recalled rejecting behaviour by their parents, but currently had an emotionally supportive marriage, expressed very low levels of negative feeling towards their child. This finding fits with others in the same study, which show that parents who had been abused in childhood but who had also had either an emotionally supportive caregiver during childhood, extensive therapy, or a supportive partner, did not ill-treat their own children.[47]

Another study followed up women in their twenties who as girls had been placed in a children's home. These women were found to be less warm, sensitive and consistent to their children than a group of mothers who had not been in care but were comparable in age and social background. Of the 'ex-care' women, those who had a supportive partner were much more likely to be good mothers. But unfortunately the ex-care women were much less likely than the comparison group women to have a supportive spouse. All these findings point to the long-term impact of insensitive or rejecting parenting, but also underline the importance of understanding the factors promoting supportive marriages, particularly for those who have had a difficult childhood.

Happy partnership, happy parent

Those who have studied the differences between happy families whose children are sociable, capable and responsible, and unhappy families whose children tend to have problems, stress that the quality of the marital relationship is 'of paramount importance' in this regard.[48] Several studies find that the level of emotional support between the couple strongly influences the emotional health of their children. For instance, one study found that women's feelings of satisfaction with their relationship as assessed before they had a child were related to their toddlers' emotional security and sociability no less than 3½ years later. Another study found that marital tension was related to the use on children of 'extreme and arbitrary discipline'.[49] Among families whose income fell sharply during the economic depression of the 1930s, the children's emotional security and affection towards their parents declined only when the parents' relationship was poor.

Several studies have found that the quality of the marital relationship tends to decline once a couple become parents. In one study three-quarters of wives felt their marital happiness had declined since they gave birth. Many husbands become somewhat jealous of the attention their wife gives the baby. Because of this one expert recommended that preventive help be offered to couples during pregnancy.[50]

A number of studies have found that a feeling of insoluble marital dissatisfaction, or a lack of emotional intimacy, contributes to depression in women. Studies which have assessed couples over extended periods have found that it is not simply that people who are prone to depression tend to be dissatisfied with their marriage; an unsatisfying marriage contributes to an individual becoming depressed beyond the effect of their personality at the start of the marriage.[51] A person is particularly vulnerable to depression when she or he is undertaking a potentially stressful task, such as caring for a baby. If a woman knows that her partner cares about her welfare and is committed to helping her overcome the problems ahead, this strengthens her motivation, reduces her anxiety, and enhances her pleasure in the task. But as we have seen many women lack such support, and therefore it is not surprising that a quarter of women suffer sustained feelings of depression for at least two weeks during the first five months of their baby's life. The unusual nature of modern parent–child relationships is underlined by the fact that in societies with a more confident approach to childhood 'baby blues' are so rare that the very concept is hard to communicate.'[52]

Depressed parenting

A large number of surveys have found that around a third of mothers of young children living in inner-city areas suffer depression. Children of all ages whose parents have depression are much more likely to have long-term behaviour or learning problems, even after taking the effects of social class into account. The episodes of depression such women suffer are rarely short. One study found that half the mothers currently suffering from depression had had the illness for at least one year, and a further quarter had had it for at least six months. Most depressed mothers have a much more detached way of relating to their babies. There is little evidence that any innate characteristics of their babies account for depressed mothers' unresponsive parenting.

In view of the central influence that having a baby has on a woman's life, it is not surprising that dissatisfaction with motherhood is related to depression. Again it is hard to judge how much a tendency to depression causes dissatisfaction with motherhood, or vice versa. But as both factors appear to be significant, the importance of new mothers having sufficient emotional and practical support during pregnancy, and as they start their relationship with their baby, cannot be stressed enough. An episode of depression can often be alleviated when someone the woman trusts enables her to share her deepest feelings. In one case this helped the woman feel 'as if a twenty-ton weight had been lifted from my shoulders'. But many parents think they ought to be able to cope with their children, or are embarrassed to seek support from others, feeling they will be judged adversely.

Parental over-involvement

Parents may subconsciously fear emotional distress if they allow themselves to reflect on the ways in which their child does not live up to their hopes. Many parents build up a strong attachment to a particular image of their child, either as he is now or as they wish him to be in the future. One woman spoke of her son using the term 'reflection of self', thus describing the relatively common tendency to relate to a child as if he or she were an extension of the parent. Certain mothers are said to feel a 'sense of depletion' in their child's absence. If they lack fulfilment in the other aspects of their life, their hopes and fears can become excessively bound up with their child. This causes great stress, because they cannot actually live the child's life.

In order to avoid this stress, some such parents may actually spend less time in their child's company than they would if they were not over-involved with him. They need to get away from the child for certain periods because they have difficulty distinguishing their emotions from those of their child. Therefore such a parent feels stress at witnessing the child living life in his own way, rather than in the way in which the parent would behave if she were in the child's shoes. Her periodic absence merely limits this problem, but does not solve it.

Another woman seems to wish to recreate herself by imagining that she can gain beauty through the imminent birth of her daughter:

> For the first time in my life I feel all round satisfaction with my appearance . . . I feel it is she who is making me beautiful. I feel a sense of complete identification with my daughter and this is expressed in our beauty.[53]

Excessive identification with one's child goes beyond a parental desire for ordinary togetherness. It is understandable that parents should wish to share common interests with their children. But certain parents have a strong desire, whether conscious or subconscious, that their child live out or embody certain aspirations, in order to give the parent an indirect taste of something they feel they cannot experience themselves. This is likely to cause both parent and child severe disappointment sooner or later.

When the mother quoted above took her 2-year-old daughter to buy a dress, the child soon got bored. After they got home she tried to persuade the girl to try the dress on again to show her father. The girl resisted, and was persuaded only when told that a neighbour she liked would admire her wearing the dress. She was persuaded to renounce her own wishes because she had been brought up to be dependent on adult approval and admiration. But as children get older their increasingly strong need to define their own identity cannot be so easily suppressed. If parents try to influence their lifestyle too much, they are likely to rebel. This may lead to them emphasising their ability to act independently by doing precisely those things their parents oppose, for instance taking drugs, or playing truant. Such power struggles commonly start at an earlier age over smaller issues, as in the case of a mother who would send her 4-year-old to bed for not eating at meal times. She felt this would teach him to be grateful for the effort she made in cooking his meal.

Dr Spock encourages parents to think in this way, saying that it is reasonable for parents to expect their children's affection, and willingness to accept parental standards and ideals, in return for the parents' sacrifices.[54]

How reasonable is it for parents to expect their children to accept their values? This question goes to the heart of one of the key issues of this book: how can we treat others so they are likely to treat us and others with respect? We must reiterate one of the main conclusions from childhood research: that children tend to imitate whichever parental behaviour seems to them to offer the best way of coping with life. If parents feel they should be able to oblige their children to accept their standards, the children will probably behave in a similarly manipulative manner once they have outgrown most of their dependence on their parents. But if parents consult their children and try to reach mutually acceptable agreements, children are likely to behave similarly and accept as many of their parents' standards and ideals as are consistent with their own. A parent who expects the child to adapt herself to him, without being willing to do likewise, is likely to lose his child's affection and respect. It is beneficial for parents to assert their rights, so their children learn not to take advantage of people. But beyond asserting such rights to a minimum standard of respectful treatment, a relationship works best by mutual negotiation.

Children will best respect parents' wishes if parents respect children's need to take their own decisions, within their level of competence, provided always that they do not encroach on the legitimate freedom of others.

Parental sacrifice

It is understandable that parents feel desperately disappointed if the way their children turn out seems a travesty of the parent's sacrifice. However parents would not run this risk if they could have enough confidence in their children to grow up to be decent people. But most parents doubt their children's ability to have autonomy and still act responsibly, and therefore feel an onerous duty to supervise them so they do not go off the rails. Moreover nowadays many parents set much higher standards for themselves than merely meeting their children's essential needs. Miriam Stoppard imposes the role of educator on parents:

All the early skills, walking, talking, socializing, intellectual development, are absolutely in the parents' hands and no one else is culpable if things go wrong.

Elsewhere Stoppard states that 'the parents are almost entirely responsible' for a child's problem behaviour, and adds to the pressure to be a perfect parent with commands such as 'try to keep all negative emotions out of your head'.[55]

Rosalind Coward found that most of the mothers she interviewed aspired to an image of an ideal mother, with 'boundless energy which she devotes to the children', encouraging them 'to find their potential in a number of stimulating and educational activities'.[56]

Such parents often subconsciously seek compensation for their devotion by steering the child towards some achievement which in fact would be more likely to gratify the parent than interest the child. As a result many children are 'dragged' to music lessons or similar pursuits. Such parents put themselves to considerable inconvenience, hoping one day to experience a glow of pride at their child's talent, while the child would usually prefer to be left alone to choose her own activity. It is ironic that parents do not instead devote some of their time and money to undertaking an activity which would bring *them* fulfilment.

A parent's desire to get the most out of their scarce 'quality time' with their children may be frustrated. The children may be absorbed in other activities, and hence the parent feels rejected. The consequent resentment adds one more twist to the negative spiral of a relationship lacking in mutual respect and enjoyment. The parent is hurt by the child not exhibiting the love they desire. The parent then hopes even more fervently to create special times of togetherness with the child. Their anxiety to do so puts a pressure on the child, who recoils from any encounters in which he feels expected to perform a parental ideal.

Parents who desire satisfaction through their child's achievements or 'love' have usually suffered disappointment in being unable to achieve their hopes, perhaps in seeking the love of a partner. The less parents are able to tackle their own dissatisfactions, especially in their marriage, the more they are likely to pin most of their hopes on their children. This increases the relatively high risk of depression for parents when adolescents cease to need them, and leave home. Parents Together, a self-help group which has had great success in helping parents achieve less stressful, more relaxed relationships with their children emphasises the importance of parents paying attention to their own needs.[57]

Children's problems are widespread

Given the stresses and anxieties I have described, it is not surprising that many children exhibit various forms of troublesome behaviour. A quarter of British preschool children are considered by their parents to have problem behaviour.[58] Three-fifths of 3-year-olds with behaviour problems have troubled behaviour five years later. During their first five months between 10 per cent and 30 per cent of babies cry to an extent defined as 'excessive' by doctors and researchers.[59] Between 20 per cent and 30 per cent of school children have serious behaviour/psychological problems. As I will show later, the psychological symptoms underlying these problems tend to persist, resulting in antisocial or other disturbed behaviour in adolescence or adulthood.

There are other disturbing signs of distress among young people. Ten thousand children now ring the British helpline Childline each day. The United States and Britain have much higher teenage birth rates than Western Europe.[60] Teenagers underestimate the risk of sexually transmitted diseases, which more and more of them are catching. Children rightly or wrongly thought to be homosexual are often persecuted by other youngsters. A high proportion of under 15s smoke cigarettes. It is not surprising that youngsters want to try those activities discouraged by adult society. But if brought up well they can learn how to take care of themselves, and respect other people. As the British Medical Journal has said, 'parenting is probably the most important public health issue facing our society'. Governments should follow the example of New Zealand and Norway, and appoint a Commissioner with clear responsibility for all children's issues.

Sensitive parent, secure child

Research has now shown conclusively that if parents meet children's needs sensitively in infancy, they are much more likely to grow up to be contented, sociable and self-confident. A child who has gained confidence in his parents' care for him, and goes to them readily when he needs affection or help, is said to be 'securely attached' to them. Having had positive experiences with their parents, such children learn to have similar confidence in other suitable people who may become 'attachment figures', e.g. grandparents, or intimate partners in adulthood. This process is conceived of as creating a conscious or subconscious 'representational model' of 'attachment figures', i.e., an habitual pattern of emotions which determine how one thinks about or relates to the possibility of attachment to different people, depending on how one perceives their characteristics as individuals. These representational models vary from being mostly positive in some people to mostly negative in others, depending on how they have been treated at critical times.

The pioneering attachment researcher, John Bowlby, concluded that a person who has formed a secure attachment to his parent

is likely to possess a representational model of attachment figure(s) as being available, responsive, and helpful, and a complementary model of himself as at least a potentially lovable and valuable person . . . influenced by those models he is likely to have been able to make further loving and trusting relationships during his . . . adult life.[61]

Parental love satisfies rather than spoils the child, and fosters responsibility to others. There is abundant evidence that babies whose parents respond sensitively to their expressed needs, especially by holding or carrying the baby, are more content and cry less. Although babies who are carried more are also fed more frequently, they feed for no longer in total, and so there is no evidence that greater parental responsiveness makes babies greedy.[62]

The key breakthrough in understanding how differences in parental treatment influence children's relationships with parents and other attachment figures was made by Mary Ainsworth. She built on John Bowlby's work to develop the 'Strange Situation'. This procedure involves an infant aged 12 to 18 months twice being separated from his parent for up to three minutes. If he becomes distressed during either separation he is immediately reunited with the parent. More than one hundred infants were videoed in the study in which the Strange Situation procedure was first tested. The videos were studied in minute detail, and three characteristic types of infant response were identified. For the sake of clarity I will describe the findings with reference to mothers, though the procedure has been found to be equally valid for fathers. Infants classified as avoidant tend not to be upset when their mother leaves the room, and avoid interacting with her when she returns. Infants classified as ambivalent are usually very upset when their mother leaves the room, but waver between wanting contact and angrily resisting contact with her when she returns. Infants classified as secure actively seek contact with and are readily comforted by their mother when she returns.[63]

Since Ainsworth's pathbreaking work there have now been many more studies which carried out frequent observations of infants and mothers at home during their first year (and a few with fathers), before they were assessed in the Strange Situation. These show that babies whose parent had the sensitivity to perceive their baby's communications accurately, and respond in a way which met the baby's needs, with affection when appropriate, were more likely to be assessed in the Strange Situation as securely attached to that parent. Babies whose parent was unresponsive at home were more likely to be assessed as ambivalent towards the parent. Babies whose parent was relatively unresponsive at home, but also behaved intrusively towards the baby, were more likely to be assessed as avoidant towards the parent. The psychologists who assessed the Strange Situation videos were told nothing of the parenting quality as observed in the home, so they would have no preconceptions. Ainsworth found that infants later classified at twelve months old as avoidant in the Strange Situation responded negatively to being put down by their mother at home both in the first and fourth quarter of their first year. Therefore their avoidant response in the Strange Stuation was not a sign of greater maturity, independence, or even-temperedness.[64]

Readers may wonder why a situation described as 'strange' should be judged appropriate to study such a fundamental aspect of behaviour as attachment. But if we reflect on the situations in which we feel most in need of our loved ones, we can understand the reason. When we have a major worry or large disappointment, such as being made redundant or failing an exam, or a tragedy, such as serious illness or death in the family, we nearly always contact those to whom we are close. So in a situation which is strange in the sense of being unusually stressful, we need to seek assistance or comfort from our loved ones. This applies to everyone except those who have had to become exceptionally self-sufficient. When life seems cruel, most of us need the concern of whoever knows and cares for us as an individual. We and our loved ones share memories or hopes arising out of similar experiences or values. Only they can readily understand what the setback means to us. If they respond with concern we are reassured that we do not need to face the problem alone.

Our reaction to stresses of the kind I have described has a major impact on our everyday life, whether we respond by trying to meet our needs in another way, downplaying the importance of the setback, or becoming bitter or demoralised. How we react influences whether we approach life thereafter with confidence and enthusiasm, anxiety, diffidence, or cynicism. Infants' attachment behaviour can only be properly studied at times when they have a similar need to turn to their attachment figure. A brief separation is the most ordinary and least stressful event which can be arranged for this purpose.

Carried babies become securely attached

I described above how in certain pre-industrial societies babies are carried frequently, treated very responsively, rarely cry, and grow up to be sociable, friendly and responsible. A pathbreaking American study found that babies who are carried frequently are far more likely to be assessed in the Strange Situation as securely attached. This study enables us to link its scientific findings of the importance of infants' need for physical contact, with anthropologists' evidence of the healthy development of children who are carried regularly as babies. Therefore the study increases our confidence in the Strange Situation researchers' evidence about the secure attachment outcome of the sensitive parenting style which evolution has selected for human beings. The particular pre-industrial societies mentioned are composed of cohesive groups of extended families typical of the societies in which the human race evolved. Such societies have stood the test of time. The study's findings help us to see that secure attachment is achieved both in modern and pre-industrial society by the same type of responsive parenting, which evolved and persisted because it promoted child development and social responsibility.

The study took care to ensure that the effects of infant carrying could be assessed separately from those of other parental characteristics. When their infants were one day old, mothers who agreed to take part in the research were assigned at random to one of two conditions. Mothers assigned to one condition were asked regularly to use a soft baby carrier (sling). Mothers in the other condition were asked to use an infant seat regularly. Mothers were only included in the study if they were willing to use whichever of the two items was assigned to them at random. Those who had already decided to use a sling or who would not consider using one were not included in the study.

Each mother was asked to use each day whichever item they were assigned, and not to use the other item. These precautions ensured that mothers who possessed any particular pro- or anti-sling feelings, and might therefore conceivably have had an exceptional parenting style, were not included. Hence the two groups of mothers were comparable in this respect. They were also comparable in socio-economic status, education, race, and other social characteristics. One set of mothers were given an infant seat in order that the two groups should be comparable in each being given an item of baby equipment.

When assessed in the Strange Situation at 13 months no fewer than five-sixths of the babies whose mothers had been given a sling were securely attached, compared to fewer than two-fifths of those whose mothers had been given the infant seat. All the mothers were asked how often they had used whichever item they were given. Practically all the 'sling' mothers had used it either daily or 2–3 times weekly. The total group of 'sling' mothers was divided into those who had used it more frequently, or less frequently. A remarkable 94 per cent of the former had securely attached babies compared with 57 per cent of the latter. The effects of sling use were apparent by two months old, when only one in five of the 'sling' babies had a regular daily period of crying, compared to over half of the 'infant seat' babies. This study clearly shows that secure attachment is strongly influenced by parenting quality, and is therefore only partly genetic. Carrying was not a response by the mother to any characteristic of the baby (inborn or other).[65]

If attachment security was due to inborn characteristics of the child, their attachment to one parent would be of the same type as that to the other parent. The limited extent to which this occurs shows that attachment security is not due to the child's genetic make-up.[66]

Secure infant, confident child

The Strange Situation procedure lasts only twenty minutes. However the fact that it assesses a fundamental characteristic of the parent–child relationship is indicated by the strong relation between security of attachment to the parent at age 1 and other measures of favourable development in later life. Research has found that infants assessed as securely attached at age 1 are more likely than other children to have:

a secure attachment to the parent, as indicated by affection and confidence shown towards the parent, at age 6;

greater empathy towards other children at age 4;

greater emotional resilience at ages 6, 10, and 15, and greater emotional openness at age 6;

less excess dependence on adult carers at age 10;

greater social skills at ages 3½, 4–5, 10, and 15;

better overall emotional health at ages 10 and 15;

a secure state of mind with respect to attachment as a young adult.

Children who were avoidant towards their parent at age 1 were found to be less co-operative and more aggressive at age 5. At age 10 they had poorer relations with other children and were more likely to feel excluded by them.[67] In all these studies each child was assessed by researchers who did not know whether the child had been securely or insecurely attached during infancy. The ratings of the 10-year-olds were made by five researchers who looked after these children for four hours daily for twenty days. The results obtained from such a thorough period of assessment provide a powerful confirmation of the expectations of attachment theory, namely that secure attachment in infancy is likely to lead to self-confidence, concern for others, and the ability to make fulfilling relationships.

Older children who were assessed as securely attached to their parent through comparable methods designed for their age group were found to have higher self-esteem, and years later as young adults to have better relationships with their romantic partners.[68]

While infant attachment has a strong influence, so do serious life events, such as acrimonious divorce, or parental death. Most infants who have been followed up in adulthood retain the same overall attachment style. However among deprived social groups the higher rate of negative life events substantially reduces the likelihood of a securely attached infant becoming a securely attached adult.[69]

It is possible at this stage to draw some conclusions about why sensitive parenting is so successful. It is important to recognise that:

> Babies have physical needs, for food and warmth, but need companionship and bodily contact just as much. This gives them confidence that others will help them cope with the unexpected aspects of life.

> Babies need warm friendly relationships with their parents, so they can develop confidence in their parents' commitment. These relationships enable them to build a secure representational model of attachment figures and therefore make supportive intimate relationships in later life.

> Parents are more likely to care for their children with warmth, respect, and sensitivity if they have company and emotional support in their parent role.

I will proceed to describe how the psychological problems which cause anti-social behaviour in adolescence and adulthood usually originate in the child's early relationship with his parents, and how these problems can be overcome. I will discuss the limited effects of income level on children's emotional development, and will outline several relatively inexpensive ways children and parents could be helped to have more fulfilling lives, to the long-term benefit of society as a whole.

Rearing co-operative children

There are many studies of young children which have not used the Strange Situation. These also provide considerable evidence that parenting which is sensitive to children's needs fosters contentment and responsible behaviour. Mothers who expressed a 'distrusting' attitude towards their infants mentioned more problems with the child's behaviour 18 months later. Children whose mothers treated them in a friendly and positive manner between the ages of 6 months and two years had many fewer behaviour problems than other children at age 4. Children aged 1½ to 2½, whose mothers were observed over an extended period to care for them sensitively, responded more caringly to other people's distress than did children of less sensitive mothers.[70] Pregnant women were assessed to see if they had a secure state of mind with respect to attachment. Of those who had, their children at age 11 were more likely to acknowledge another person's distress more readily, and more able to suggest how that person could relieve it.[71]

Many studies have found that children who have a warm relationship with their parent, or whose parents are fairly unrestrictive, more often fit in willingly with parents' and others' wishes. Another study found that the more mothers had responded caringly to their young child's dependency, and the more the fathers had been involved in the care of the children, the more concern for others these children had when followed up in adulthood.[72] Helena Norberg Hodge's uplifting account of the people of Ladakh shows how a pattern of responsive parenting leads to many benefits for society. In Ladakh babies are cared for with great affection. From the age of about five children lovingly help care for babies, and spontaneously show generosity to those around them. Adults are hardworking, cheerful, and even-tempered, and fights are practically unknown. Adults have good relationships with each other, but without the excessive emotional dependence, anxiety, and resentment which is prevalent in our society. Ladakhi women are noticeably happy compared to women in other societies.

These favourable features of Ladakhi personality are clearly not due to the conditions there. The winters are long and bitter, there is no electricity or running water, and transport is primitive. But the Ladakhis have not developed a merely stoical acceptance of their situation; they enjoy a positively happy community life, singing while working together, and celebrating regularly at parties and religious festivals.[73] Given the findings mentioned in Chapter One that (a) happiness in childhood, and (b) satisfaction in family life, have the strongest relationship to adult happiness or satisfaction with life, the most convincing explanation of Ladakhi well-being is one which emphasises the importance of family relationships.

Responsive parenting promotes school progress

Parenting quality also has an important impact on children's intellectual development. There has long been controversy on the size of the relative contributions of 'nature' and 'nurture' to intelligence. Michael and Marjorie Rutter reviewed the research on this question and concluded that genetic factors and the quality of the child's social environment had roughly equal effects.[74]

Many studies have found that warm, responsive parenting promotes children's intellectual and language development, even after taking into account the influence of the family's social class and the mother's intelligence.

Responsive parenting is related to children having greater task persistence at age 4, and at age 6 having more initiative, choosing more challenging tasks, and being more confident with adults. Children aged 4½ became more involved with a task if their mother sensitively helped them engage with it by asking non-directive questions, rather than issuing instructions. Children assessed as securely attached at age 7 were able to think more logically at various ages from 7 to 17, even after the effect of intelligence at age 7 had been taken into account. On most measures secure attachment had this effect chiefly because securely attached children had more self-confidence. They were also more able to pay attention.[75]

Parents influence babies more than vice versa

As stated above, some people doubt the extensive evidence on the ill-effects of unresponsive parenting, and suggest that a child's problem behaviour often arises from her or his innate characteristics. Such commentators believe that children whose nature is difficult or unresponsive are harder for parents to love and look after. Therefore their parents are less attentive, the child may misbehave to try and gain more parental attention, and the parents' negative view and treatment of the child is reinforced.While children vary in their inherited characteristics, there is considerable evidence that parents have more influence on children than vice versa. In saying this I stress again that parents should not be criticised for behaviour which hinders their children's development. Many parents have practical or emotional problems which impair their ability to do as well for their child as they wish. Later I will discuss services which have been shown to help parents both respond to their children's needs more sensitively and enjoy parenthood more. But sweeping the issue of parents' influence on children under the carpet performs a disservice to both.

An analysis of many studies compared the rate of security of attachment when infants had particular problems, and when mothers had specific problems. Infant problems included handicaps such as Down's syndrome, deafness, and cystic fibrosis. Mother problems included mental illness, alcohol abuse, and ill-treating the child. In the samples of children with problems, the rate of secure attachment was only very slightly less than that in ordinary samples of children. But when mothers had specific problems, secure attachment was much less common. The researchers concluded that while ordinary mothers could adapt their behaviour to compensate for a child's handicap, children cannot compensate for an unresponsive mother.

A similar ability to make up for a baby's problems with sensitive caring was shown by certain mothers of premature babies. The mothers were asked to complete questionnaires about their baby's behaviour. Mothers whose baby's behaviour was rated difficult at 6 months and easy at 12 months were observed to be much more sensitive and responsive towards the baby than were mothers whose baby's rating changed from easy to difficult.

In general, studies which measured the irritability and responsiveness of babies up to a few days old have found no consistent pattern regarding whether these factors relate to secure attachment at age 1. One study found that such measures had a weaker effect than that of the social support enjoyed by the mother. Another found that while maternal sensitivity at 2 and 6 months was related to secure attachment at age 1, newborn alertness had no influence on maternal sensitivity at either 2, 6 or 10 months.[76] It is rarely the case that a baby's difficult behaviour evokes insensitive care from a parent who would otherwise have been adequately attentive. Babies' behaviour patterns are liable to fluctuate quite a lot before the age of 4 months. By that time the more powerful influence of the parents' personalities and behaviour has shaped the baby's behaviour to a large degree.

The impact of the parent's attachment pattern, independent of any influence of the newborn baby's temperament, is also shown by the Adult Attachment Interviews of women during their first pregnancy. Those assessed as being secure were much more likely than insecure women to go on to have a baby who was securely attached to them.[77]

The importance of parental influence was further demonstrated by findings that the amount of a mother's positive behaviour towards her child between the ages of 6 months and 2 years had a stronger impact than the nature of the child's behaviour during that period on the child's freedom from behaviour problems at age 4. Another indication that children's innate characteristics are not a major influence on problem behaviour was suggested by the emergence of conduct problems in previously well-behaved children after the onset of marital discord.

Does divorce harm children?

Children whose parents either divorce or suffer marital distress have high rates of a range of problems, including depression, behavioural and school difficulties, and physical illness. Some research has found that it is the effects of pre-existing marital conflict, more than separation or divorce itself, which contributes most to the link between divorce and children's behaviour problems. But another study gave a different picture. It found that children's self-esteem, psychological health, and social well-being is poorer in lone-parent families than in two-parent families with high marital conflict. These qualities are greatest when children are living with both parents and marital conflict is low. This study casts doubt on the assumption that children's situation may improve after separation or divorce because it brings an end to marital conflict. Couples who had had major conflict during their marriage were in fact likely to have conflict after divorce.

In many couples who later divorced, open marital conflict had begun only just before the separation. At least four years later considerable conflict persisted; only four out of ten couples could discuss arrangements for their children without feelings of anger, resentment or frustration. Two-fifths did not speak to their former partner at all. In view of this, it is not surprising that partners' health and feelings of well-being decline after marital breakdown.[78] This is thought to damage parents' ability to respond to their child's needs, at a time when they also have to try and agree with their ex-partner new arrangements concerning both finance and the children.

Post-divorce conflict is damaging to children, who have lower self-esteem if their divorced parents have a poor relationship than if they have made amicable arrangements about contact with the children. Very few children 'felt positive' about the arrangements for contact with their other parent. Less than a fifth of lone parents whose child lived with them said their child had regular, problem-free contact with the other parent. A high proportion of children had more bad moods after the divorce. Children in lone-parent families have more 'major disagreements' with their resident parent than do children in two-parent families.

The problems of children in disrupted families are due not only to parental conflict, or to the effects of having only one resident parent. Adults brought up with one parent and a step-parent are far more likely than other adults to say they were abused or neglected.The step-parent is in a very difficult position, as children may feel that they have usurped the parent's position.

Trying to judge from the research evidence whether couples suffering marital distress should divorce, or stay together for the sake of their children, is rather academic unless we as a society decide to provide the resources to help distressed parents make an informed choice. By the time a person takes steps to seek a divorce, they usually feel deeply hurt by or alienated from their partner. The painful emotions are then far too strong to permit calm consideration of the best course of action. Marriages need help at an earlier stage.

Although governments continually stress that the breakdown of family life harms society, they do little to improve the quality and stability of marriage. Marital breakdown in the United States has been estimated to cost a massive $41 billion annually.[79] Examples of such costs are the fact that adults whose parents divorced during their childhood have fewer qualifications, and are much more likely to smoke, than others of the same social class background. Governments should commission TV advertisements on the effectiveness of marital counselling, and ensure that it is much more promptly accessible than at present. We should also help people end irreparable marriages in ways which reduce children's and parents' distress. Family mediation assists divorcing couples to reduce conflict by making sensible agreements about children and finance.

Social support for parents

Of course we must remember that being married or cohabiting is no guarantee of having sufficient support in the parental role. Moreover the influence of social support on parents' morale goes far beyond having company or assistance in performing the physical tasks of parenting. A parent also needs understanding and to be valued as an individual. The higher the quality of emotional support individuals feel they receive, the less they experience symptoms of depression or other distress. A person's perception of the quality of support they receive influences emotional well-being more their actual amount of social contact. The crucial impact of the partner relationship on emotional well-being was shown by a study which found that a mother's level of intimacy with her partner had the strongest influence on how much she was satisfied with the social support she received.[80]

Social class and child development

Another factor that is commonly thought to have a strong impact on children's development is social class. It is known to affect school attainment. A review of the literature found that low social class, conflict between the parents, maternal depression and stress, and being brought up by a single parent, all had an important impact on the level of children's behaviour problems. Ways in which lower social class could contribute to children's problems are suggested by various findings:

a) unemployment and other life stresses, which are more likely to strike working class people, tend to lead to increased marital conflict and thus reduce parenting quality and harm some previously secure attachments;[81]

b) working-class and less educated mothers tend on average to be less sensitive and positive towards their children, and provide less mental stimulation;[82]

c) on average working-class mothers receive less social support before and after giving birth;

d) large family size, and low family income during childhood, are associated with children's behaviour problems and later delinquency;

e) in poor or high-crime neighbourhoods, or those which lack playspace and community facilities, parents are less warm to their children, who do worse at school and have more behaviour problems. This influence operates in addition to the impact of the parents' own characteristics.[83]

In the same way as adult health and life expectancy appear to be linked to feelings about one's income compared to that of others', rather than the direct physical effects of lacking certain material goods, it appears that parents' low income has a negative influence on children in certain families in which it tends to lower parents' morale. Incomes have increased considerably in the last few decades, but still many families suffer disharmony. Therefore it appears that absolute income levels, once a certain minimum has been passed, exert relatively little influence on family well-being.

Some research found that social class had a relatively slight influence on various psychological features of parents and children. A major study of children from age 1 to 3 found that measures of parental sensitivity, and provision of a stimulating home environment for the child by way of freedom to play, toys, and books, had a greater influence on child development than did social class and employment status. This study also found evidence that young children living in disadvantaged areas had seriously inadequate levels of various nutrients. These children often ate quite expensive non-nutritious snacks. Other poor families who had received a new model of health visiting which encourages parents to identify their own priorities for their child, provided a much better diet for their children, showing that the difference was not due to financial factors.[84]

Parents who feel stressed, and lack positive feelings for their child, are more likely to abuse their child. It might be thought that being working-class, as manifested by low income, would contribute to parental stress and hence to child abuse. However to understand this it is important to distinguish the effects of social class as conveyed through low income, from other factors related to social class. For instance there are higher rates of teenage motherhood and disrupted families among lower social classes. Research shows that younger children, first-borns, and children of teenage mothers, are most at risk of abuse, and social disadvantage in itself is a less significant factor.[85]

Overall it appears that the material stresses suffered by many working class people affect the parenting quality only of some working-class parents. For psychological reasons people vary in the way they react to such stresses.

Insensitive parenting, problem children

There is abundant evidence that unresponsive parenting is related to children's serious anti-social behaviour, depression, and difficulty in making friends. The parental factors identified include lack of supervision of or involvement with the child, harsh or inconsistent discipline, rejection, child abuse, marital discord, maternal depression or stress, paternal criminality, above-average family size, and single parenthood. Most of the parent factors research has found to be related to children's anti-social behaviour have that effect because they are signs of parents' difficulty in finding sufficient sensitivity, energy, or commitment to care for each of their children. One example of this is the fact that when the age differences between the children of a family are small, they are punished more. This is probably because when they are young the children all need a lot of parental attention simultaneously.

The effect of parents' lack of commitment to their child is demonstrated in a particularly stark form in those who did not want the baby initially. Research programmes have compared children who were born as a result of their mother being refused an abortion, with a sample of babies who matched them in social status, father's presence or absence, and other important characteristics. The children studied all lived with their mothers. At age 21 more than twice as many of the children whose mothers had been refused abortion had a history of delinquency. They also had achieved less at school and were more likely to be dependent on social security. Another study found that at age 14 to 16 children whose mothers had been refused abortion were less successful in school, and had a poorer emotional adjustment. These findings reflect the severe distress of most women who request an abortion at the prospect of continuing the pregnancy and having a baby at that stage of their life.[86]

Schools should give girls the chance to meet women who have had an abortion, and adults whose parents did not really want them. This would help them understand the impact of unwanted pregnancy and thus reduce the chance of their ever being in that predicament.

Problem behaviour persists

Young children with behavioural problems tend to have further serious anti-social behaviour, or psychological difficulties, as they grow up. Aggressive or ill-tempered 8-year-old boys were found still to have these traits at age 30. Childhood ill-temper had as strong an influence as intelligence on the men's educational attainments, and as great an impact as social class background on their adult occupational status.

Women who had behavioural problems as girls are more likely to suffer from depression.[87]

Why do such patterns of behaviour persist? One factor affecting children is that the nature of their parents' behaviour tends to persist, thus tending to reinforce the child in her existing style of conduct. While exceptional events can change an existing behaviour pattern, this is offset by the fact that one's reaction to such an event is strongly influenced by one's existing personality. Children whose parents treat them sensitively tend to have positive expectations of life and therefore to bounce back after a setback, while emotionally fragile children take it much harder.

Another crucial factor in the persistence of individuals' behaviour patterns is that some people are given negative labels by those around them. Whether someone is clearly labelled and disliked by those who know him, or simply treated with coolness, he comes to expect such a reaction from most people. Therefore he tends to behave in a less confident or friendly manner towards them either because of anxiety, or a lack of warmth towards them. The other person's reaction then reinforces the child's general expectations of people. Sometimes we have largely subconscious fears of encountering in relationships disappointments similar to those we have experienced in the past. This often leads us to get involved with people who present similar problems, as if we are subconsciously hoping that *this* time things will turn out well so that we avoid further disappointment. Freud termed this pattern the 'repetition compulsion'.

Those who work with children in care believe that the repetition compulsion often explains the way such children commonly misbehave soon after being placed with a new foster family or children's home. Having felt rejected by their original family, they expect, without realising it, to be rejected again. Therefore they cannot relax until they have indulged in bad behaviour, in the hope that this new family will not reject them for it.

The aggression of abused children

If we are to help aggressive children improve their behaviour, it is important to understand how they get caught in the spiral of increasing hostility I have described. There is a vast literature detailing the fact that most seriously aggressive children have been abused or neglected. Having thus learned from their experiences to expect negative reactions from people, they become hypersensitive to the slightest suggestion of such rejection. For instance, an aggressive boy staying at a treatment centre yelled 'You hate me!' at a nurse when she did not respond immediately to his mumbled 'goodnight'.[88]

While in some ways such children have a desire for adult acceptance, their previous negative experiences ensure that even with caring adults they rapidly disown this desire if they perceive, usually mistakenly, a lack of acceptance. Then this desire seems dangerous as it exposes them to the risk of crushing disappointment if they were to be rejected.

These children usually model their behaviour on their uncaring or cruel parents, who appeared strong because they did not need others' affection. From this perspective aggression seems like a strength, and the desire to be liked by understanding adults a weakness which must at all costs not be indulged. Such children were said by Anna Freud to 'identify with the agressor'. Mantel's book about Green Beret commandos gives a fascinating description of how this leads to such children becoming authoritarian adults.[89]

Repeated punishment causes defiance

Some may hope that severe punishment could correct aggressive young people. Many of us who have been victims of their crimes understandably feel angry at their unrepentant attitude. Clearly those who are really a danger to the public must be locked up for a time, and given expert help. But in the case of most aggressive youngsters, who have already been given harsh physical treatment by their parents, further severe punishment will only harden their anti-social attitude.

The common practice of smacking children has been shown to be counterproductive. Children whose parents smacked them at least once weekly at age 7 or 11 were more likely to have acquired a criminal record by age 20. Children who had been smacked at least weekly at age 11 were more likely at age 16 to be rated 'troublesome' on the basis of dishonesty, regular involvement in fights, or truancy. 4-year-olds whose mothers smacked them more often than average were less able to take account of the emotions and expectations of others with whom they had contact. By contrast, mothers who responded to actual or potential disagreements by bargaining with their child in an understanding way had children who were more aware of others' wishes and feelings.

Research on children from ages 1 to 4 showed that smacking actually harms the development of intelligence, having a direct effect separate to other factors such as social class.[90]

While it is understandable that parents smack children who seem unreasonable, this gives them the message that stronger people are able to get their own way. Therefore when they become stronger, they will probably use force to impose their will. Making a child comply by smacking him is tantamount to admitting defeat in appealing to the child's good nature. It reinforces the view that parent and child are in conflict, and that co-operation between them is impossible.

A 1994 survey of adults up to age 45 found that four out of ten remembered a childhood punishment which had 'felt humiliating and degrading'.[91] The fact that so many adults remember an event which occurred so long before indicates the emotional impact some punishments can have. If regular smacking or other severe punishments continue, before long the child's attachment to his parent is likely to weaken. Like the aggressive children discussed above, the child will eventually lose his desire for others' love. Then the child has lost the strongest incentive to co-operate with the parent, and many issues will instead become a battle of wills. He is no longer affected by the emotional pain the smack used to inflict, and the parent finds herself escalating the level of punishment to try and enforce her wishes.

I have spoken to many parents who have said that their child seems determined not to show pain when smacked, but to laugh off the punishment defiantly. Such children have learned to identify with the strength of the smacking 'aggressor', and to disown both their former desire for parental love, and any wish to attain it by behaving as requested.

Troubled children need help when young

How can we respond to anti-social behaviour constructively? We now know enough about the path towards serious adolescent misbehaviour to be able to identify preadolescent boys likely to become aggressive youths and adults. A 1963 survey of boys aged 6 achieved a remarkably high rate of prediction of later delinquency. The researchers measured the parents' affection for the boy, the standard of their supervision of him, and the cohesiveness of the family. Four-fifths of the boys whose families obtained poor scores on these criteria went on to become serious or persistent delinquents. I describe help available for young offenders in Chapter Five.

Several studies show that children who start problem behaviour at a younger age, and whose misbehaviour is more frequent, especially if they are hyperactive or have poor concentration, are likely to persist in anti-social behaviour into adulthood.[92] The younger the child, the more successful therapy for these problems usually is, as I will describe in due course. This is in part because younger children have a higher level of dependency arising from their need for help. Younger difficult children are therefore less advanced along the path of renouncing their needs for the adult acceptance and affection which is their lifeline to the assistance they require. Such children are more likely to respond positively to therapy, because if treated respectfully they will wish to please their parents and teachers by achieving the goals of therapy.

The younger the child, the less entrenched his educational problems have become, and the less his consequent alienation from the aspiration for school success and social acceptance. Therefore governments should introduce a system of discreet screening checks by teachers so that parents of children showing signs of having serious future educational or behaviour problems can be helped as soon as possible. Teachers can play a vital role in helping troubled children, and should be given administrative assistance with their heavy workload so they may do so. The better the child's relationship with his teacher, the more interest he will take in school activity. Abused children are less likely, when parents, to abuse their own children if they have received emotional support from an adult during childhood. Teachers are in the best position to establish a supportive relationship with such children.[93]

Emotional support during pregnancy

As many insecurely attached infants have various problems in later life, the most effective kind of help for families would be to assist parents to establish a secure attachment with their baby from the start. Children under 2 are most likely to suffer severe physical abuse. If emotional support can give parents confidence in their ability to care for their baby, and hence enjoyment in doing so, they are far less likely to abuse the child. In addition the baby is more likely to reward the parent with friendly and contented behaviour, thus further reducing the likelihood of receiving poor parenting.

Overall personality strength, whose origins lie largely in childhood experience, had the greatest influence on whether mothers of 6-week-old babies suffered 'parenting stress'. However the level of stress mothers had suffered during pregnancy also had a strong impact on their level of parenting stress, as did the quality of social support they enjoyed. Both of these measures had a much stronger impact than that of any stress the women suffered during labour and delivery. When all the factors were analysed together, social support seemed to be particularly helpful in reducing stress *during pregnancy*, and thereby preventing parenting stress.[94] Women with good social support also have fewer pregnancy complications.

Recent research found that the children of women who suffered anxiety during pregnancy are much more likely to have difficulties such as hyperactivity, even after taking into account the effect of mothers' problems after the birth.

This evidence shows us why mothers who were visited regularly by a child development worker from early pregnancy until their child was aged 15 months, were more responsive to their children, and provided them with more freedom to play, than comparable mothers whose visits began 6 weeks after the birth. Their children also had fewer accidents, and a better immunisation record at one year. A review of the evidence on special support schemes for mothers and infants found that most successful schemes began during the pregnancy. The children of mothers who were visited by a nurse from pregnancy till age 2 had fewer behaviour problems at age 4, and had had since birth fewer injuries and accidents, and fewer visits to hospital accident and emergency departments.[95]

The success of these programmes, which are available to very few women, highlights the need for extra health workers to contact certain pregnant women and assess if they would benefit from inclusion in such a scheme, or from assistance with any problem causing stress. Special resources are needed to increase the proportion of women who attend antenatal care, which sharply reduces the likelihood of premature birth. Intensive care for a premature baby, depending on the period for which it is needed, costs between 15 and 300 times more than a normal course of antenatal care.

Support for mothers starting in pregnancy could potentially yield great benefits by reducing the rate of smoking. Smoking ten or more cigarettes daily during pregnancy leads to a reduction of over 4 percentage points on intelligence scores when the child is aged 4. Ceasing smoking during pregnancy would also reduce the baby's risk of various birth problems and other illnesses, including asthma.

The value of extra support for mothers during pregnancy is also shown by the results of a discussion group for pregnant women run by a psychologist and a health visitor, focusing on the stresses of motherhood. It significantly reduced the incidence of depression in the women who attended.[96] Postnatal depression impairs the development of many children, due to the fact that between 10 and 15 per cent of mothers suffer from it. All pregnant women with risk factors for depression should be given the chance to take part in such a group.

Health visiting to improve parenting

Another scheme starting in pregnancy which offers extra support to parents is the Britsh Child Development Programme model of health visiting, as described on page 96 above. The chief difference from standard health visiting is that the health visitor aims to empower parents to take responsibility for finding solutions and making their own decisions. The numbers of infants in the programme who were abused was reduced by half from the expected rate for children with their social characteristics.[97]

Health visitors are a crucial lifeline for parents, especially those who lack confidence or support in caring for their children. Most women have little experience of caring for young children before becoming a mother. A survey has found that health visitors are 'the health professionals most valued by mothers of young children', and that mothers wanted more contact with their health visitor than was available.[98] Increasing the numbers of health visitors would entail only a tiny rise in the overall health budget. Investing this small amount would yield substantial benefits by helping parents bring up healthier and more responsible children.

Nursery education is cost-effective

Another investment in children which would yield great benefits for society is high quality nursery education. The most successful

American scheme, the High/Scope programme, randomly assigned children aged 3 to 4 either to receive or not to receive nursery education for 2½ hours daily. All the children studied came from the same poor neighbourhood. At age 27 those who had received nursery education were more likely to be employed, to have undergone college or vocational education, and to have done voluntary work. They were less likely to have needed special education, caused someone a serious injury, committed a crime, or had a teenage pregnancy. Careful estimates showed that every dollar spent on this programme had saved $7 of public money.

This particular programme is distinctive in giving the children maximum opportunity to plan, perform, and review their own activities. This promotion of autonomy must play a key role in the children's later achievements. It also includes a weekly home visit by the teacher, thus promoting parents' interest in their child's development. Other research has found that the more parents feel involved with their child's education, the more supportive and sensitive their parenting, and the better progress their children make.[99]

Volunteers helping families

Support from non-professionals can also be of great benefit to parents. The Dublin mothers visited monthly by trained 'community mothers' (see above) during their child's first year had more positive feelings and fewer negative feelings for their child at age 1 than other comparable mothers. Unlike professional workers, whose intervention can be experienced as stigmatising, volunteers are more likely to be seen as having the genuine commitment of a friend. Some disadvantaged parents are reluctant to share their worries with health visitors and social workers, whom they often perceive as potentially hostile. The trained volunteers with the organisation Home-Start become both friends and confidantes to the parents they visit. About two-thirds of families referred to Home-Start were assessed to have improved 'considerably' after Home-Start's involvement.[100] Home-Start's costs are just over £1,000 per child per year. This is very modest when we consider that a high proportion of children helped by Home-Start might otherwise end up in care, costing many thousands of pounds per child.

Another very effective organisation using mostly volunteer labour is Childline (see above). As it cannot afford enough telephone lines it can only answer a third of the calls children make. Another charity, Parents Together, runs courses that help parents to communicate better with their children, and respond to their behaviour more effectively. It also depends largely on voluntary labour, and receives little public funding. If ordinary people make their voices heard and insist that governments fund charities such as Childline, so they can meet the needs of children and families, the moral pressure and long-term financial logic would be irresistible. Governments should pay for TV ads for groups like these, to inform children or parents who are suffering great distress of the help these groups can give.

Assertive parents

Self-help groups such as Parents Together are harnessing the insights of assertiveness training to help parents improve their relationships with their children. Rather than seeking directly to control the behaviour of an awkward child, an approach which usually leads to confrontation, the key aspect of the strategy is for the parents to state their wish, and how they feel about the child's behaviour, and give the child the chance to devise a solution. Being given more influence over the resolution of the disagreement evokes a much more positive approach from the child than if his only influence lies in stubbornly resisting the parent's proposal.

Birth companions

Just as the friendship of fellow Parents Together members, or of Home-Start volunteers, gives distressed parents an enormous boost, companionship has also been found to be of great benefit for women at the particularly stressful time of giving birth. In most cultures it is usual for a woman to have an established close bond with the woman who is helping her give birth. Research found that women who were invited to have a female companion during labour had, on average, a shorter and less painful labour, were less likely to need a caesarean section, and more likely to breast-feed for longer. Hospitals should encourage women to bring a female friend, as well as the father, to the birth.

The value of breast feeding

The failure to help many new mothers breast feed confidently and effectively costs large sums of public money. If breast feeding rates increased just a little, health services could save millions of pounds a year in treating diseases which afflict bottle-fed babies more than their breast-fed counterparts. This saving could be achieved relatively easily if the large number of women who try to breast feed but give up due to various difficulties were given the straightforward help which would enable them to avoid these problems. Breast-fed babies have been found on average to have higher intelligence and better eyesight, due to the effect of certain fats contained in breast milk. This suggests that the low breastfeeding rate is costing millions of pounds by retarding children's education. Breastfed babies are also much less likely to die from cot death. In Norway and Sweden breastfeeding has become more popular recently, thanks to government support.

Curing problem behaviour

Yet another area in which a relatively small investment could yield great benefit is in training programmes for parents of children who show signs of behaviour problems at a young age. These programs operate in groups of about 10 to 15 parents meeting weekly with one trainer for about 10 to 12 weeks. Many studies have reported beneficial results which were sustained when the families were followed up between one and three years later. One of the leaders in the field has achieved a success rate of 75 per cent with children under 9. These programmes have also cut levels of depression among parents.

Research has also reported positive results for parents who simply watched presentations of the treatment on video regularly.

While they did not achieve such good results as the parents who attended sessions with the trainer, who also had the benefit of mutual support with other parents, the study shows that for parents who are unwilling to attend groups, self-administered video treatment is a very good alternative.[101] Such parents could also be offered the chance of informal contact by telephone or in person with other parents facing similar problems, and with a trainer.

Another very cost-effective programme is anger control training for parents who have abused their child, which has helped parents reduce the level of their angry and insensitive behaviour towards their child, and improve children's behaviour.

Different types of therapy for children and parents vary in effectiveness. Sceptics have in the past suggested that certain forms of therapy are no more effective than no therapy at all, as some individuals overcome their problems without treatment. But a thorough analysis of studies of family and marital psychotherapy found that nearly two-thirds of those treated showed a significant and sustained improvement, while of those who were not treated, fewer than two in five showed a comparable improvement.The most successful therapies, such as the training for parents discussed above, show a much greater advantage over the no-treatment option.[102] The British government is considering providing this training on the National Health Service.

Helping families in extreme distress

Even parents who suffer acute emotional turmoil, and appear likely to abuse or abandon their children, can be helped. Only one parent in 14 who had abused their children did so again after receiving treatment through one American project.[103] It is usually only when understanding and concerned therapy enables such parents to express their own memories of childhood distress that they become able to show warmth towards their child consistently. Once they are helped to face and bear their own repressed pain, they no longer feel anger towards their baby for crying and thereby unwittingly reminding them of that pain, as a well-known and moving study shows.[104] Intensive short-term support for families whose children appear to be on the verge of being taken into care has been a great success in the United States. Social workers assigned to such families spend up to twenty hours a week with the family, who can call for help at any time, day or night. During the year after the planned support ceased only one quarter of these children needed to be taken into care. It has been estimated that every dollar spent on such *Family Preservation* schemes saves $3 on foster care, and $13 on specialist residential care.[105]

Another group of children at risk are those whose mothers suffer domestic violence. One-third of such mothers say their partner has also beaten the children, while nearly as many say that their children have become aggressive themselves. I describe the remedies for their situation in Chapter Five.

Deprived girls and teenage mothers

Some people imply that certain young single women become pregnant in order to get public-sector housing. Some have suggested that an atmosphere of stigma should be recreated to deter single women from becoming mothers. This would not only be a futile attempt to turn back the clock in the face of changes such as improved contraception which have altered attitudes towards sex, but would also be cruel and ineffective. Girls who become teenage mothers tend to lack any sense of control over their own lives, and therefore often fail to think before they act. A very high proportion of teenage pregnancies are unintended.

Most teenage mothers come from disadvantaged or relatively unsupportive families, and have done badly at school. They are more likely to come from large or lone-parent families. Such girls' educational failure has damaged their confidence in seeking the goals valued by other teenagers. Therefore some of them view motherhood romantically and consider it the one opportunity for fulfilment they have. As they lack both emotional support and knowledge of the demands of parenthood, for many 'a baby represents something in the world that is theirs to love and be loved by'.[106] It is only by being helped to gain confidence in their ability to plan their lives successfully that they are likely to avoid pregnancy. Few are influenced by the level of welfare benefits; teenage birth rates are actually lower in those American states whose welfare benefits are higher. They are higher in states with more unemployment and divorce.[107]

We have good reason to help such young women. Babies born to teenage mothers grow up to have poorer health and educational attainments than those of mothers five years older from similar social backgrounds. They are much more likely both to die in the first year of life, and to be abused (not necessarily by the mother herself). In general teenage mothers are more punitive and less responsive towards their babies.[108] The younger the single mother, the less likely she is to cope well with the stress of unsupported parenthood, and the more likely she is to fall into a pattern of excessive punishment. As I will describe later, children subjected to physical punishment are more likely to exhibit behavioural problems and delinquency.

Preventing teenage births

Another small investment which would save considerable sums of public money would be to improve sex education in order to reduce our teenage birth rate. It is much lower in some Western nations, such as Holland, than others. The factors common to countries with low rates include good sex education, and easily accessible contraceptive services for teenagers. Dutch sex education has been widely praised, including by Britain's Chief Medical Officer.

Many people are anxious about sex education, and believe that it leads to young people having early sexual experience. But in fact a number of researchers have found that this is not the case. The proportion of young women who have had sex at various ages up to 19 is very similar in the Netherlands, America, Britain, and France. Teenage men who have had good sex education tend to have a lower number of sexual partners, and to be more consistent in using condoms. Countries with low teenage birth rates generally have low abortion rates as well. Moreover Dutch teenagers who have sex are more likely to do so out of a sense of love and commitment to their partner.[109]

Lack of proper information about sex merely increases curiosity and irresponsibility. Our mass media are so obsessed with sex it is hardly surprising that young people want to try it, especially if no one clearly explains the full emotional and physical consequences to them. Many British girls have been sexually active for at least six months before seeking contraceptive advice. Carelessness is rife even among older teenagers; only four out of ten sexually active 16- to 19-year-old women always use contraception. The conclusions should be clear: as in all aspects of childhood children tend to meet adult expectations. If adult society conveys to young people the idea that they are too irresponsible to be allowed to have sex, many will be irresponsible, and will have sex without regard to the risks involved.

British young people who were surveyed stated that the sex education they received was inadequate. Governments need to ensure that teachers of sex education are well trained, and are not inhibited from answering children's questions. While schools should consult parents about how to cover the topic, they should not routinely tell an individual child's parents what the child has asked. Two-thirds of 13- to 15-year-olds would not talk to a teacher about sex if their parents were likely to be informed. While it would be preferable if young people felt able to seek this advice from their parents, few can do so. Parental embarrassment is a major obstacle; only a third of parents teach their children about sex.

Education for parenthood

Teenagers are likely to exercise more care about contraception if they have a realistic idea of what parental responsibility involves. British young people rated parenthood as the second most important topic about which they felt school should teach them more. Certain classes in Personal and Social Education have been very effective in helping teenagers learn about children's needs. A New York teacher who developed a successful Child Development and Parenting course found that initially most teenagers punish young children very readily. But the course enables them to see the need to make allowances for young children's level of understanding and limited capabilities in teaching them acceptable behaviour. These courses are extremely popular, and stimulate youngsters to reflect on their own experiences in a way which helps them understand how emotions influence behaviour. This also enables them to enjoy better relationships with their parents and siblings.

Some American schools with day care centres attached assign each 11- or 12-year-old a toddler to look after for certain periods. This impresses clearly on the child that toddlers need a great deal of parental time. The toddlers become attached to the particular child allocated to them. This has proved to be an especially important experience for boys, enabling them to see caring for children in a positive light, even in districts where the macho youth culture exerts 'intense pressure' on them 'to repress their interest in the subject'.[110]

Improving parenthood, improving society

I have discussed society's vital need that children are brought up with secure attachments to their parents, able to contribute to the common welfare. As family life is the major source of personal fulfilment, making it more enjoyable and relaxed would over time create greater social harmony. If parents can gain confidence that children would respond sensibly to being given more autonomy, this would transform parenting from the containment of demands to a united journey of discovery. As I have described, children's well-being and development depends crucially on their parents' positive outlook and emotional security. These qualities are fostered by a committed intimate relationship. In the next chapter I will consider how male–female relationships can become more supportive, fulfilling, and durable.

Chapter 4
Promoting Loving Partnerships

How fulfilling can a relationship or marriage really be?
Can women and men ever really understand each other?
How can we prevent the stress of modern life harming marriage?
How does personality or personal history affect the quality of one's relationships?

In answering these questions, this chapter illustrates: how to assert one's wishes in ways which evoke a positive response; how expectations arising from childhood affect interaction in adult relationships; and how fear of rejection erodes the commitment which is the best guarantee of a good marriage. I describe how various people have broken through emotional barriers to find intimate fulfilment. Nearly all the issues discussed are of equal relevance to lesbians and gay men as well as heterosexuals, married or unmarried. I also explore the impact of income and social class on marital quality.

Commitment and intimacy

On average the quality of a person's marriage makes the largest contribution to their happiness.[1] Most of us have a strong need for a committed partner with whom we can face life's ups and downs. Being single even shortens one's life: separated or divorced people suffer higher rates of illness, and are more likely than married people to kill themselves or others, or to have car accidents.[2]

Divorced people have lost what one researcher concluded is the strongest attraction of marriage:

the promise of not being left alone in a very cold and competitive world.[3]

This sense of security depends on the partner's commitment to continue caring for their spouse. A woman who had a loving husband said that the most precious aspect of her marriage was

the intimacy of knowing you are the most important person in the world to someone.[4]

This is why studies have found that people's perception of the depth of their partner's commitment has the strongest influence on how satisfied they are with their marriage.[5]

Fear of divorce, fear of commitment

Few marriages attain the degree of emotional security enjoyed by the above woman. Research found that of couples married for seven years only one in four were satisfied with their marriage, while among couples with children three marriages in every ten were fragile.[6] Present trends suggest that four new marriages in every ten will end in divorce.

Clearly a couple can have a committed and loving partnership without being married. But for most couples the decision to make a permanent commitment to each other is best expressed by marriage. In some cases reluctance to marry may be perceived as lack of commitment, damaging the trust needed to sustain the relationship. Although some may think that a promise to stay together is no more likely to be broken than a marriage vow, in fact cohabiting couples are more likely to split than married couples of the same age and with the same number of children.

Although people are finding intimate relationships harder to sustain, which is partly why many more are living alone, most people still believe strongly in marital commitment. Four-fifths of British 18-year-olds intend to marry. Two-thirds of American single mothers consider marriage preferable to cohabitation.[7] Among under-35s fewer say they would forgive their partner for having an affair than among the over-55s. Britons consider faithfulness the most important ingredient for a successful marriage.

Increased expectations of marriage

So why is divorce so common? Its frequency has risen since the early 1960s, both in countries where legal changes have made divorce easier, and in countries where the law has not changed. This is partly because many people have higher hopes for their relationships, for intimate communication and happiness, and are no longer prepared to tolerate those which fall seriously short.

Expectations of marital intimacy have increased as relationships with extended family members have weakened, partly because they are less likely to live nearby. Since the extended family has declined, and the working class has shrunk, the previously distinct social worlds of husband and wife have become somewhat merged. As people now have less contact with other relatives, and women friends are busy as they are more likely to be employed, many husbands and wives have only their partner to turn to for the bulk of the emotional support they need. After a hard day at work most partners are too tired to meet this need adequately. As a result, many people build up a degree of disenchantment or resentment towards their partner.

I will proceed to discuss three major reasons why many people are dissatisfied with their intimate relationship:

lack of intimate communication, often due to the emotional differences between women and men;
fear of rejection inhibiting true intimacy;
wanting perfection due to fear of disappointment.

Mars and Venus?

Most men give priority to different aspects of marriage than do most women. In general, men particularly value the stability of marriage, as embodied in their wife's presence: 'having someone to come home to', as one man put it. On the other hand most women regard intimate communication as the most precious aspect of marriage. Women who share emotionally supportive and open communication with their male partner are rare. On average women are less satisfied than men with their marriage. Far fewer women than men say that they would turn first to their partner for help if they were feeling depressed.[8] The dependence of many men on their wife is heightened by the fact that they receive less social support from their friends and relatives than women do.

The emotional support women receive from their male partner may decline further after marriage because, having 'gained' a wife, many men no longer feel the need to try and win her love. For many women, their disappointment is magnified by the fact that on starting to live with their partner, they reduce their contact with those women who had given them emotional support previously. Most women invest most of their hopes for fulfilment in the relationship with their male partner. This is partly due to the deep need to feel held and secure, 'wrapped up in pounds of strong muscle', as one woman put it. But because of male reluctance, such moments of bliss are rare. As a result, many women develop an anxious craving for intimacy. The common pattern in which the woman puts pressure on the man to be emotionally intimate, while he reacts by being distant, is likely to result.

The difficulty of many men in intimate communication causes disappointment in women, in response to which men often feel bewildered. Such incidents often begin with a woman sharing her feelings about something which happened to her earlier. Men tend not to realise the importance of such remarks, often perceiving them as 'pointless moaning'. The man is also likely to feel the woman wants him to rectify her discontent, a pressure he resents. Alternatively he may feel he can calm his wife's complaints by solving the problem for her. However, wives often complain that their husband tries to do so without having properly heard and understood her point of view.[9]

Men's difficulty in providing emotional support is related to their reluctance to recognise and confide their own feelings. This is one reason their suicide rate is four times that of women's.

Research shows that a blend of traditionally male qualities of self-confidence towards the external world, and traditionally female emotional connectedness, promotes secure attachment, and high self-esteem.[10] Later I discuss ways in which many men and women have become able to communicate with each other much better.

Emotional distance and the fear of rejection

The second obstacle to gaining intimate happiness is a fear of loss or rejection, based on a lack of confidence in human love. Past setbacks in close relationships make many people wary of further disappointment. Consequently such people may not reveal the depth of their true desire for love to any other person, and may not be aware of it in themselves either. They do not trust their partner, or a potential partner, to respond sensitively to their emotional needs. These anxieties therefore inhibit them, either from sharing their feelings with their partner, or from ever establishing an intimate relationship. Rather than take the risk of pinning high hopes on a rewarding relationship or family life, such people keep in check the natural human need to be accepted and loved despite their faults. Instead they seek other types of ego boost, possibly immersing themselves in other activities, such as workaholism. Some women find a relationship in which they are needed as a helper. If they chose a partner who wanted to relate to them as an individual, they would fear he would reject them because the extent of their emotional needs would then become apparent.

I interviewed a man who once used to devote practically all his time to his business. After he had started to doubt whether he really wanted to be a company director, he dreamed one night that he spoke to his dead grandfather, to whom he had been very close as a child. When he reflected on the dream later, he realised that ever since his grandfather's death, he had cut himself off from the pain of losing him. It was only by finally facing the distress and anger he had repressed at that time that he was able to recover the confidence to make close relationships. By reminding him of the sense of security he had once gained from his grandfather's warmth and attention, the dream showed him that this had given him the ability to love other people in the future. He regarded the dream as his most happy and precious experience ever. It helped him to see that his over-involvement in his business had been a way of distancing himself from any close relationships, thus avoiding the risk of further devastating loss such as he had suffered when his grandfather died.

When one partner is reluctant or unable to be emotionally intimate, the marriage is likely to be unsatisfying for both. This often leads to at least one partner starting an affair. Half of married men and nearly half of married women admit having been unfaithful. Nowadays people know how common both adultery and divorce are. This strengthens the fear of rejection, and reluctance to risk true intimacy, of the high proportion of people who are somewhat emotionally distant.

It is surprisingly common to have a profound and possibly unacknowledged fear of rejection by one's partner. Deep down such people either believe themselves not to be loveable, or believe other people incapable of committed love. This may lead them to try and control their partner in ways they consciously or subconsciously feel will reduce the risk of the partner abandoning them. However, possessiveness will probably damage the warmth and trust between the couple.

The perfect partner?

The third common reason for disappointment in marriage and family life is hoping for unrealistically perfect love and harmony. This subconscious longing for unconditional love implicitly seeks to compensate for past disappointments and present frustrations. This pattern is also rooted in emotional disappointment. Typically, someone, in this example a woman, feels that she had been loved once, but the parent or other person who loved her either left, or was perceived to have stopped loving. Therefore she can only feel secure with a love which appears certain never to cause the devastation of further disappointment. Unfortunately this wish often leads people to idealise their loved one, seeing them as completely dependable or perfectly loving, and hence able to 'transform' their life. One author who had 'searching conversations' with a large number of women concluded that a great many still have such unrealistic hopes of their intimate relationships with men.[11]

Once someone invests such high hopes in a perfect beloved, they may suppress their partner's true personality. But before long the partner's behaviour will shatter the myth of their perfection. This may stimulate deep disillusionment or rage which can blind a spouse to whatever good points the partner actually has. I tended to overreact when my wife behaved in certain ways. Fortunately as she was so understanding when I lost my temper I was able to see that the behaviour to which I had taken exception was trivial compared to her loving patience in response to my anger. I also realised that I had been troubled by certain minor aspects of her behaviour because I feared that they indicated an inability to love me. The way she reacted to my anger proved this was not so.

Partners can only achieve a contented and dependable intimate relationship if they each believe that :

I am lovable enough for my partner to make the effort to treat me as I wish. My partner is loving enough towards me for me to make the effort to treat him as he wishes. As he appreciates me, I can be confident he won't reject me. As I can be confident of his love, I can tolerate the ways in which he disappoints me sometimes.

Unfortunately many people lack the confidence to discuss their needs frankly with their partner. Most women have been brought up to feel that they need to accommodate themselves to others, and hence many are unable to assert their own views sufficiently. Voicing one's wishes or discontents usually raises the fear of conflict, which can arouse hate or bitterness if either partner feels they may be rejected. If partners lack confidence in each other's commitment to the relationship, they tend not to raise contentious issues. This may avoid friction in the short term, but will lead to trouble sooner or later. If a partner feels unable to state her discontents, she is likely to behave less lovingly. This hastens the day when the warmth between the couple has declined so much that any hope of true intimacy has been lost.

Secure attachment and commitment

Couples are likely to suffer a mismatch between their respective needs for intimacy if one or both of them lack confidence in emotionally secure attachments, as described in Chapter Three. Pioneering studies suggest that only between a third and a half of young adults have an emotionally secure approach to intimate relationships. The most prominent features of this secure approach are valuing intimate friendships, and being able to maintain close relationships without losing personal autonomy.[12] Social class, educational level, and sex appear not to have a strong influence on the likelihood of an adult having a secure approach to attachment.[13]

People assessed as having emotionally secure attachments are more satisfied with their relationship. They also suffer less loneliness, depression, anxiety, flu, and psychosomatic illness. They have more commitment towards and trust in their partner, to whom they are more empathic.[14] Therefore their marriages or relationships are more likely to last than those of insecure people. A secure state of mind in relation to attachment is most likely to derive from having received sensitive and affectionate care in childhood. This gives individuals a positive view of themselves, and a generally positive view of other people.

Those who have had positive relationships with their parent(s) have experienced the parent(s) soothing their distress, and thus have confidence that ultimately love is stronger than sadness. Those whose parents were unable to be patient enough towards their sadness or anger lack this trust, unless they have been lucky enough to meet someone in adult life from whose example they have gained a more hopeful view of love. A boy who was crying on his birthday was told that he should not, because crying on one's birthday leads to one crying each day for the whole year. People rarely analyse such experiences, but they give rise to deep, often subconscious beliefs that one's emotional distress is likely to evoke others' rejection or indifference.

Insecure attachment styles

Studies show that those whose past life has led them to feel that people have little tolerance for others' distress may respond to this in a few different ways. Researchers have described these reactions as three different insecure attachment styles. As stated above, some people distance themselves from intimacy, tending neither to recognise their own repressed needs for close attachment, nor easily to accept others' emotional needs. This is called an avoidant, or dismissing attachment style. Avoidant people may marry or have long-term sexual relationships, but do not relate to their partner in an emotionally intimate way. They rarely reveal any of their most profound feelings or worries.

Although some avoidant people may appear reasonably content in their relationship, this does not mean they have no desire for true intimacy. As stated above, they are less satisfied with their relationship than are secure people. When shown descriptions of the different attachment styles, and asked which one described the kind of partner they would ideally like, they, like other insecure people, chose the description of a secure person.[15]

The second insecure attachment style is called preoccupied, or ambivalent. Such people are extremely anxious to find love, but tend to attach themselves to a partner who cannot give them the emotional support and acceptance they crave. They are preoccupied with relationships, and are considered ambivalent because while they value intimate attachment enormously, they doubt whether their excessive desire for emotional union can be satisfied.[16]

Researchers have fairly recently identified a third insecure attachment style, named fearful. Like avoidant people, those who are fearful lack confidence in others' ability to care for them, and find it difficult to make intimate relationships. But unlike those who are avoidant they are unable to repress their attachment needs, and still wish for intimacy. Unlike preoccupied people, their image of others is generally negative, and therefore they are fearful of forming relationships because they expect disappointment.

In fact most people have elements of each attachment style in their personality, to varying degrees. However my discussion of the effects of the various styles is informed by research showing the powerful influence of a person's predominant attachment style on their personality, behaviour, and emotional well-being.[17]

Attachment and expectations of others

Our understanding of the effects of attachment style is borne out by research findings that people's close relationships are usually with others who see them as they see themselves.[18] This explains why most secure people have a secure partner, and also accounts for the tendency for preoccupied (ambivalent) people who are in a relationship to have an avoidant partner. The preoccupied person has low self-esteem, in line with the negative view of others held by their avoidant partner. The latter has high self-esteem, in line with the positive view of others held by their preoccupied partner. We can see, for example, that an avoidant couple would probably soon split, as each individual's negative view of their partner would clash with the partner's positive view of himself.

The above phenomena occur because our general expectations of other people both lead us subconsciously to choose partners who confirm these expectations, and to relate to those partners in line with our expectations. Someone whose parents lacked warmth, and were rarely able to listen to any distress with patient concern, is likely to lack self-esteem as her parents' behaviour made her feel she was of little value. Hence she would believe, possibly subconsciously, that an apparently loving person would not want a long-term relationship with her. She would feel that their loving nature would make them so attractive that they would be able to choose a more gratifying partner than her.

Rather than build up her hopes of a truly loving partner, and risk severe disappointment, she would be much more likely to end up with a partner who had some of her parents' flaws. In doing so she would be following the well-known 'repetition compulsion' (see Chapter Three). This seems to be a subconscious way of trying to perfect as an adult the crucial ability one could not attain as a child, namely to obtain love and understanding from a partner who, like one's parent, seems unable to give it regularly. Why should this fixation come about? Children know that they cannot exchange their parents for others. Experience has shown them that their parents are the only people who consistently give them the necessities of life. They are dependent on their parents for survival, but often fear parental rejection. This childhood anxiety leaves an emotional wound which, as adults, draws them towards people who resemble their parents psychologically, as if they need to try and master the situation they felt defeated them in childhood.

This pattern is most common among those with a strong preoccupied element in their attachment behaviour. Their efforts to get the love they crave inevitably lead to disappointment.

A child's attachment style may change if the quality of her relationships with her parents, or how she generally perceives them, is affected by some type of disruption. When she was aged nine Usha lived apart from her father for about a year while the family were in the process of emigrating. He had to stay in England temporarily both to work and to sell their home. Usha, her mother, and her sisters were abroad living near her grandparents. She had been 'very, very close' to her father. At first Usha was in touch with her distress at his absence, feeling rejected and thinking 'Why has he left me?' This led to her becoming ill repeatedly. Eventually, because of her illness one of her father's friends advised him to arrange for the family to return to England. By then Usha's previously secure attachment to her father had been damaged and become avoidant. On returning to England, when her father appeared

> I wanted to run up to him and give him a hug like I used to when I was little, but I thought, I'm grown up now, I'm not my Daddy's little daughter any more.

Although Usha's relationship with her father was tolerable for the rest of his life, her trust in love and emotional support had been severely damaged. She had developed the fear of dependence which as an adult has prevented her from making any fulfilling relationship. She became excessively self-reliant to the extent that when she was desperately sad for the three years that her own marriage lasted, she hid this from her parents.

Childhood, attachment, and adult personality

As attachment style is based on deep and lasting feelings about the nature of the self and of other people, it is not surprising that it has been shown to be related to three of the five most commonly measured aspects of personality. Securely attached people are more extrovert, have higher self-esteem, and are less neurotic than insecure people. They are also more agreeable and generous than avoidant people. Partners' personalities have been found to be similar to that of their spouse. This is to be expected given that most secure people have secure partners, and most insecure people have insecure partners. On average individual personality changes little over many years.[19]

Evidence shows that the more a partner's personality resembles that of his or her spouse, the less it is likely to change over time. These are the major reasons behind the tendency for the quality of a marriage to persist over many years. These factors would also account for the fact that many marriages which end in divorce experience problems from soon after their beginning.[20] Beliefs about whether one deserves love, and whether other people are generally loving, are integral to the personality. These beliefs are linked to attachment style, which determines whether one shares secure intimacy with a well-chosen partner, is avoidant or fearful due to distrust of love, or chooses partners who cannot meet one's yearning for intimacy (the preoccupied attachment style).

Insecure attachment and the fear of anger

Insecure attachment does not necessarily lead to divorce. Avoidant people react to an unfulfilling marriage by being too busy for true intimacy, or becoming emotionally distant. But as they subconsciously fear their own anger, they may not face the full extent of their dissatisfaction. A woman who had devoted herself totally to her family consulted a therapist about her insomnia. The therapy revealed that she had suppressed enormous rage about her own needs being neglected. This enabled her to begin to assert herself, and balance her needs with those of her family.

A man who had had a domineering mother had repressed a great deal of anger that he had not received enough love from her. When he married a woman whose personality was somewhat similar to that of his mother, his repressed anger came out in the form of criticism towards his wife. This sapped her self-esteem, reducing her ability to dominate him. This is an example of how behaviour which damages intimacy can nonetheless help an insecure person sustain a relationship of a limited type. If his wife had not been inhibited from domineering by his criticism, his anger at her would have harmed or ended the marriage. After this man joined a therapy group he began to understand these processes and became more assertive. He was relieved to find that his wife continued to care for him even though he was angry sometimes. As he saw the depth of her commitment, he was at last able to commit himself fully to her. His attachment style had completed the change from avoidant to secure. His new ability to assert himself was a critical aspect of this process; secure people tend to be more assertive, both because their high self-esteem makes them feel their wishes should be respected, and because they expect a generally reasonable response from others.[21]

Some people, particularly women, direct their anger towards themselves rather than take the risk of upsetting their partner. This has been shown to contribute to them becoming depressed. People develop the tendency to turn their anger inwards when they have encountered situations in which they felt powerless to achieve their key goals. Childhood is a critical time for the development either of self-confidence, or of a wide ranging sense of helplessness. One study found that for nearly three-quarters of women who had felt an overall sense of helplessness as a girl, this feeling persisted long into adult life. Being abused is an important reason why some children develop a sense of helplessness.[22]

Emotional support fosters hope

The key problem for all those whose relationships do not give them the intimate acceptance they need is to gain the confidence that they *are* a lovable person, and *can* find love. Too many people either blame their unhappiness entirely on their partner, or on themselves, concluding that they are unlovable. They neither weigh up their actual strengths and weaknesses, nor reflect on the reasons they chose an unsuitable partner. Such people have rarely experienced someone taking a personal interest in them in a way which conveys real respect. When this happens, it can release years of buried grief. The stimulus can often be a simple remark or gesture. One woman describes how a counsellor said to her

Why do you hate yourself so much? And who made you?

She began to weep, with the relief people feel when at last they find someone trustworthy to help them face their distress. She explains that this was the first time anyone had suggested to her that her plight was not her own fault. Before then she had felt ashamed of her despair and tried to hide it.[23]

Friends are another source of help in overcoming emotional distress. But they often lack the awareness or confidence to point out that their friend is stuck in a pattern of self-defeating behaviour. Many women want affinity and acceptance so intensely that they tend to relate to their close friend's experiences exactly as she does. But occasionally a friend may depart from the safe response of unquestioning sympathy to help her friend consider how she might surmount a chronic problem. One woman would often tell her friend of her husband's many faults. One day her friend said they should consider why she stayed with him. This led to a much deeper conversation than the pair usually had, in which the first woman revealed the reasons for her profound pessimism about marriage in general. Thereafter she abandoned the fantasy that one day her husband would truly love her, and began to develop deeper friendships.

When subjected to exceptional stress, the need for attachment and reassurance of even the most avoidant or fearful person can be aroused. A shy academic named Laura avoided the slightest hint of intimacy. But when her brother became seriously ill, she found herself leaning on the support of a colleague. This eventually led to her colleague helping her see that she had cut herself off from intimacy because the grief she suffered at losing her parents as a child made her fear another overwhelming loss. After a period of emotional turmoil, she realised that as an adult, she did not need to feel so vulnerable. She decided to accept her colleague's love, and was revived in every aspect of her life.[24]

A 60-year-old man who had also repressed his attachment needs for many years dreamed that he heard a cry, and then saw a hand sticking out of the ground. He began digging urgently, and unearthed a boy aged about four, who was barely alive. After reflecting on this in psychotherapy, he then realised that he had kept his attachment needs buried ever since that age because his fear of abandonment had been so strong.

Being true to oneself

As I said above, in order to build a secure attachment relationship one needs confidence that before long somebody will love one *for oneself*. Being true to oneself can often involve asserting oneself so one does not feel aggrieved or taken for granted. Various incidents with my wife showed that my periodic sarcasm was due to anger arising from difficulty in asserting myself. This occurred because I was nervous of stating my reluctance to join in certain activities, fearing wrongly that she would be annoyed if I opted out of them. My expectations of her were in line with the way I had always perceived intimate partners before, namely that they would be too demanding to value and accept me unless I always fitted in with their wishes. Until we clarified this together I had lacked the confidence to discuss these issues with her.

Many people have benefited from assertiveness training. I studied the written feedback given by 50 people who had attended assertiveness courses. Almost without exception their comments were very positive, stating that they had gained confidence in dealing with potential conflict constructively.

Another way for people to be true to themselves is to ensure that they have enough peace, and solitude if they want it. Periods of solitude enable many people to relax and get in touch with their innermost self. This underlines the importance of protecting ourselves from stress to ensure that we do not begin to experience other people as too demanding. This enables us to be with our loved ones in a receptive and relaxed frame of mind.

Fear of rejection and the power struggle

Asserting oneself in order to resolve disputes with one's partner is often far from simple, largely because many people bring huge needs and fears to their intimate relationships. Fear of rejection often leads people to present the best side of their personality during the early stages of the relationship, until the couple have made some kind of commitment to each other. At this point the self-control to repress one's unlovable characteristics may be sustained only at great cost.

At the same time, each partner begins to notice their spouse's previously hidden faults. Consequently resentment and anger arise in reaction to the fear that the partner may shatter one's hopes of loving acceptance. Awareness of one's dependence on the partner stimulates both fear of rejection and further anger. This can lead either to a degree of withdrawal from intimacy, in which one partner or both begin to invest their energy in other activities, or to a power struggle between them. In this case each tries to control the other, fearing subconsciously that any deviation by their partner from the behaviour they find acceptable indicates a lack of love, and a potential to disregard or hurt them. At the same time the fear that one might feel betrayed by the partner's behaviour leads to doubts about whether one should seek another partner instead. These doubts have corrosive effects on the commitment of both partners.

A power struggle of this kind cannot be resolved by ordinary negotiation, largely because the expectations of each other which such couples have developed are unrealistic. Therefore even if negotiation leads to agreement on a certain issue, another dispute will soon arise because by this stage one of the couple or both repeatedly find fault with each other. Each needs to understand that their partner will inevitably disappoint them from time to time, but that to consider rejecting them for that reason is a response to exaggerated fears. The partner's imperfections have to be seen in perspective. If they cause disappointment only occasionally, the anger or distress they provoke can be contained if each partner is willing to make a commitment to the relationship.

The power of listening

At this point it is crucial 'to recognise our rage at the power the loved one has to hurt us.'[25] This rage does not indicate evil, but the depth of the fear of rejection, which haunts us through memories of our infant impotence. But as adults we are much more able to influence our situation, provided we have enough confidence in our partner's capacity to co-operate in addressing the problems. If a couple recognise that anger is an understandable response to fear, and can be calmed by patient listening, they can understand and accept each other, thus deepening their relationship.

People are unaware that anger can soon lead to increased understanding; they believe that someone who is angry or complaining can only be satisfied if they get everything they want. In fact, people's discontent usually soon passes once they feel they have been heard and understood. Such understanding has long-term benefits; video observation of couples found that when partners showed approval and understanding of each other's feelings, they were more likely to remain married.[26]

An imperfect partner can be tolerated

The fact that acknowledging one's partner's feelings helps cement a marriage underlines again how a secure approach to attachment, based on a sympathetic view of oneself and others, can build trust and reduce friction. In the absence of a secure attachment, the first major breakthrough in ending the power struggle is to give up the anxious illusion that only a perfect partner is tolerable. One needs to take stock carefully of all the times one's partner has been loving and patient, and all the happy or peaceful occasions one has shared with them. The purpose of doing so is not to distract oneself from the extent of one's distress. It is important to recognise that the happy times may not have been as frequent as one would wish. Nor am I suggesting diluting the desire for such experiences. But one's judgement will be flawed by the pain of disappointment if one does not clearly remember them, and consider how one would miss them if the relationship ended. Soon after remarrying, a majority of men actually wish they had not divorced their former wife.[27]

One also has to bear in mind the tendency to project one's negative qualities on to one's partner. This means that if one is scared or ashamed of certain of one's impulses, one has a subconscious tendency to try and reduce one's unease by blinding oneself to their presence, instead perceiving them to an exaggerated degree in one's partner.

My wife helped me see how my fears of her rejecting me persisted partly as a means of my downplaying my occasional impulses to reject her. Although this mechanism caused me anxiety, deep down I was less scared of her rejecting me than of the impulses which might have caused me to reject her. Clarifying these points can help each partner strengthen their commitment to the relationship, which is the best confidence-building measure of all. The more that a couple can make a permanent commitment to each other, the less fear and alienation any dispute between them causes. This means that they each respond with less hostility or coercion to any complaint their partner makes about them. The complaint can be seen as a request to improve the relationship, not as an attack or threat of abandonment.

Drifting into marriage

Commitment to a marriage is much more likely to last if it is based on a shared and deep knowledge of one's partner and oneself. However many couples probably lack sufficient affinity with each other because they have married partly as a way to 'secure the future' or 'be recognised as a normal, independent adult'. If they had reached the same stage of the relationship at an earlier point in their life, they would not have felt sufficiently confident of their partner to marry. However once they have reached the age group in which marriage is usual in their social class, any reservations about their partner tend to be overridden by the strong wish to gain the stability which marriage seems to offer. This adherence to conventional social roles accounts for such a high proportion of people marrying for the first time at around the same age.[28]

Few young married couples discuss or take a clear decision about how they divide the tasks of married life between them, even though they know that the conventional roles have been questioned in recent years. This is another example of how so many people fall into a pattern of behaviour without considering how it fits in with their hopes. Earlier I suggested that one reason for the greater prevalence of divorce in recent years is that people have higher hopes for a satisfying marriage. However for most people there are still many inhibitions discouraging them from talking in depth with their partner about what they each want from the marriage, and how to achieve these goals. In view of this, efforts to help more couples achieve intimate fulfilment need to focus on ways of enhancing young people's overall self-awareness, so they do not stumble into marriage, only to feel a few years later that they have little in common with their partner.

Social class and planning the future

How much do practical stresses, for instance money worries, affect the course of marriage? Some studies have found that low income has the strongest relationship of various socio-economic factors to divorce. Others have found that youth at marriage has the strongest influence.[29] Working-class people have a higher divorce rate than those of the middle class. These three factors are interrelated. Younger people almost always have relatively low incomes. Most working-class people marry at a younger age than middle-class people, who have higher incomes. However each factor also has an independent effect, and from a policy-making point of view should be considered separately. Trying to understand why these factors increase the likelihood of divorce is complex. Middle class couples tend on average to communicate more openly with each other, and to respect each other's feelings more. This suggests that their relationships would probably be more intimate, and promote a more secure attachment.

Another important element in the process is that working-class couples have children sooner after marriage, and generally have more children in total. Having a baby before marriage also increases the likelihood of divorce. Middle-class people have been found to choose their partner more carefully. Partner choice, and the timing both of childbearing and of marriage (or committed cohabitation), are all crucial issues in relation to which different people apply widely varying degrees of reflection and planning. The evidence overall suggests that most middle class people have a greater ability to plan their lives. In addition, having postponed marriage and childbearing until they are somewhat older, they have had a greater chance to explore the excitement of youth, and hence are more able to devote themselves to family life. With maturity, they acquire more self-awareness, and thus are able to decide on these commitments with more clarity. Working-class people have had fewer options of all kinds throughout their lives, and have therefore not developed the capacity and confidence to plan their lives to the same extent. Otherwise they would be likely to have fewer children than middle class couples, as they would realise that due to their lower income and generally smaller homes, a greater number of children would be likely to put more strain on their marriage.

A society with no class or income differences may never exist. However it would not be hard for our society to give working-class people more control over their lives, for instance more choice about where to live or how many hours to work. This would enable them to develop the ability to plan carefully.

Financial setbacks and marital stress

As risk factors for divorce, how important are early childbearing, and poorer communication, compared to low income? In Chapter One I outlined how it is income inequality, much more than low income itself, which leads to poorer people having somewhat worse health and higher rates of offending. This is due more to people's frustration and resentment at not being able to afford the same goods as others, than to the direct physical effects of lacking those items. This process may well operate in a similar manner in relation to marriage and divorce. Research has found that men, but not women, tended to become hostile or withdrawn if their income fell or they were under 'economic pressure'. Neither overall income in relation to family size, nor the amount of a fall in income, was related to negative behaviour towards the partner. But the more that a family *felt* they were having difficulty in making ends meet, the more likely the husband was to be negative towards his wife. The wife was not affected in this way.[30]

Other research showed that the aspirations of unemployed young men for marriage were connected to wanting enough money for a home, a car, children, and a little extra.[31] The level of income a couple consider high enough in order to marry depends on the aspirations of the time. Clearly in the 1930s and 1940s very few men would have been discouraged from marrying because they had no car, as only a minority owned cars then. People who doubt that they can achieve an income to match their hopes also doubt that they and their prospective partner could be satisfied enough to remain content together.

This evidence suggests that the higher divorce and lower marriage rate among those with lower incomes is due more to them feeling deprived or inadequate compared to better off people within the mainstream of society, than to a shortage of money for essentials. Their feelings of dissatisfaction undermine the emotional stability needed to sustain a committed relationship. While people on low incomes do face serious stresses, it is the tendency either to blame one's partner, or to feel inadequate in their eyes, which translates these stresses into marital discord. Even if a couple's income is high, if they are dissatisfied with it the consequent stress may put their marriage at risk. In all social classes, it is secure attachment which enables a couple to encourage, tolerate, and appreciate each other, thus making married people more able than single people to withstand stress.

Many men feel under pressure to provide a certain standard of living for their family, and gain a strong sense of pride if they achieve this. But if they fail to do so the blow to their self-esteem can be so humiliating that maintaining the relationship becomes almost impossible. However if they tell their partner of their anxieties, and feel accepted despite the financial problem, this strengthens the relationship. Other men are so focused on their work, that their partner feels unfulfilled and eventually seeks a divorce. This is traumatic for the man who felt he was fulfilling his duty by earning a good income.

Overall it is the way the couple *manage* their money that influences which partner dominates in decision making. This is more significant than factors to do with the income and employment status of one partner compared to the other.[32] So the balance of power or degree of co-operation between a couple depends on a range of complex factors, including emotional and psychological ones, and not only on income. Secure attachment is relevant here, as it fosters trust, positive emotion, and a constructive approach to potential conflict.

How can the information I have outlined be summarised to provide a policy to strengthen marriage and committed relationships? The evidence suggests that secure attachment promotes satisfying marriage. A secure attachment style is most likely to derive from having received warm and sensitive parenting. However those who did not may develop a secure approach to attachment if their emotional isolation or distress is acknowledged by a warm and reliable person. Being respected and liked for one's true self can give a person a positive self-image, and a generally positive view of others. This fosters confidence in their capacity to find love. I will describe a few strategies and resources which could build on this knowledge to improve the quality of marriage.

Starting marriage well

Couples can avoid years of misery and frustration if they can set their relationship on the right track from the start. 'Marriage Preparation' events give groups of couples many listening and communication skills. Couples planning to marry were asked to take part in research, and then assessed on various commitment and relationship quality factors associated with successful marriage. This enabled the researchers to split the total group of couples into two halves which they had matched on these factors. Therefore neither half appeared more likely than the other to have successful marriages. One half was offered the chance to take part in a five-session Marriage Preparation programme, while the other half was not.

Three years after the start, couples who had been offered the programme had greater marital satisfaction, better communication, and less marital violence than couples not offered it. The couples who completed the programme were about six times less likely to split up before marriage than the other group who were not offered it. Couples expressed great satisfaction with the programme, with most saying they would strongly recommend it to other couples. They particularly appreciated the section on the effect of their own childhood relationships on the quality of marriage.[33] This is to be expected, given the link research has shown between childhood attachment relationships and adult attachment style.

Governments should help get Marriage Preparation established more widely. They should take account of the fact that at present few people would attend an unfamiliar activity such as this. However I described above how parents who watched videos about how to improve their relationship with a difficult child benefited nearly as much as parents who attended professionally run sessions on the topic. The same principle should be applied by presenting Marriage Preparation on video, both to help couples learn its techniques, and to spread awareness of Marriage Preparation events. Couples applying to marry in certain districts would be loaned a video which the government had commissioned. The video would show couples having typical rows, and other couples discussing their conflicts constructively using the active listening and non-blaming styles of communication they had learned. The video would not preach. At the end the video would show Marriage Preparation events in action, with couples explaining how they had benefited from taking part.

Research could show how effective such videos were, by comparing the separation rate of couples loaned the video with that of other couples from a comparable range of social backgrounds in districts where the loan scheme was not operating. All these couples should be followed up after a few years to see how satisfactory their relationship was then, or whether and why they had separated.

At present one can marry in a British Register Office for the minimum fee having given only 22 days' notice. This is far too short a time for reflection on what is probably the most important decision of one's life. If the research showed that the video was effective, the law should be changed to require people to give at least three months notice if they wish to marry. All couples applying to marry would then be loaned the video. An adapted version could also be offered by doctors to women when they became pregnant, in view of the findings outlined above that the birth of a baby puts great strain on many relationships.

Some people may doubt whether the expenditure needed to commission a video, and research a large enough sample of couples, is justified by the research described. However studies involving observation of marital interaction have achieved largely consistent results in several countries including the USA, Germany, Britain, and Spain. Amazingly, one study was able to predict with 94 per cent accuracy which couples would divorce on the basis of a brief interview, a few questionnaires, and a 45-minute observation of their interaction.[34] Given the high divorce rate, it would be irresponsible for governments not to make this information available to couples in an accessible form.

Enriching marriage

A Marriage Enrichment event involves a small number of couples in various exercises to help them gain the ability to listen to each other more caringly, discuss their feelings more openly, and resolve conflicts more creatively. These events are suitable for any couple except those suffering severe marital problems or seeking therapy. They create a wonderful atmosphere because the trust which individuals show by confiding their deepest feelings evokes love and concern from the rest of the group. Couples leave the event with the ability to build a deeper sense of commitment and union, and are also more able both to be themselves and accept their partner's individuality. One man described the first Marriage Enrichment weekend he and his wife attended many years earlier as 'a watershed' in their marriage which bestowed on them long-lasting joy.[35]

Marital therapy works

Marriage Enrichment is beneficial for couples who have a reasonably strong commitment to each other, and who are confident that sharing emotions which they would generally keep private could enhance their relationship with their partner. However there are a great many couples to whom one or both of these factors do not apply. If such couples seek help, they tend to do so only when their relationship is close to breaking down. It is only then that they realise how deeply they want a fulfilling relationship, and become more determined or more desperate to find intimacy. This can cause their predominant attachment style to change, either in the short or the long term.

I will outline this process in the case of a person preoccupied with attachment, who for ease of explanation I will make female. This change might involve starting to see that making her relationship fulfilling should not have to depend entirely on her own efforts, and at the same time facing up to the extent of her partner's shortcomings. As already discussed, a preoccupied person has a generally positive view of others, but a negative view of him or herself. When that person begins to face up to the possibility that her relationship may bring her acute disappointment, she may blame herself even more than usual. However, she may also become more inclined to share her deepest fears with others, and if they are understanding she may realise how she has unwittingly chosen a partner who tends to avoid intimacy.

Similarly for ease of explanation, I will describe a person whose attachment style is avoidant as male. He might get more in touch with his attachment needs because of some kind of anxiety, arising for instance from illness, bereavement, or the threat of redundancy. Such stresses undermine his feeling of stability, and show him he is not as independent and capable as he likes to believe. This can reawaken his need to seek comfort from others.

However the ingrained beliefs of people with an insecure attachment style, either that other people are incapable of love, or that one is unlovable, are usually too strong. They tend to prevent such a person finding the hope to take concrete steps to improve their relationship. This is unfortunate, as couples who seek marital therapy or counselling are much more likely to save their relationship. Studies of all types of therapy show that when followed up two to four years later about half of couples have a happy relationship. This compares with an extremely low improvement rate among couples who received no such help. Some studies of certain types of therapy have found much greater success.[36]

Freeing oneself

Marital therapy can help people feel safe enough to face their deepest emotions, repression of which led to the anger, depression, or other problems which damaged their marriage. In his moving book, *Getting the Love You Want*, Harville Hendrix describes the first step with which a couple named Marla and Peter began to revive their lifeless marriage. Hendrix helped Marla to free herself from a lifetime of passive reserve by enabling her to express anger without blame. Before the exercise, Hendrix helped Peter prepare himself so he could remain calm, and encourage Marla to say whatever she might feel appropriate. Initially she recalled having felt sad recently when she tried to tell Peter about an important event and he was not listening. With Hendrix's help, she was able to identify her fear of getting angry on such occasions. She said:

If I get angry at you, you're going to hate me.

The therapist did not lead Marla, but merely encouraged her to develop her own thoughts. Soon she said:

I have a right to be angry!

This statement brought to mind anxious thoughts of her father. She fought the fears which had briefly weakened her, saying:

I have a right to be who I am! And not try to be somebody else because I'm not good enough!

She hesitated, realising her anger was breaking the 'rules' her father had imposed on her, saying:

if I break the rules, I'll be alone, and I won't have anyone to take care of me.

After wondering what would be the consequence of being true to herself, Marla found the confidence to say:

I'm myself. I deserve to be loved

and finally to shout:

I'm me and I'm alive.

Exercises such as this cannot at a stroke conquer the fears which destroy autonomy. But they are a great leap forward towards the self-acceptance one needs in order truly to love another. By asserting her right to be herself, Marla felt much more positive both about life, and her husband. He too was elated at her new joy and vitality.[37]

When a couple can communicate constructively, expressing their emotions without blame, they can build the commitment which brings both joy and security:

When we are together I feel full and content, free to express whatever it is I'm feeling – anger, sex, silliness, humour, anxiety, general values, and sensitivity to a situation. We learn from each other – listen to one another, and accept one another. On top of it all, I get excited when I see him![38]

Chapter 5
Preventing Crime and Reforming Offenders

Will crime lead to anarchy?

In Chapters Three and Four I have described how families can improve the quality of their relationships; in the final two chapters I will discuss how we can build relationships, across communities and across society as a whole, to tackle our most serious social problems. The most urgent of these is crime, not only due to the trauma it causes, but also because it could irreparably harm the trust and social cohesion needed to address our other problems. The fear of crime engenders suspicion between neighbours and erodes sociability, as described in the Introduction. This fear is not surprising; there is in fact *thirty* times more violent crime than in 1950. Victim surveys, by far the most reliable measure, suggest that in the United States between a fifth and a quarter of adults suffer one crime or more each year; and in Britain the rate is more than a quarter. In most other industrialised nations it is similar. Crime has fallen slightly across the developed world since the mid-90s; however it remains much higher than in the 1960s and earlier decades of the 20th century.[1]

A few months after the crime, victims of even non-violent crimes show increased levels of anxiety, hostility, and other symptoms. A quarter of victims of violence had 'extremely' high levels of depression, hostility, and anxiety. They were still more prone than non-victims to these symptoms a whole year later.[2]

In recent years crime has consistently been either the chief or one of the major concerns people mention when questioned by pollsters. While Americans' fear of crime has been overtaken by fear of terrorism, crime was the biggest concern of the French during their 2002 election. The regularity of shooting massacres in America, such as that at Columbine High School, has prompted a large gun control movement. Politicians must respond with radical measures to the distress and fear caused by crime. It is also an appalling waste of resources, costing as much as one-tenth of national income.[3]

Recent falls in crime may in part be due to government policies. However the sustained expansion of the economy in the late 1990s, and the fall in the proportion of young men in the population may well be more important reasons. Young men commit most crime, so the fact that they will become a slightly larger proportion of the population over the next few years will contribute to crime rising once more.

How we can really cut crime

Tony Blair's famous soundbite 'Tough on crime, tough on the causes of crime' struck a chord as it spanned the gulf between what are sometimes perceived as two opposed reactions to crime: punishment, and prevention through social improvement. For too long the crime debate had portrayed these as alternatives, obscuring the fact that for all but a few zealots they are both essential parts of a sensible crime policy. The ideologues have given a misleadingly negative impression of the feasible options. Those who are fixated on tougher sentences, which they believe will deter criminals, underemphasise the evidence that reducing educational failure, improving the prospects and facilities for youth, and improving security, will prevent much crime. Others say that tougher sentences are not the answer, because only about one recorded crime in 50 leads to a conviction. But these people give too little weight to the fact that a very small number of offenders commit between two-fifths and two-thirds of all crimes, and an even higher proportion of serious crimes. Therefore by focusing more police surveillance on them, imprisoning the most dangerous for longer once they are convicted, and devoting more resources to proven rehabilitation programmes, we *will* be able to reduce crime. In this chapter I will explain how being tough on crime and its causes really could work in practice.

Governments must be frank with the public and explain that a sustained fall in crime will require a small increase in taxation. This will be a most worthwhile investment, one that we would be foolish *not* to make. Otherwise we will continue to pay a huge bill for police, courts, and prisons every year. Later in this chapter I describe some of the inexpensive programmes which have been shown to prevent crime and reform some offenders. These schemes should be much more widely available. First I will consider the most widespread reaction to crime, namely the desire to punish.

Understand the criminal mind

Feeling outraged by crime, it is understandable that we want to punish criminals severely, and think this will deter them. But we cannot hope to devise a sound crime policy unless we recognise that presistent criminals differ from us in many ways; we have to understand how their minds work.

The more professional criminal, rather than being deterred by prison, plans his crimes with great care so that he does not get caught. Most frequent offenders lack such self-discipline, and cannot resist the chance of what seems to be an 'easy' crime when they come across it. Given that the chances of being arrested for a burglary are around one in thirty, and for a robbery around one in twenty, this is not surprising. Moreover most 'petty' criminals enjoy the excitement and sense of power at defying social rules. One shoplifter said that his first crime gave him much greater excitement than losing his virginity, and thus got him addicted to it. Some offending is so exciting, and confers such high status within a criminal peer group, that even severe punishment is no deterrent. Joyriding persisted in Northern Ireland despite the high risk of joyriders being shot in the knees by the paramilitaries.

The motive to offend can outweigh the risk of punishment even when the potential gains are small. To be 'one of the lads' it is essential to ignore the risk of being caught, rather than be seen as soft by refusing to join in a crime.

Such young men are aware of the reality of imprisonment; most have relations who have been in prison. But even the imminent threat of a jail sentence hanging over them deters very few. Many offenders sentenced to attend a day centre as a last-chance alternative to prison continued regular offending during their period of attendance.[4] Sexual and violent offenders are less likely than property offenders to be deterred, presumably because their behaviour is more deeply rooted in psychological disturbance. In 1982 California brought in longer sentences for repeat offenders. Comparison of its crime rate with that of other American states shows that only a small part of the reductions in crime which followed were due to deterrence.[5]

But we should not go to the other extreme and imagine that tough sentences have no deterrent effect. Several young offenders stopped when they realised that as they got older, courts would consider tougher sentences appropriate for them. The compulsive shoplifter mentioned above made the effort needed to cease offending as he feared being imprisoned if convicted again. Young people are more likely to stop offending if they value some aspect of their life, for instance a job, or a relationship, which they do not want to jeopardise. Gaining a sense of direction or meaning may help such young offenders begin to think about the consequences of their actions. And of course the prospect of punishment deters many relatively sensible people who might be tempted to commit crimes otherwise.

Public protection comes first

It is understandable that politicians have stressed the supposed deterrent effect of tough sentences, rather than saying that we need to make large investments in order to root out crime. As we are the innocent victims of crime, it seems unfair that we should be told to pay the cost of preventing it. Indulging in rhetoric condemning the criminal, and colluding with the popular wish for revenge, seems an easier way of gaining public support. But people will accept the need to spend public money on crime prevention provided that politicians show concern about the stress crime causes, and the firmness to imprison those criminals who cannot be reformed. Too many liberals have emphasised miscarriages of justice, and the conditions of prisoners, without recognising that every crime is an injustice against the victim. The public will only tolerate the substantial expenditure needed to rehabilitate those ex-offenders who can benefit from training and treatment, if government also takes a tough line to detect and restrict serious or prolific criminals.

But when people hear repeatedly of cases such as one boy having appeared in court 120 times before he was finally sent to secure accommodation, and another having an incredible 128 convictions at the age of only 12, it is hardly surprising that they demand that punishment be severe, and lose confidence in those who devised such a crazy system of 'justice'. Unless governments take effective anti-crime measures, such feelings will lead to an increase in vigilante action and revenge attacks.

Are criminals born or made?

It is important to consider whether any tendency to criminal behaviour may be inherited. A study of adopted Danish boys found that having a criminal birth parent increases somewhat the likelihood of committing property offences, but not violent ones. Overall research shows that heredity has a modest influence compared to parenting quality and family size. The one gene which has yet been found to affect violence does so only when a person has suffered cruelty or rejection in childhood.[6]

An important partially inherited characteristic related to crime is low intelligence. Low intelligence slightly increases the likelihood of offending, compared to other people from the same social class. This does not merely show that less intelligent criminals are more likely to be caught. Research in which criminals revealed the actual number of offences they had committed found that offending *is* linked to intelligence.

However, the limited impact of low intelligence is underlined by a study which compared its influence with that of a poor home environment in childhood. Children who suffered both went on to have levels of aggressive behaviour four times greater than for those who had only one of these disadvantages. This underlines the importance of remedial education, financial support, and help to improve parenting quality.[7]

In comparing the impact of heredity with that of life after conception, it is important to be aware that some of children's developmental problems, including low intelligence, can be due to hard to detect brain injuries caused by parental abuse. Many children who have been abused develop learning problems which contribute to them becoming delinquents. Such offenders tend to be more violent than criminals who were not abused in childhood.

Why inequality causes crime

In order to make our society more law-abiding, we need to heed the thorough research showing that economic inequality is a major cause of crime. For instance, the amount of inequality within an American state accounts for no less than half of the difference in the murder rate between states. Comparison of 15 developed nations shows that inequality has a particularly strong impact on crime in nations where many people have self-centred values. National income per head had no influence on the international comparisons either of crime rate, or self-centred values. Inequality has a particularly close relationship to violent crime.[8]

Inequality has this effect because of the discontent it arouses, particularly in those on low incomes. The 1992 international victim survey found that the proportion of young men in each nation who were dissatisfied with their income was related to its crime rate. But the fact that people want more money does not mean that they lack material necessities. A British study found that physical need was the motive of only one crime in ten.[9] When asked why they commit crimes, young people most often mention boredom, a clear sign of dissatisfaction. Obtaining drugs is another common reason, as I discuss below. Drug addiction usually arises as a reaction to discontent with life.

The way the discontent caused by inequality arises through comparison with other people is shown by the words of a young street robber. He was not prepared to tolerate low social status which had been the lot of his father, whom he said had been paid 'peanuts'. He said he would not 'slave out my guts to build up this country', for even if he did society would keep him and those like him 'at the bottom of the pile'. It is a similar resentment which leads disaffected youngsters to choose expensive cars such as Mercedes or BMWs to vandalise. Nowadays both well- and poorly-qualified young people have very high aspirations, leading one research team to dub America's teenagers 'the ambitious generation'.[10] As the middle class has grown, more and more people from working-class backgrounds aspire to join it. Hence unskilled wages are now much less acceptable than when the majority of people received them. As it is impossible for most of these teenagers to fulfil their ambitions, resentment will continue to be widespread.

Another aspect of inequality which causes the demoralisation of potential criminals is housing; many young criminals live in housing estates widely considered 'awful'. These estates have become unpopular largely for social reasons; their physical condition is not the basic problem. Those who moved out of slums into the first modern British housing estates in the 1960s were delighted to have a warm and relatively spacious home. At that time few working-class people aspired to own their own home. Many estates which are now regarded with horror were perceived very positively by their first residents, as one recalls:

> [I]n those early days there was a great sense of community among the people who came to live on Providence . . . they all knew what sort of background they'd come from and what sort of background everyone else must have come from, and it gave them a big feeling of all being in the same boat . . . It was like being put to live in a palace . . . The people who lived in the tower were all very nice polite people.

Such estates deteriorated largely due to vandalism and increasing youth crime, provoked partly by a lack of play space for youngsters whose homes were overcrowded.[11]

Impersonal cities breed crime

But inequality is probably not the primary cause of crime. Offending rates rose significantly during the period 1950 to 1973 although inequality fell then. Many criminologists believe that a major factor behind this post-war growth in crime is what they call the decline in informal social controls.[12] These are the sanctions or disapproval potential offenders would face from relations, acquaintances, or other non-official people if they were to violate social norms. These controls are stronger in societies in which people know a high proportion of those in their district, and thus recognise those they see behaving in an anti-social manner. Informal social controls have weakened since the 1960s as far more people have moved to live in areas where few people know them.

The decline of informal social controls is clearly a factor in the much higher crime rate in large cities. The international survey mentioned above found that families are less cohesive in cities.[13] This is probably because family members are less likely to live close to each other. The frequency of moving house contributes to crime, as it tends to cause a fall in parenting quality, possibly because it often involves moving away from supportive relations. Attachment to one's family, and secure employment, are two of the main sources of meaning and stability in a person's life. People do not want to jeopardise them by commiting crime and incurring social disapproval. But once people's attachment to their family has weakened, or they feel estranged from society due to unemployment, something else will fill the vacuum as they look for alternative sources of meaning in life. In our consumer society, money is the prime candidate.

Research sheds light on the link between young men's financial dissatisfaction, and the higher crime rate in large cities. The international crime survey found that young men in urban areas are less likely to be satisfied with their income than those in the country.[14] Cities are places of social mobility, where people go to pursue their ambitions, or because their settled rural way of life is no longer viable. City life makes extremes of wealth very noticeable, particularly as most people one sees are strangers of whom one can tell little but their approximate social status. In rural areas other people are known as individuals, and therefore their income is only one influence on the level of respect they enjoy in the community. Self-centred values are more prevalent in cities, and among young men, and unemployed people.[15]

Social controls and family cohesion

Another critical way in which family cohesion has declined in modern urban society is the rise in divorce, which often results in children seeing much less of their father. As mentioned in Chapter Three, crime is higher in societies in which children have less contact with their father. Children from lone-parent families are more likely than others to offend, but research shows that this is due chiefly to them being less likely to have strong relations with both parents. This underlines the importance of helping separating couples to maintain a reasonable relationship with each other as otherwise the father is more likely to lose contact with the children. One study of persistent young offenders found that less than one-third lived with both parents.[16] This helps explain one link between the strong informal social controls and the much lower crime rate of Japan, where divorce is uncommon.

The strength of family ties helps sustain social controls in Japan despite the fact that it is a largely urban society. The crucial factor maintaining the influence of informal social controls is that most Japanese people feel a strong sense of belonging. One expert on Japan comments that from an early age children 'learn that fitting in brings warmth and love'. Japanese people adhere to the expectations of their families, schools and workplaces 'because in exchange they are nurtured, supported, and cared for'. Young Japanese refrain from delinquency partly because they do not want to suffer the shame of having their misdeeds reported to their teachers, parents, and peers. Informal social controls are also exercised by the 57,000 volunteers who support youngsters at risk of delinquency, and gently warn adolescents who are behaving wrongly in public.[17]

Unfortunately in recent years Japan's economic crisis has increased inequality, contributing to a decline in social integration, and increased youth crime. However the factors I have described still exist much more than in the West.

Although Japanese society exercises more control over the individual, it is rarely harsh. Japan imprisons many fewer offenders than America and Britain. Many offenders are not prosecuted provided they apologise. Often prosecution is suspended, trusting the offender to refrain from further crime. Offenders rarely take advantage of such leniency. Instead they feel ashamed of their offence, and grateful that they have been forgiven and enabled to regain social approval.

People are much more likely to feel these emotions in a society like Japan which has a high level of social consensus. One important reason for this is that its income inequality is much less than that of most industrial nations. In addition, given that they feel a strong sense of belonging to the groups of which they are members, individuals do not need to compare themselves with others as much as we do in the West. Japanese society respects effort at work regardless of the status of the worker. Its relative equality fosters respect for social norms, and enables informal controls to prevent much anti-social behaviour.[18]

Unemployment and crime

Many people believe that unemployment influences crime rates. This is a complex issue. When incomes cease to grow, this leads to a temporary rise in crime. However when incomes rise as unemployment falls, people go out more as they have more money to spend. They are then more likely to be mugged, to drink too much and get into fights, and to be burgled in their absence. While these effects offset each other, on balance unemployment does seem to contribute to a slight overall increase in crime.[19]

While a high proportion of frequent offenders are unemployed, evidence suggests that it is mostly the nature of their personality which both inclines them to crime and makes it hard for them to hold a job. Certain programmes which tried to give offenders employment found that this did very little to cut their rate of offending. Delinquents who were given military employment during World War Two were ten times more likely than nondelinquents to turn out to be unemployable. Many young offenders lead chaotic lives which make it impossible for them to keep a job even if they wanted to. Moreover most frequent offenders do not want the low-paid jobs which they might be able to obtain, regarding work as capitulation to authority.

Less than a quarter of young offenders who had not served a custodial sentence said getting a job would help them stop offending.[20] However, other research has found that some schemes to help offenders find work have reduced their offending. But if unemployment had a strong influence on offending, we could expect the link between criminal behaviour and social class to be much stronger than it is, as most unemployed people are from lower social classes.

However, a cut in unemployment would reduce crime somewhat, chiefly by decreasing inequality. This particularly applies to areas of high long-term unemployment, in which a culture of demoralisation ensures that many youngsters under-achieve at school. They lack both the basic numeracy and the self-discipline needed to hold down even an unskilled job. Their progression to delinquency often follows truancy; two-thirds of offenders were habitual truants. I make detailed proposals to rectify this below.

In considering the relative impact of unemployment and inequality on crime, we should note that white-collar crime, by definition undertaken by employees, costs as much as forty times more than other types of property crime.[21] Many such crimes go way beyond the theft of a few envelopes.

Social class and crime

Most high-crime areas are large council estates, few of whose residents have made a positive choice to live there. If they do have a job, they also have less control over their conditions of work than is the case among more educated workers. Having continually to fit in with others' decisions about work and other important matters gives unskilled workers the feeling that they control few aspects of their life. Research shows that this also makes their thinking about how their life could be improved less open-minded, and therefore more influenced by social conventions such as the wish for money and status.[22]

Young offenders also have little control over their lives, for instance in relation to their schooling and their neighbourhood. As I have shown in Chapter Three, most children are also obliged to fit in with others' wishes in most aspects of their lives. They are rarely consulted about where they and their family should live. On average working-class parents are less sensitive than middle-class parents to their children's wishes. They use more physical punishment. They give fewer explanations geared to the specifics of an issue, and to the child as an individual. They also make less effort to avoid conflict with the child. Moreover most working-class parents are less consistent than middle-class parents; while they demand obedience more and negotiate with the child less, they also exercise less supervision and take less interest in the child. This is not a criticism of working-class parents, who suffer greater stresses than the middle class. Their parenting style is due largely to the sense of lack of control over their lives due to their place in the social hierarchy. Their experiences give them less confidence that they can achieve their goals, for instance in influencing their children to behave well.

Research has shown that children of working-class parents are more likely to commit crime. This is due in part to their awareness of their poor future job prospects, and also to the parenting style I have already described. When parental behaviour is understanding, concerned, and consistent, social class makes no difference to the likelihood of offending. Young men whose relationship with their father was poor were more likely to commit crime than others of the same social class. Ten-year-olds from poor families whose mothers were non-authoritarian were nearly six times more likely than other poor children to be performing well at school and to be well-adjusted. As will be outlined below, such children would be most unlikely to become criminals.[23]

Due to their parents' greater inconsistency, working-class children have more difficulty learning how to meet parental expectations. They have fewer chances to learn how to negotiate and reach mutually acceptable agreements. This leads to two important factors which make working-class children more likely to commit crime. One is that more of them feel resentment towards authority which, as embodied first in their parents, they found relatively unsympathetic. The second is that the quality of their lives appears to fluctuate according to the unpredictable behaviour of others. Therefore they tend not to invest energy and hope in longer-term goals, but to apply a more short-term perspective to their actions. If they see a chance to get something they want, they are more likely than a middle-class child to take it even if it is against the wishes of authority. This is because they lack confidence in being able and allowed to create alternative satisfying experiences for themselves, and believe that the reaction of authority tends to be unpredictable. Children whose written stories showed that they tended not to look far into the future were more likely to take advantage of an easy chance to steal.[24]

Educational problems and crime

The tendency of many working-class children to resent authority strains their relationships with teachers. A well-known American study investigated the factors which influenced the amount of crime a person had committed by age 19. A low level of attainment at school-leaving age had the strongest direct relation to the number of criminal convictions. However, the child's misbehaviour in school at ages 6 to 7, twelve years earlier, had nearly as great an impact. [25] If children's progress in the early years of school is poor, it is very likely to remain poor throughout their school career. Two-fifths of American young offenders have learning difficulties which were not addressed at school. This underlines the need to make children's first few years of school a particularly positive experience.

Some commentators insist that it is children's intelligence which almost entirely determines their educational attainments and future life outcomes. Such people suggest that intelligence is largely genetic, and therefore there is no point in trying to enrich the early education of disadvantaged children. In America this position is associated particularly with Herrnstein and Murray's book *The Bell Curve*. In fact it appears that Herrnstein and Murray's bias led them to underestimate the impact both of children's family background, and their school experience, on their intelligence and overall success in life. They used a limited measure of parental social class, which later analysis of the same data shows failed to register the large influence of other aspects of family background on children's outcomes. They relied on a measure of intelligence at age 15 to 23, while failing to recognise that the children's school attainments exerted a strong influence, independent of this intelligence measure, on their adult outcomes. Other studies have shown that excellent pre-school education can have lasting effects on intelligence and educational attainment, both measured at age 15, as discussed in Chapter Three.[26]

Children can become disaffected from school and adult influence at a very young age. Working-class children are more likely to lose interest in school for a few interconnected reasons. On average they achieve significantly lower educational standards than middle-class children. Their parents often have negative memories of school, and therefore tend to transmit lukewarm attitudes about education to their children. Moreover some lack the confidence to help their children with pursuits which would further their education. It is vital that we provide extra help for children with behavioural or learning problems in the first couple of years of school, including enabling their parents to assist them to learn. This could ensure that they do not feel increasingly alienated from education.

The estrangement of such children from school is magnified in areas of chronic high unemployment, where many teenagers consider trying to pass exams pointless as job prospects seem bleak. Most working-class teenage boys feel negative about school and their teachers, some vehemently so. If youngsters become so demoralised at school that they play truant, they are particularly likely to get involved in crime. While absent from school they can find little to amuse themselves. Crime is both an exciting pastime, and a way of obtaining money for activities to relieve boredom.

Investing to cut crime

In order to reduce inequality and cut crime, it is vital that schools in disadvantaged areas receive extra resources for smaller classes, and to attract top quality teachers. Governments should invest in poor areas, for instance by improving housing, including its security, and providing better training programmes, youth recreation facilities and public transport. By enhancing the quality of life in these areas, and providing more employment at reasonable pay rates, this would boost community morale, helping parents to bring up their children with a more positive outlook. Governments could also cut one of the most damaging aspects of inequality by giving substantial tax credits to low-paid workers. This would increase the incentive to find work. Knowing that their children had reasonable future earning prospects, more parents would encourage them to try hard at school. These measures would help to make employment appear a more attractive option for school students who might otherwise begin to feel alienated from society. A further vital step is to provide immediate professional help for parents who are having difficulty raising their children, as described in Chapter Three.

The emotional insecurity of young criminals

The primary shortcoming in the lives of most persistent criminals was in the parenting they received, which for most of us is the basis of both our self-esteem, and respect for others. Most seriously aggressive children have been neglected or abused by their parents, and persist in anti-social behaviour as they grow up, as described in Chapter Three. Most persistent young offenders experience regular emotional distress. Most drink and use drugs often, perhaps to blot out their feelings. One major reason they offend is to gain the admiration of their mates, perhaps to compensate for their lack of self-esteem. This lack of self-esteem causes them great distress if they feel someone has insulted them, and therefore they are always ready to fight anyone they believe has done so.[27]

Having received little respect and concern from their parents, such offenders have no concern for the suffering of their victims. They feel alone in trying to cope with life, having alienated most people who had been willing to help them. Perhaps this explains why they have a fatalistic attitude to their future.

Children needing special help

Children who persistently misbehave in primary school, and have poor educational results, are more likely to commit criminal offences later. It is vital that such children and their parents are given expert help as soon as these problems become apparent. The effectiveness of such treatment was described in Chapter Three. If governments are too short-sighted to devote enough money for these services, children who also have one of the following problems should be given priority, as they are even more likely to become delinquent: hyperactivity; poor quality parenting; father with a criminal record; poor relationship between the parents; one parent with psychological problems. In addition, children who suffered complications at birth are particularly likely to become violent by adulthood if they were either unwanted before or after birth, separated from their mother during their first year, or hyperactive as children.[28]

Hyperactivity is probably the strongest sign that a child may become criminal if not given adequate help. Hyperactive boys of normal intelligence, compared to other state school boys matched on intelligence and race, were found to be nearly 30 times more likely to go on to commit more than one serious crime. A Californian study shows that hyperactive young men probably account for a remarkable two-thirds of admissions to Young Offenders Institutions.

Children with minor physical abnormalities, usually due to problems before birth, or to head injury, are also more likely to become violent later if their home life is below par. One study found no fewer than nine out of ten persistent offenders had some degree of brain damage.[29] This damage is usually evident in childhood, well before the individual has committed any offences. If services cannot be provided for all children with behavioural problems, such children should be examined to see if they have suffered any of the above symptoms. If they have, they and their families should receive specialist help without delay.

Parents receive little help

Many countries' specialist services for such children are so under-funded, they can respond only to the most pressing cases, mostly those where the child has been abused, or has become unmanageable. Yet these services could be extended to many other families who need them, at relatively modest cost. If parents are offered help *before* their child has become involved in truancy or crime, a positive outcome is much more likely, for the following reasons: firstly, the parents have more confidence than they would if the child was a few years older and therefore harder to manage, and secondly, the parents would be less likely to feel let down by the authorities, or that the latter blame them for their children's misdeeds.

Politicians should take care not to speak of such programmes in ways which stigmatise parents, who respond best to encouragement rather than criticism. However, some parents whose child has commited serious or repeated offences may refuse to undertake parenting training. Compelling them to do so has proved successful in most cases, as they have found the training beneficial. But imposing other sanctions on young offenders' parents is rarely helpful. The Magistrates' Association warned that doing so could 'damage such little cohesion as may survive in already fraught and vulnerable families'.[30]

Services for children at risk of abuse and neglect, many of whom become offenders, need to be better resourced. Their shortage of staff in many districts means they can do little beyond investigate whether the child needs to be removed from home. Such families need comprehensive and intensive support. This will save money by preventing both crime, and the need for many children to be taken into public care.

Disruptive drop-outs

Probably the most vital crime prevention issue concerns adolescents who feel alienated from school. Nearly all such children get involved in crime. Children excluded for serious misbehaviour, and persistent truants, many of whom are later excluded, make up two-thirds of those who appear in British youth courts. These children urgently need help with their behavioural problems, and education geared to their special needs. One pioneering project gives such children an individually tailored programme of work experience and attendance at a further education college. The young people's attendance was surprisingly good. Their attitudes to education and employment improved considerably. By the end of the year's course, three-quarters moved either into further education or employment, a much higher proportion than would have done so otherwise in view of the problems they had before.

Another programme matches an adult volunteer with each teenager to provide encouragement for the youngster to get back into education or work. The young people's rate of offending fell by nearly two-thirds during the year of the scheme. This project costs only £3,000 per youngster annually, a very modest investment in view of the high risk that such young people will embark on a life of crime, become unemployed, or need regular psychiatric care. A similar American programme lasting for ten months provided a counsellor who supported male school drop-outs on a one-to-one basis in finding and keeping work, and tackling any other problem they had. Ten years later, these young men had a much lower arrest rate, and were more likely to be employed, than comparable young men who had not been offered this programme.[31]

In Britain there are about 16,000 children at risk of exclusion from school. Providing services like those described would require only a tiny increase in taxation, for instance by raising tobacco tax by less than one per cent. We will regret it in the future if we do not invest this modest amount now.

Giving young people hope

The final two years of compulsory school are a crucial period if youngsters are to become positively integrated into adult society. Until recently the peak age for delinquency in the United States and Britain was the year before the end of compulsory schooling. In order to reduce crime, young people need to feel valued as individuals, and that they are on the way to achieving a respected role in adult society. Not only must we ensure that all young people are engaged in fulfilling education during their final two school years, but we must provide employment opportunities which they do not consider 'slave labour' for failures. The status of training schemes for unemployed youth is very low because most of those who went on them felt they had not been helped to get a job. This is a vital factor in relation to welfare-to-work programmes, which I discuss in Chapter Six.

A lot is at stake in trying to improve the youth employment situation. In the more settled economic era of the 1950s and 1960s, the vast majority of delinquents ceased criminal activity once they had left school and found a job. But nowadays young men are taking longer to mature out of crime. While the proportion of young women who had committed a crime in the previous year fell steeply from the 14–17 to the 18–21 age group, and even more steeply to the 22–25 age group, among males the proportion rose. For young women who had committed previous offences, leaving home to live with a partner played a part in them ceasing to offend, but this did not apply to young men. Men aged 17 to 25 account for nearly three-quarters of adult convictions.[32]

Youth wages have been badly hit by the growth in inequality of recent years. The longer young people remain on low incomes, the more likely they are to commit crime. Fortunately most offenders cease regular crime by age 31.[33] But the prospect that more and more of our young males will lose interest in school and embark on a criminal career lasting around seventeen years should make the public demand urgent government action to improve education and training.

Constructive leisure for youth

The contribution of education to reducing crime is not only by helping youngsters pass exams. As we have seen, much youth crime is committed due to boredom. Schools need to develop youngsters' ability to concentrate, and introduce them to a range of activities they can enjoy without being dependent on expensive commercial leisure. Youth clubs and youth workers are also an important crime prevention investment. Teenage males at risk of offending who were invited to take part in youth activities committed much less crime thereafter than comparable young men from a nearby district. Youth workers need to target such youngsters, most of whom do not otherwise attend clubs. A programme of activities for Canadian children aged 5 to 15 led to a large reduction in vandalism; the cost of the programme was much less than that of the vandalism.[34]

Drug-related crime

Another important cause of crime is drug addiction. Most heroin users fund their habit through crime. In Britain drug-related crime, which is thought to include a third of burglaries and street robberies, is estimated to cost a massive £19 billion each year. Alcohol is probably even more destructive, being a factor in two-thirds of violent offences and a third of road traffic deaths. As many as 40 to 80 per cent of offenders, in various studies, feel that alcohol or drugs play some part in making them offend.

While drugs play a crucial role in crime, very few people who experiment with drugs become addicted. Most drug-using criminals start on drugs or alcohol a few years *after* they have started frequent offending. The same factors which seem to propel young people into crime, namely poor relations with parents, low self-esteem, psychological problems, and educational failure, also appear responsible for them becoming addicts. Like these factors, drug abuse is much more common in poor areas.[35] As stated above, we need to invest far more on helping such children and their families as soon as their problems become apparent, which is usually long before they commit offences or try drugs.

But the question remains, what should be done specifically about the contribution of drug and alcohol use to crime? None of these substances show much sign of becoming less popular. No less than 87 million Americans have used illegal drugs. Over a third of Britons under 25 have used drugs, nearly a quarter during the preceding year. Drug use has risen considerably since 1989. The number of heroin users has increased enormously. This is despite police efforts to keep drugs out of circulation, and stiff penalties being imposed for possession. Although America is very tough on drugs compared to many other countries, the rate of heroin addiction there is eight times that in Holland. Seizures of all types of drugs have risen about threefold since 1988, but drugs are still fairly cheap.

Although hard-liners try to suggest that marijuana and cannabis lead to hard drug use, United States government research shows that for every hundred marijuana users, there is only one cocaine user, and one heroin user.[36] Most drug use takes place in the late teens, and half of Britons have tried drugs, so it is only a tiny minority who become addicts.

The American government persists with its 'War against Drugs' despite all the evidence. Many American and British judges favour legalisation of certain drugs.[37] At stake are the billions spent on police attempts to restrict the drug trade. The American drugs tsar's annual budget is $19 billion. Much of this is wasted arresting no less than 700,000 Americans each year for possessing marijuana. There are an incredible 400,000 Americans in prison for non-violent drug offences, constituting nearly two-thirds of federal prisoners. Keeping all drugs illegal merely prolongs drug trade violence. This has led to dealers giving guns to local couriers aged as young as 11.

If thorough study led to the legalisation of certain drugs, this would give the warnings against the really dangerous drugs greater credibility. As cannabis is tolerated in Holland, Dutch young people probably understand that government warnings against hard drugs are not due to any anti-drug bias. This may explain why less than one Dutch teenager in a hundred has tried hard drugs. While ecstasy is not addictive, regular users, especially women, are much more likely to suffer mental illness later. However young people will not heed such warnings from an establishment they perceive as anti-drugs.

If drugs could be made legal without any serious consequences, the vast amounts of money saved could be used for a radical attack on the social and educational disadvantages that are at the root of crime. Treatment could be provided for many more addicts. By reducing crime, treatment saves three times as much money as it costs. And if more drug addicts could be given a hygienic supply of their drug, or a safer substitute, this would remove their need to find huge sums through crime. In Switzerland, offending fell drastically among heroin addicts once the government allowed doctors to prescribe heroin to them. This policy has been shown to save the government £20 per addict daily.[38]

Biological signs, social causes?

In recent years low levels of the brain chemical serotonin have been shown to be linked to criminal behaviour, being found in many violent offenders. Low serotonin levels lead to irritable and impulsive behaviour. It is also linked to excessive alcohol use. Alcohol initially boosts serotonin levels, but then it falls beneath the 'sober' level, contributing to the desire to drink more. Therefore medication which raises serotonin could help cut crime both directly, and by helping offenders reduce the drinking which plays a large part in violent offences.

Biological research shows that brain chemistry which relates to crime has both genetic and social origins. Studies of animals show that low serotonin is often found in those which are low in the status hierarchy. Such creatures tend to be violent towards any weaker animal they encounter. The illness and other physical signs of stress low-status animals show are not due chiefly to heredity; if a dominant animal is moved to a different group in which it becomes subordinate, it too develops these signs, as described in Chapter One.[39]

Levels of serotonin and other brain chemicals are related to poor diet, and thus provide another link with social factors. Working-class people suffer more stress, and hence are more likely to smoke and eat 'comfort' foods which are high in sugar and fat; as inequality increased during the late 1980s, obesity among people of working age became much more common. Offenders became much less violent when they were given a diet with less sugar and more fibre. Governments should increase the numbers of health visitors, who can help parents get their children into a good pattern of eating, which need not be expensive. Governments should also ensure that drug therapy to raise serotonin levels is evaluated and publicised as soon as possible.

Will zero tolerance cut crime?

Improving education and helping young people will gradually reduce crime on a long-term basis. However many people hope that the police could become more effective and cut crime immediately. Their hopes have been raised by the emergence of 'Zero Tolerance', a strategy suggesting that if the police refuse to tolerate lawbreaking of any kind, but crack down hard on even the most minor offences, serious crime will fall as a result. The idea is that the more that 'anti-social elements' are prevented from 'developing the feeling that they are in charge', the less confidence they will have to commit serious crimes. In addition Zero Tolerance is supposed to keep neighbourhoods in good condition, so that people are less inclined to cause, or tolerate, vandalism.

Many commentators have attributed New York's remarkable fall in crime over the past few years to Zero Tolerance policing. But the evidence for this is weak. The murder rate has fallen significantly in nearly all of America's great cities in recent years. In San Diego it has fallen nearly as much as in New York, yet there the police have concentrated far more on preventive and longer-term strategies. Other reasons for the drop in American crime include falling unemployment, the decline of the crack cocaine epidemic, and a fall in the numbers of young men.[40]

However one clear benefit of Zero Tolerance is the way it reduces the number of people carrying weapons, and hence the injuries they cause. An increase in police searches of those likely to carry a weapon led to a fall in crime in the Strathclyde area of Scotland.

Whether the increase in police stopping and searching resulting from Zero Tolerance is beneficial depends on the quality of police–public relations. In some areas the police have become unpopular due to racial discrimination by some officers. A study in one such area, requiring officers to stop and search people only when they had valid reasons, led to a halving of such searches, with no rise in crime. In Britain ethnic minority citizens are five times more likely than whites to be stopped and searched. There is in fact no relation between the amount of stopping and searching, and the level of street crime in different areas, probably in part because in some areas much of the stopping and searching constitutes police harrassment.

We need to bear in mind that nearly a fifth of British 13- to 16-year-olds 'regard the police as people to be ignored', while an alarming eight out of ten do not think that police behaviour sets a good example. Many of the British riots in 1991–92 followed an unusually high level of police activity in the area.[41] This shows what could happen if the police introduced a Zero Tolerance policy in an area in which many local people saw them negatively.

Most people obey the law because they agree with it, not because they fear punishment. If the police abuse their authority, respect for the law will decline. The consent the police need to fulfil their role will be lost, and an upsurge in crime will result. However in most areas where the police are viewed positively, young people will not object to being stopped and searched occasionally, provided they feel others are being treated similarly. In fact, this would probably make them feel more safe. But where the police have lost the trust of significant parts of the population, more intrusive policing will make matters worse.

More police on the beat?

In drawing attention to the risks of Zero Tolerance, I am not suggesting that we should tolerate minor crime. But the police can only target regular offenders by not paying attention to every act of littering or graffiti. The idea that our response to crime should be simply to have more police on the beat takes no account of the calculation that an officer would have to walk the streets for no fewer than 35 years before catching a burglar red-handed. Unexpected arrests are rare because an officer on foot patrol is single-handedly covering an area with 140 miles of pavement. Therefore it is not surprising that experiments show that even fairly substantial increases in foot patrols have no impact on crime levels.

However, very large increases in patrolling *have* been shown to cut crime, though often only in the short term. In any case, this would prove to be far too expensive in the long term.[42] The only proven policy is to focus on known offenders and known trouble spots. But targeting frequent offenders is not a panacea, as there are so many of them, and the surveillance required takes a lot of police time. Some will move their criminal activity to relatively crime-free districts where they are not known and the level of police patrolling is less.

Poor districts have much more crime

Nevertheless increased surveillance, with particular attention to frequent offenders, is one vital part of the comprehensive strategy needed to tackle crime in disadvantaged areas. The British Crime Survey shows the scale of the problem deprived areas face. The rate for offences involving violence or robbery is over twice as great in the most deprived tenth of districts compared to those which are slightly less deprived. It is a remarkable *34* times higher than in the least deprived tenth. The rate of property crime is over ten times higher.[43] The increasing concentration of poverty in certain districts is a major factor in crime.

Many such areas are plagued by gangs of young people who, by their sheer numbers as well as their behaviour, are intimidating to local residents. Intensive policing is necessary to prevent them dominating an entire council estate, and persecuting anyone who dares to report their misdeeds.

In many countries racism and fear lead to the perception that crime is more common among ethnic minorities. Research shows that in fact it is poverty, ghettoisation, and the family disruption associated with it which raises crime rates among people of all races.[44]

Improving deprived areas

Research shows that policing has a limited impact on the amount of crime. It has to go hand in hand with more fundamental policies to improve such districts. These are in addition to the longer-term employment creation and education improvements I have already described on page 154. A package of cost-effective measures which have been shown to reduce crime on an estate quite quickly would include the following:

(a) security improvements, such as strengthened doors, entryphones, and in the most disorderly areas concierges to prevent unauthorised entry to blocks of flats. Improved security should be available especially for victims of burglary, who are more likely to be burgled again;

(b) acceptable behaviour contracts to correct anti-social tenants or their children, eviction if they infringe them, and court orders, such as Britain's Anti-Social Behaviour Orders, forbidding known troublemakers from entering certain areas;

(c) assistance in forming residents' associations to represent residents' wishes to the landlord, foster a sense of belonging on the estate, and promote norms of decent behaviour. Schemes giving certain young people a special role to liaise between their criminal contemporaries and the authorities, thus reducing their disaffection, have been very successful;

(d) promotion of youth work and play schemes;

(e) provision of local services of particular value to residents, such as financial advice centres or credit unions;

(f) closed circuit television cameras in high-crime locations, and undercover 'professional witnesses' to observe suspects.

By improving the quality of life these measures lead to a increased sense of community, encouraging residents to put pressure on the potentially anti-social not to cause further damage. Evidence shows that these initiatives do not simply lead to the same amount of crime being 'displaced' to a neighbouring district.[45]

Targeting troublemakers

Court orders, as described above, are necessary because, while residents are usually well aware of the identity of local troublemakers, they are often terrified to give evidence against them. In the first British case of its kind, two brothers were ordered not to go within a mile of the estate on which they had previously lived and committed numerous crimes. Such an order gives local residents easily enforceable protection, because the offender can be imprisoned for infringing it. The likelihood of any injustice is small, as no court would grant such an order unless there was a considerable volume of credible evidence against the person in question. These orders last only for the period specified by the court.

These court orders have a strong deterrent effect even on relatively impulsive offenders, partly because breaching them can lead either to the whole family being evicted, or to a youngster having to leave their home area. A sentence for a common crime which did not involve breach of a court order would not have such a dire consequence. The threat of eviction has also succeeded in getting perpetrators of racial harassment to refrain.

There are also simple ways in which the police and local authorities can use the criminal law to restore peace to problem areas. In parts of South London the police have persuaded magistrates to impose a curfew as a bail condition on certain young offenders. The British government is planning to widen the circumstances in which witnesses are allowed to testify without their identity being made public. Such witnesses should be allowed to give their evidence by video link, so that only the judge, jury, and lawyers can see them. Otherwise they would be too frightened to attend court. These steps would not prevent defendants getting a fair trial, as anyone giving false evidence would still be subject to punishment.

Neglecting crime prevention

The reason that the measures I have described have been applied comprehensively in very few of the districts which need them probably reflects the limited priority governments give to crime prevention. Out of each £1000 of the British criminal justice budget only £2 is spent on prevention. It is mostly businesses and individuals who try to fill this gap, with a massive £2 billion being spent each year on security equipment and personnnel.

In many countries crime prevention has not been given due priority, partly because no single agency has both the resources and the incentive to tackle it fundamentally. To do so would require a comprehensive approach to housing, education, employment, and other policies. The police service usually has no responsibility for any of these, and its predominant culture is to fight crime which has already occurred. As its limited resources are already stretched it is not surprising that its crime prevention activity has been fairly marginal.

Crime prevention which depends chiefly on physical security to make offending harder is of course only one part of a crime reduction strategy. Sooner or later criminals will find ways round such security, and then new and potentially costly measures will be needed.[46]

The logical answer is to make local government responsible both for crime prevention, the costs of crime, and the police. As I describe in Chapter Six, councils elected by Proportional Representation would no longer be under predictable long-term one party rule. Hence local politicians would know that unless they were seen to be doing a good job, they could be voted out at the next election. Knowing that their council would have to pay prison, probation, and court costs for its convicted citizens, local people would put pressure on politicians to improve crime prevention. As the council would have comprehensive control over all local services, they would be able to allocate funds among their various departments, such as education, police, health, etc., in order to cut crime as much as possible.

The police need public confidence

Confidence in the police has fallen in recent years. British surveys have found that only about two-thirds of people are satisfied with the policing in their area. Active public support is vital to the effectiveness of the police, who discover less than one-tenth of known crime themselves. I will show how making the police democratically accountable is important in this respect, and would help protect ordinary officers.

In recent years 'unprovoked attacks on police officers have become commonplace', often involving large gangs. Nearly half of the British officers who took part in a survey had been injured in the previous two years.[47] Two of the major causes of hostility towards the police are the number of deaths in police custody, and brutal incidents such as the beating of Rodney King. These incidents harm the reputation of the vast majority of decent officers. Justice must be seen to be done in these cases. Otherwise public co-operation with the police, especially on the part of the young, will decline.

An important first step would be to make the system for investigating complaints against the police clearly independent and effective. New York has improved public confidence in the police since it transferred its police complaints investigations to an independent body in 1993. While some critics have suggested that civilian investigators are less effective and 'have difficulty penetrating police culture', there is no reason why police complaints investigation bodies should not employ some ex-police officers, who could soon help their colleagues overcome any such problems.

Another major factor damaging public confidence in the police is the prevalence of racist behaviour by certain officers. The vast majority of those who die in police custody or due to unjustified police shootings are from ethnic minorities. It is difficult to assess the prevalence of racism by officers towards the public. However in both America and Britain ethnic minority officers suffer regular racism from certain colleagues, who probably inflict similar or worse treatment on members of the public.[48]

The police must be accountable

In certain countries the political structure exerts too little control over the police. Hence when their actions offend local people, there is more likely to be a riot than any normal political response or peaceful protest. In addition their strategy may not be sufficiently focused on the public's needs. Past attempts to reorganise officers to collaborate with the public in addressing long-term problems have been hampered by the tendency to prioritise crises and detection over more mundane preventive work. In addition, without strong public pressure, some forces will be complacent, and fail to apply best practice.

Democratic control of the police by local government could lead to improvements in these and other areas by ensuring that police managers' work was closely monitored, giving them incentives to achieve local goals, and enabling the police to gain greater public support. In many parts of Britain official police–public liaison groups have had little impact on police priorities. Most police forces have failed to give these groups a high enough profile to encourage many people to attend. But one group was much more effective. It had been set up as a sub-committee of the local council, which provided a full-time adviser, and integrated its work into the council decision-making process.

Local councillors include some of the most committed and able citizens in their area, and would do to a greater extent if councils were given greater responsibilities. They are in the best position to stimulate an improved working relationship between police and public. They are also best placed to bring together knowledge about the local causes of crime, and thus decide on the most effective strategies both for long-term crime prevention and current policing. Local authority management of the police would encourage citizens to demand that elected officials tackle crime effectively.

The very slow progress the police have made in trying to root out racism in the ranks provides another reason for making them truly accountable within the local authority. While councils are not free of racism, they have been operating equal opportunity policies for many years, stimulated partly by the need to seek black votes, and also by the efforts of many ethnic minority people in political parties and trade unions. Councils would be more effective in rooting out police racism and recruiting more ethnic minority officers.

Why most crime is committed by men

One of the clearest, but most neglected, facts about crime is that most of it is committed by males. No less than nine tenths of those found guilty of indictable (serious) offences are males. Women are increasing their criminal activity, but it remains at a much lower level than that of men. While some people may say the tendency to crime is an inevitable aspect of male biology, the fact that female crime is increasing suggests that changes in gender roles have also had an impact.

In recent years the suicide rate of men under 40 has increased, while that of women has declined. Women are gradually gaining more control over their lives, with a minority stepping out of role to the extent of becoming criminal. In comparison, men are losing control over their lives, with more becoming unemployed and ill. Men are much more likely to be alcohol or drug addicts, and those under 25 are three times more likely to die than women of that age.

Now that earning a good wage is no longer a viable way of achieving self-esteem for many working-class young men, criminal behaviour can give them a taste of the power they identify with the male role. This is illustrated by the difference between delinquent middle-class as opposed to working-class gangs. The former drink to excess, and undertake minor vandalism and theft. By contrast working-class gang behaviour tends to be much more violent. The middle-class delinquents are more likely to have a secure sense of masculinity as they are confident they will achieve high status at work. But for the most poorly educated young men, any employment they may find is a painful reminder that they have to take orders from middle-class bosses.[49]

Male insecurity and crime

Having a good relationship with their father has a crucial impact on boys' self-esteem. However, many adolescent boys from poor families receive little attention from their father, and also feel resentment at their low place in the social hierarchy. Some seek experiences of power which bolster their sense of masculinity, for instance by beating up gays, or raping women. In all Western societies, nearly all rapists are those 'most removed from the confirmations of manliness derived from wealth or position'. Such men are said to experience attacking a victim as 'a public ceremony of domination and humiliation of others'.[50]

World economic pressures have led to most people feeling less secure in their job. If we are to cut crime, we must help male self-esteem become less dependent on the work role. We must also educate boys from an early age to be more sensitive to their feelings so they do not need to deny their emotional pain by inflicting distress on others. Aggressive boys are likely to become aggressive men.

Emotional security in infancy has a continuing influence in this area. Children who had been assessed at age 1 as securely attached (see Chapter Three) were more sympathetic to their peers' distress at age 3½. This is another reason why the programmes to improve parenting described above and in Chapter Three would help reduce crime. Research has also found that children as young as 1½ to 2½ are more sympathetic to others in distress if their mother is generally sensitive towards her children, and regularly explains to them, when someone becomes upset in their presence, why it is wrong to hurt others.[51] This would also apply to fathers, and to primary schoolteachers, who need to regard such moral education as a central part of their job.

Positive role models for boys

Recruiting more male primary school teachers should be a priority in the effort to teach boys a more caring male role. In primary school it is the boys who are most likely to become offenders, namely those who have been maltreated or have difficult relations with their parents, who most want a close relationship with their teacher. As children get older, their wish for such a relationship with the teacher declines.[52] The type of man with whom a boy is able to identify has a strong impact on the type of man he grows up to be. The primary school years are a key period during which a boy's attachment needs are still strong enough to make him want a relationship with a father-type figure. Therefore he will be able to identify with a supportive and responsible male role if he is fortunate enough to have a relationship with a man who embodies those qualities. But if he has no such male role model, because of his father's absence or shortcomings, and because his teachers are all women, he is likely to renounce his need for adult affection and grow up identifying with a tough or egocentric model of masculinity.

Men make up less than a sixth of those starting primary teaching. Adverts for trainee teachers and classroom assistants should target men. Unemployed over-25s, many of whom are men, should be offered generous packages to train if they can show the potential. The pay of classroom assistants should be enhanced as it is at present too low to attract enough high quality applicants.

In addition, schools should build relationships with their children's fathers, and encourage them, especially in areas of high unemployment, to help in school regularly. With the right preparation they could help disaffected boys perceive education more positively. Their experience of life could make a particularly useful contribution in careers and personal/social education, helping boys address these topics with more enthusiasm. Such men should be offered training so they could feel confident this would be a role they could usefully fulfil.

Increasing respect for women

If disaffected boys see school as a largely female environment, they may develop negative feelings towards women. Many women teachers face regular sexual harrassment from boys, who make 'degrading comments' and references to pornography. British MP Clare Short received thousands of letters of support when she protested about the everyday use of pornography in newspapers. Many came from women who had been sexually abused as children, who said their abusers had used pornography to present their behaviour as normal.

One survey found that a third of men under 45 believe that pornography makes rape more likely, and two out of five feel it turns women into sex objects. Two surveys of London women found that nearly a quarter in one district, and an eighth in another, had been raped by a husband, partner, or former partner. Whichever figure is more typical, it represents an appalling level of distress.[53]

The vast majority of men have used pornography. Even if it does not affect most men's behaviour, its possible impact on as many as one-third is a cause for great concern. There has been rather little research on the effects of pornography in recent years. However one study showed that it was pornography which presented women in a degrading manner which promoted attitudes in men conducive to rape. Pornography which was not degrading did not foster these attitudes. Research has also shown that watching violence on TV or video leads to an increase in aggression. In addition men shown violent films became less aware of the effect on the victim. Pornography with a coercive element is similarly likely to influence the actions of men with a predisposition to sexual violence, encouraging them to act out their fantasies.

Further research should be undertaken to clarify the effects of different types of pornography. This may show that some are probably harmless, while others should be banned. Steps should also be taken to prevent children being exposed to pornography. As many as a quarter of American children age 10 to 17 have come across pornography on the Internet. A very high proportion of French children have seen pornographic films, which are very easy for children to access there.[54]

In order to combat male aggression towards women, boys need to see male teachers, and their own fathers, treating women teachers as equals. This will make them less likely to perceive women in a distorted manner. We need to ensure that men play a prominent part in schools with women, so that boys learn to look up to men who respect women's autonomy, while also enjoying their company. This will help gradually to erode the male hostility which generates serious crime against women.

Violence in marriage

Much male violence is hidden within the home; the British Crime Survey found that less than a third of incidents of domestic violence are reported to the police. The extent of domestic violence varies somewhat between different surveys in America and Britain. An American survey found that nearly one woman in four has been asssaulted by a partner or ex-partner.[55] Each year one woman in ten is the victim of violence by her current or ex-partner, and about one hundred women are murdered by him. And, as stated above, one third of wife-beaters also abuse their children. If men were being terrorised on this scale, there would be a public outcry.

Research is needed to clarify how this level of violence can be reduced. Women should be given help to separate from a violent partner. Courts should be prepared to order such men to leave the home in serious cases, with arrest for defiance. Housing should be available for women who need to move out due to domestic violence. In Britain many such women want their partner to receive treatment for his behaviour, but courts rarely arrange this. Most women feel that the penalty imposed on their partner did not reflect the seriousness of the assault.

The inadequacy of the legal options may be part of the reason why on average a woman has been attacked 35 times by her partner before she reports the assaults. It is partly due to her fear of the consequences of doing so. However there is also considerable stigma attached to the issue; a quarter of women who reported their partner's violence to the police had told no one else at all. This probably applies even more to those women who have not yet contacted the police. The issue should be brought out into the open by government-funded TV ads emphasising that no woman should have to tolerate violence, explaining the remedies briefly, and giving the number of a helpline.[56] There should be a series of ads, some showing a woman mentioning briefly how she took steps to deal with her partner's violence, and others with a man explaining how he learned to cease his violent behaviour. Such ads would be very beneficial now that the success of re-education programmes for violent men has been established.

In addition professionals need better training about the various options for victims of domestic violence. Deciding to resist her partner's violence, particularly after some years, carries major risks for the woman. She or her children may suffer even worse violence, or it could hasten the end of a relationship she may still want to improve. Taking the first step is very daunting, so it may not be enough just to be given the number of a helpline. Doctors, police officers, solicitors, and others need to understand the hazards a woman faces in this position. This will enable them to help her address it in an informed manner.

Courts should also take note of indications that the man may attack the woman again. If a man infringes a court order he should be imprisoned. In one British case the court was guilty of appalling carelessness. A man twice broke bail conditions imposed for causing damage at his ex-partner's home. Incredibly he was again released despite the police warning that he was a danger to the woman. A few days later he murdered her.

Paedophile panic

Although domestic violence affects so many women and children, it receives far less attention than paedophilia. It is understandable that men who traumatise defenceless children become objects of hate. I believe strongly that those who have committed a serious offence against a child should receive a reviewable prison sentence. They would be released after a specified minimum period only when experts had assessed that they were no longer dangerous. They would then be closely supervised, and returned to prison if experts thought they were showing signs that they might reoffend.

Unfortunately outrage towards paedophiles seems to hamper understanding of the best way to protect children. The desire for public disclosure of paedophiles' addresses has become a panacea for those whose fear has clouded their judgement of the issue. We must recognise that this demand actually *detracts* from efforts to reduce sexual abuse of children, as 'Megan's Law' has shown in the United States. This is because the more that sex offenders are known as such to their neighbours, the more threatened they feel, and the more of them move to districts where they are not known. Nearly a sixth of offenders subject to Megan's Law have done so.[57] This gives them the confidence to offend again.

Another unintended consequence of public disclosure of paedophiles would be that it would compound the psychological isolation which contributes to their offending. Research on rapists shows how isolation, and difficulty in making sexual relationships, leads to offending. If paedophiles feel driven to leave whatever sources of friendship or support they have, they will be more likely to offend. As one put it:

The more we're shamed, the more we're outcast, the more we're gonna go into our deviant thinking, and the more we're gonna feel separated, and once we feel separated, we can become dangerous.

Another said that if social outrage threatened paedophiles' jobs and family ties, they would lose the incentive to obey the law, and would reoffend.[58]

Implementing Megan's Law by informing neighbourhoods of convicted paedophiles living in their midst, and policing the vigilante consequences, takes a lot of police time. This could instead be spent preventing crime. Rather than asking for a public register of paedophiles, concerned parents would do much better to exert pressure on government to make sure that offenders get lengthy sentences, and are given treatment in prison, as I will describe below.

The understandable demonisation of sex offenders blurs the distinction between those who have a high rather than a low risk of re-offending. International research shows that only about one paedophile in eight is reconvicted within four years, a much lower rate than for those convicted of other crimes. Only a minority of child sex offenders reoffend repeatedly. Fortunately they can usually be identified. As with other offences, those with more previous convictions are more likely to reoffend. Some offenders have a definite sexual preference for children, as opposed to those who prefer sex with adults but who have abused children because they were more easily available. The former are more likely to reoffend.[59] This knowledge enables the authorities to identify the high-risk offenders who need really close supervision. Chemical castration should be considered for them on release from prison.

The ultimate irony is that *more* children would be put at risk, from vigilantes, if paedophiles' identities were disclosed. Already a child has been burned to death after vigilantes set fire to a house in which they believed a certain paedophile was living. Vigilante attacks have 'soared' in the United States since Megan's Law was introduced.

Part of the reason for the concern about paedophiles is that we feel safer if we can pin all the evil which scares us onto a few outcasts. If we just keep an eye on them, we think, things will be OK. But this lulls us into a false sense of security. In fact nine out of ten child abusers are not convicted monsters, but trusted friends and relations, most of whom are never reported.[60] It is difficult to face this fact, because then how can we feel confident that our children are safe? But if we over-protect our children, they will not develop the judgement to deal with risks which they must face, sooner or later. In addition, they will resent us for confining them. If parents severely restrict their child's social life, for instance by not allowing her to 'sleep over' at a friend's house, fearing that the friend's parents could be abusers, the child will be handicapped in developing the capacity to distinguish trustworthy from untrustworthy people. The risks of children being abducted have not increased in the past twenty years. If we show our children they have the right to be treated kindly, and give them the confidence to assert themselves, they are most unlikely to be abused. Of sexual abusers who are not family members, the vast majority will back off if a child firmly says no.

In addition, governments should set up helplines for child abusers. In its first 18 months of operation the helpline in Vermont, USA, took more than one hundred calls from abusers seeking confidential help to prevent them reoffending. Contrary to the myth, many such offenders can be reformed. Sex offenders given treatment had a reoffending rate half that of comparable offenders who received no treatment.

Offenders *can* be reformed

Once a young person has started offending, too little is done to tackle his problems and get him back on the path of decent behaviour. There is strong evidence, which I outline below, that certain programmes can reform offenders. Yet funds available for rehabilitation are grossly inadequate. The British Prison Service's aim is that about one prisoner in forty completes an approved rehabilitation programme each year. Too little rehabilitation means that more of us will become victims of repeat offenders.

There have now been a great many comparative studies of various rehabilitation programmes. This ensures that offenders have committed the same average number of offences, of equivalent gravity, as the non-offenders. The two groups are matched on other relevant factors such as age. The most extensive analysis of this research shows that 45 per cent of offenders treated were reconvicted within six months, compared to 50 per cent of those who received no treatment. This may seem a small difference, but it is highly significant considering the volume of research evaluated. Many costly established medical treatments, such as heart bypass surgery, have no greater success rate.[61] Moreover, some of the rehabilitation schemes are consistently much more successful than others. If we therefore extend the most effective programmes we could save a considerable amount of money and personal distress by reducing crime.

One of the most successful programmes is called 'Reasoning and Rehabilitation'. It gives offenders a greater sense of control over their lives by teaching them how to understand others' motives, and to weigh up situations rather than act impulsively. Having experienced little sensitivity towards others' wishes, any attempts they may have made to think before acting were unlikely to have led to the outcome they sought; they therefore developed the belief that their fate is determined by others whom they are powerless to influence. Hence they acquired the habit of reacting with egocentric fatalism to any frustration. Canadian offenders considered very likely to reoffend who received 'Reasoning and Rehabilitation' had a much lower reconviction rate than comparable offenders who had received other programmes teaching skills such as money management and employment seeking. A similar programme was also very successful among prisoners in Vermont.[62]

'Reasoning and Rehabilitation' is successful partly because offenders enjoy it. They do not find it emotionally intrusive like other types of therapy, and are able to pick up the skills quite quickly.

Teaching offenders mutual aid

Programmes such as these also try to create within the group a caring climate which can generate shared moral norms. One such programme uses straighforward terms such as 'assuming the worst', and 'authority problem' to teach offenders how their distorted thinking causes problem behaviour. This programme stresses the need to challenge offenders' common tendency to displace the blame for their antisocial behaviour on to other people. It devotes one whole meeting to each member in turn, focusing on his view of the problems he has in interaction with others. The group are influenced by the respectful way the worker relates to them, and by the attention they each receive from the whole group when it is their turn to consider their own issue. Thus a supportive atmosphere gradually develops. This programme has cut reoffending among imprisoned American young offenders. It has also been run in some Chicago schools, and has reduced violence there.[63]

The way such programmes help young offenders begin to exert a positive influence on each other is probably their greatest achievement. When delinquents are asked why they commit offences, the most frequent answer, given by two in every five, is that they have friends or relations who do.

Politicians should be aware that the public in general, and victims of crime, support spending on rehabilitation. In Britain's first 'deliberative poll' a representative sample of the population voted on various crime questions both before and after a weekend of expert presentations and group discussion. At the end a narrow majority believed that the penal system should concentrate more on reform than punishment. Before the weekend there had been a slight majority for punishment.[64]

Many offenders are hard to reform

Factors which contribute to reoffending are now well known. Younger offenders who have committed a large number of offences compared to their contemporaries are more likely to reoffend, especially if they started offending at a particularly young age. Those who have an unstable way of life are even more likely to reoffend. Abuse of drugs, alcohol, or solvents increases the probability, as does unemployment, poor school attainment, and having delinquent friends or relations. The more of these factors apply to an offender, the less likely he is to be reformed by any rehabilitation programme.

Other types of offender who are unlikely to benefit from rehabilitation include psychopaths, and offenders with severe psychiatric problems. Judges should also be aware that when interviewed, only one rapist in twelve expressed any remorse. This suggests either callous indifference, or denial of responsibility. Nearly a third of rapists released on parole are convicted of rape again.[65] Considering that rapes are often not reported, and only one case out of every ten reported results in a conviction, the number who actually rape again could be much higher. The likelihood that only a minority will benefit from treatment should inform decisions about sentence length.

Many prisoners, even some chronic serious offenders, can be reformed. A sample of Canadian prisoners, whose average sentence length was 3.9 years, were given Reasoning and Rehabilitation. Nearly all were thought likely to reoffend, but some were considered to have a relatively high, and the remainder a somewhat lower, risk of reoffending. It was only among the relatively lower risk prisoners that 'Reasoning and Rehabilitation' reduced the reconviction rate.

Compulsory treatment can work

Courts and probation officers need to bear this evidence about risk in mind. Moreover offenders at liberty are much less likely than prisoners to attend for rehabilitation, largely due to their chaotic lifestyles. Therefore it is noteworthy that those who undergo rehabilitation programmes either under a court order, or in prison, are only slightly less likely to be reformed than those whose attendance is voluntary. There is considerable evidence that compulsory treatment for drug dependent offenders is very cost-effective. Some studies have actually found that treatment is equally or more effective in prison than in the community.[66] Rehabilitation staff can emphasise to prisoners who are compelled to attend that within certain basic limits, the way in which they take part is completely up to them. This approach 'promotes mutual respect and the conditions of genuine co-operation between "us" and "them".' The pioneers of Reasoning and Rehabilitation stress that since most compelled participants arrive with some resentment, it is important that the programme is enjoyable, and explains clearly the value of what it offers.

Shame and reintegration

One of the most positive crime prevention innovations is the family group conference, as used in New Zealand and Australia. These meetings are an alternative to a court appearance for a young offender. The conference enables the offender and his family to propose steps which should be taken both for the purpose of reparation, and prevention of future offences. The conference aims to induce in the offender genuine shame for his crime. Rather than condemn him, however, it formally reintegrates him into society by requiring him to make amends, whilst recognising his good qualities. It also tries to create a climate which strengthens his bonds with his family, thus motivating him to behave more responsibly in future. The victim can veto the family's proposal, provided they attend the conference, but in nearly every case a consensus is reached.

Nearly all conferences agree a penalty of some kind. The conferences have resulted in a fall of nearly three-quarters in the number of custodial sentences for juveniles, without any increase in youth crime.[67] The 'teen courts' of Florida and San Francisco also utilise offenders' need for social approval in order to promote group norms of decent behaviour. They are official courts in which former young offenders sit in judgement on current minor offenders. The reoffending rate for teen courts is very low.

Ruthless criminals

But many of the most persistent offenders are beyond the influence of their parents or their civilised peers. Instead they revel in their notoriety. A football hooligan told of how he and his mates took 'revenge' on rival fans, leaving a scene he described as 'a bloody casualty ward'. At his first court appearance he was 'let off with a warning or something'. He had no intention of complying with the sentence he received for a further offence:

> The bastards put me on community service or some such shit. Fuck that for a laugh.

Such offenders have contempt for those they consider soft, which includes the criminal justice system if it fails to punish them.[68] They need whichever punishment will make them realise that society will not tolerate such behaviour in future.

However in proposing longer sentences for persistent and violent offenders, I would disagree with those who want prisons to be more punitive and austere. Prisoners need high-quality education and training. If activities which give hope are cut back, aggression among prisoners will increase, and more will be brutalised by their time inside. Young offenders are most at risk in this respect. Mixing with those who have hardened themselves to the violent atmosphere of most young offender institutions tends to make youngsters who might have been reformed become more hostile and anti-social. America will cause itself serious problems in future through its growing practice of sending youths to adult prisons, where conditions are often brutal. Many such youths are sexually abused by adult prisoners. Young offenders serving a first custodial sentence should generally do so in institutions or secure accommodation catering only *for first custodial sentences.*

Such youngsters should be placed near enough to home to receive regular family visits and thus maintain good family relationships. A prisoner who has family support is six times less likely to reoffend during the year after release.

The bias against prison

Those who stress the shortcomings of prison emphasise its high reconviction rate. However alternative sentences are no more successful in this respect. By far the most comprehensive study of this issue followed up 18,000 offenders either released from prison or given community sentences in 1987. It showed that being male, relatively young, and having a greater number of previous convictions were positively related to being reconvicted. But once these factors were taken into account, sentence type made no difference. The same result was found for all those either released from prison or given community sentences from 1991 to 1993, and also in a separate study of young offenders. Those given custodial sentences were expected to have a higher reoffending rate than those given intensive community supervision, given that they had a more serious previous criminal history. Taking this into account, follow-up fourteen months after they had left custody showed that sentence type made no difference to the reoffending rate.[69]

Prison is cost-effective

Those who emphasise that prison does not reform criminals stress that it is also very expensive. Such people rarely consider whether prison may save public money by preventing offenders committing frequent offences, causing great expense and human distress. Making this assessment is extremely complex. It is necessary to estimate how many crimes per year the average prisoner would have perpetrated if he had *not* been imprisoned. The most convincing and meticulous study in this area compared the crime rates and prison populations of different states in the USA, showing that for each additional prisoner, nearly 15 crimes per year were prevented. This excludes minor crimes such as vandalism.[70]

In 1997 the British government estimated that crime cost the country a massive £31 billion each year. This includes the costs borne by victims, including death, pain, and suffering, and also extra costs such as security.[71] By looking at the total number of crimes recorded by the British Crime Survey, in equivalent categories to those used by the American study, I have calculated that the average non-trivial crime costs £2,554, at 2004 prices. Another study found that the average youth crime, many of which are relatively minor, cost only a little less than this. This suggests that my calculation of the average cost of a non-trivial crime is not excessive.[72]

On this basis, remembering that the average prisoner would commit nearly 15 crimes per year if at liberty, society saves £37,941 for each person in prison. This is more than the £36,651 annual cost of keeping a person in prison.[73] The loss of the taxes paid by formerly employed prisoners, and the saving of benefits paid to those who were unemployed before being imprisoned, probably balances out and makes little difference to the overall cost borne by society.

Four other studies show that 15 crimes prevented for each prisoner per year is not an underestimate. The most comprehensive American study suggested that the average prisoner was committing about 37 offences per year before imprisonment. This research was based on interviews conducted in 1976-78, before many American states started sending less serious offenders to prison. The prisoners were asked roughly how many crimes of various types they had been committing monthly during the twelve months before they were imprisoned, in order to help the researchers make accurate estimates. The statistics were adjusted to offset the effects of any exaggeration by those who reported particularly frequent offending. Estimates by British persistent young offenders suggested they committed nearly 98 crimes per year. A larger British study found that juveniles given custodial sentences admitted an average of more than 300 offences in the previous year. Drug addicts with a recent criminal record had been commiting a remarkable 400 plus offences per year.[74] A high proportion of frequent offenders are heavy drug or alcohol users. The varying prevalence of addicts in these studies probably accounts for some of the difference in the estimates; most addicts have no choice but to offend.

If we compare the cost of various crimes we can see how society could save far more than the cost of imprisonment if those who had committed certain types of offence were kept in prison for longer. A very careful American study calculated the typical costs of pain and suffering involved in various crimes by analysing thousands of court compensation awards to accident victims. The calculation, converted to pounds sterling at 2004 prices, shows that the material loss, pain, and suffering caused by the typical rape amounts to £67,279. The average robbery causes harm to the value of £12,130, and the average assault costs £7,669. The young offenders mentioned above admitted on average having committed slightly more than one assault each in the previous month. On an annual basis, this would have cost society no less than £95,708.[75]

Most serious offenders reoffend

Evidence shows that the more crimes an offender has committed, the more likely he is to commit further offences. For instance, once someone has got six convictions, there is about a 75 per cent chance he will obtain another. In addition persistent offenders are more likely than other offenders to be violent. Long-term studies of offenders show that on average the annual number of offences for which they are convicted begins to fall significantly only after the age of 25. About two-fifths appear to cease offending around the age of 20. However only a small proportion of the remainder cease as they move towards age 45. From that age the proportion who cease offending rises significantly.[76]

In considering sentencing policy, it is particularly important to note that violent offenders are less likely than offenders against property to cease crime after a relatively brief period of offending. Criminologists call this ending their 'criminal career'.

In proposing the sentencing of certain criminals for a longer period than others who have committed the same offence, on the basis of a more serious previous record, we need to consider how likely an offender is to continue his previous offending pattern in the future. The research on the length of 'criminal careers' is incomplete because individual offenders' records have not been checked over a long enough period to judge whether a conviction-free period of, say, three years is an indication of a career ending, or merely a lucky spell during which the offender has not been caught. However, the information which is available shows that while the average criminal career lasts for about three years, that of the most frequent 10 per cent of offenders lasts at least 11 years.[77]

Therefore the argument that longer sentences may be a needless expense for many offenders because the average criminal career may be only about three years is a very weak one when considering a frequent offender. Studies which have investigated all the young males in a district, tracking them from adolescence into adulthood, have found that the minority of frequent offenders account for no less than nine-tenths of the offences committed by the whole group. One study found that 90 per cent of the serious crimes in California were committed by the minority of offenders whose above average criminal record was characteristic of those in prison.[78] Given that such criminals are caught for only a minority of the offences they commit, it is vital that their criminal history is taken into account to ensure that they are given realistically long sentences once they are convicted. In addition, governments should sponsor long-term research on persistent offenders to investigate the factors which encourage them to cease regular crime.

Those who are biased against prison imply that the rise in the British prison population represents a mistaken following of the American example. In fact prison populations have risen in most European nations, due to the massive rise in crime over the past 30 years. While British crime reported to the police has increased an incredible twelve-fold since 1954, the prison population has merely doubled. We should also note that in countries such as Germany, where the prison population has fallen, crime has nonetheless risen steeply. Overall in Europe prison populations have risen by much less than the crime rate.[79]

I would certainly oppose the American practice of 'three strikes and you're out', whereby anyone commiting a third offence is given a life sentence. This leads to locking up many people for minor offences. In addition comparison of those states using 'three strikes' with other states suggests that it raises the murder rate, presumably by encouraging a few offenders to murder a victim to try and avoid that victim reporting them and getting them imprisoned for life.[80] Using the system of 'reviewable' sentences (as described above) for repeat violent offenders would not cause them to feel that the risk of being kept in prison for life would make murder a better option.

Protect the public

The British government has been wise in increasing minimum sentences for serious offences. Among a sample of young offenders who were arrested three or more times in 1992, nearly half had committed burglary. They admitted to having undertaken an average of nearly one and a half burglaries in the previous month, as well as other offences So a persistent burglar is likely to average around 17 burglaries annually. Of British burglars sentenced in 1993–94, less than three-quarters of those convicted of a *seventh* offence were imprisoned. Of those, their average sentence was only 19 months.[81] In view of the distress most people suffer when they are burgled, this represented an appalling failure to protect innocent people.

British sentences for violence also needed to be raised. In 1994 the average sentence for wounding with intent to cause grievous bodily harm was only three years, and that for threat or conspiracy to murder less than five years. Less than a quarter of those convicted of violent offences received custodial sentences. I am not suggesting that everyone convicted of any violent offence should be imprisoned. However it is well-known that the vast majority of those who appear in court have committed several previous offences, even if few have been detected. Once an offender has been convicted of nine previous offences the chances of him being convicted again is over 80 per cent. This is not merely an indication that certain offenders are less able than others to evade capture. Offenders' reports to researchers also show that those who have committed offences often in the past generally continue frequent offending.[82] If the courts take these facts seriously, they will imprison higher proportions of persistent serious offenders in future.

We still have the chance, if we act wisely now, to ensure that crime does not regain the peak it reached in the mid-1990s. I have described a range of relatively inexpensive measures to prevent youngsters starting crime, and to reform those offenders for whom there is hope. But as I have shown, certain offenders are unlikely to be reformed, and the public needs protection from them. The degree of extra imprisonment I favour is only one-tenth of the scale of the American prisoner increase of recent years. In British terms, it would take about a third of the proceeds of a new 50 per cent tax rate on those earning £100,000 or more, or alternatively, an increase in petrol tax of less than one twentieth. Practically all voters would consider this a small price to pay to stop nearly 450,000 crimes each year. In fact, a 1996 poll showed that 90 per cent of Britons were willing to pay more tax in order to cut crime.[83]

Longer sentences for those convicted of a second violent offence are just, even if such people were not psychologically responsible for their actions. It is just that they are given help to overcome their problem in a way which protects society as a whole, provided they are not kept in custody longer than necessary. The parole system has proved its success; those released on parole have substantially lower reconviction rates than would be expected on the basis of their criminal history.[84] However it is unjust that so many prisoners become homeless on release. While society has a right to protection from dangerous people, once we have decided that it is safe to release them they should have the right to a stable home. In addition they will be less likely to reoffend if they have a decent home.

The reforms I have proposed take account of the evidence that if crime does not fall significantly, the public will continue to put pressure on politicians to be much more punitive towards offenders. Arguing for more expenditure on rehabilitation is unlikely to succeed unless tough steps are also taken to curb crime. The proposed reductions in inequality, and improvements in education, help for parents, run-down neighbourhoods, and rehabilitation, all require relatively modest increases in public spending. These will only be achieved if their advocates understand the process of building popular support to influence political decisions. It is this area to which I now turn.

Chapter 6

Community Empowerment and Political Co-Operation

Can we use politics to improve society?

I have described various ways in which our quality of life could be improved. Relatively small amounts of government money devoted to better support services would boost parents' morale, and help them to bring up their children to be happier and more responsible citizens. Agreements by the better-off to exercise pay restraint in return for shorter hours and greater job security would reduce stress throughout society. A fairly small increase in taxation on non-essential items and higher earners could improve education for disadvantaged children, generate more jobs, and cut tax rates for low earners. These measures would decrease inequality, and thus reduce crime. In this chapter I discuss how we can make our society less divided by showing politicians the breadth of support for such policies, thus moving them away from their obsession with seeking votes by cutting taxes. I will also address the origins of the ability to co-operate effectively in democratic groups. Unless we cultivate this ability and arrest young people's disaffection with politics, democracy will become an empty charade.

It *is* possible to influence politicians in this way. Cynics say that once elected they do whatever they want, blatantly ignoring their election promises. Clearly we should be conscious of politicians' readiness to go back on their word. But detailed research on ten countries since 1945 shows that in fact parties' published programmes do have a strong, though not complete, relationship to the policies they follow in office. Even losing parties' manifestos have some impact on government policies, due to the government's need to address issues which concern many of their opponents. In all but the most unusual circumstances governments' main aim is to build up the popularity they need to be re-elected. Hence they would be most unlikely to make any radical change from a policy supported by a majority of voters, unless none of the other major parties were advocating that policy.[1]

So even losing parties have some influence on government if they gain significant support for their policies. But when the opposition is weak or divided, as in Britain during the early 1980s, governments may make radical changes to areas of policy on which there had been a long-standing consensus previously.[2] For instance, soon after taking office, the Thatcher government cut spending on public housing severely.

Rarely are political decisions based on the whims of party leaders. They are strongly influenced by activists both within and outside parties. Environmental groups brought concerns about pollution to politicians' attention, leading to a ban on dumping nuclear waste at sea, and an international treaty curbing ozone-depleting chemicals. In 1960s' America the Civil Rights Movement led to the ending of legal segregation, and to the allocation of substantial funds to inner-city improvement. Any of us can contribute a little time or money to help such groups highlight or influence public opinion, which politicians take care to observe. Citizens' ability to publicise such campaigns has now been enhanced by the Internet.

Many people believe that ordinary citizens, even working together in their thousands, have only a slight influence on politics compared to that of the media. Some say that the media shape public opinion in line with the wishes of the rich and powerful. In fact, research on this point suggests that the media have surprisingly little direct impact either on political views or election results. This is largely because people's overall political outlook develops in their youth, influenced chiefly by their relations and friends. Hence they are rarely receptive to information contrary to their established views. In addition, many people pay little attention to reports on politics. Over a third of the regular readers of some papers are not aware of the paper's attitude towards major political parties. Insofar as they are interested in reading about politics, readers' choice of paper reflects rather than shapes their views. This was well illustrated by the editor of Britain's *Sun*, who said that his paper switched to support Labour in the 1997 election 'because we wanted to be in step with our readership'. Rather than being influenced by parties' views as reported by the media, most people are very dismissive of political claims. For instance, just three weeks before Britain's 1997 election only one person in six thought that taxes would not *rise* after the election, despite both major parties stressing their plans to cut tax.

During exceptional periods, there may be a strong consensus in the media on certain issues. In the first few weeks after the September 11 terrorist attacks, practically all American newspapers backed both President Bush's labelling of the attacks as an act of war, and his plan to attack Afghanistan. It was the dearth of significant opposition to Bush's "war on terrorism" line after 9/11 which led to the media backing his plans so unanimously. By contrast when Bush was preparing to invade Iraq, opposition by several former government members led to the American media putting forward both sides of that argument. [3] When the vast majority of opinion in a country subscribes to one position, it is not the fault primarily of the media for reflecting this. America's electoral system, which I discuss below, and the overall nature of American society, bear much greater responsibility. However if America had a strong independent non-commercial TV channel, like most West European countries, its media would cover non-majority viewpoints much better.

While few people are gullible in response to media reports, the media have considerable power in choosing which issues to cover. And as only a minority scrutinise media coverage of politics carefully, it is vital that the law ensures that citizens are not misinformed. No country can be truly democratic unless the actions of the powerful are exposed to informed public criticism. Otherwise citizens' voting choices are based on false premises. As Tony Blair said, 'the first right of a citizen in any mature democracy should be the right to information'.

With the growing possibility of corporate power compromising balanced reporting by commercial broadcasters, top quality public service broadcasting is vital in making this right a reality. The BBC enjoys one of the highest levels of public confidence of all British institutions. It is because the commercial media have had to compete with the BBC's high standards that British TV is acknowledged to be among the best in the world. Public service broadcasters such as the BBC should have sufficient income from public funds, and the independence to provide comprehensive and authoritative news and current affairs coverage. They should be managed by directly elected governors to ensure that they remain accountable to public opinion. In addition, no individual or company should be allowed to own more than a small portion of any nation's media. The trend for certain companies to acquire ever-growing shares of the press, television, and radio needs to be reversed if we are to achieve true democracy. The media should be diverse enough for all relevant opinions to be aired, enabling electors to cast an informed vote.

Fewer people now watch or read the news regularly. This largely reflects the disengagement from politics which I discuss below. In this chapter I propose several measures to extend democracy. If only a few were implemented, many people would come to relish their increased influence over government, and would be eager for media reports to inform their revived interest in politics.

Public investment will boost the economy

In Chapters Three and Five I have outlined steps to improve education and cut crime. In many advanced nations there would be a consensus in favour of doing so through relatively small increases in taxation. As many as seven out of eight Britons, and around two-thirds of Americans, believe that the gap between rich and poor is too large.[4] Taxation narrows this gap because the better-off pay more tax, and the resulting government spending reduces unemployment and poverty.

A former Director of the British employers' federation (the CBI) has said that the share of national income given to wages should not continue to decline indefinitely. This is because if people spend less, business will not be able to sell its products. It is well known that people on lower incomes spend a higher proportion of their income than those who are wealthier, who are more likely to save. Therefore as taxation redistributes some money from the better-off to those on below average incomes, more money is spent, which helps to create more jobs. It is unwise for governments to insist that they will not increase income tax rates even for those on higher incomes. Ruth Lea of the (British) Institute of Directors pointed out that the government could easily raise personal taxes significantly without troubling the financial markets, which are

> in a way indifferent as to the make up of tax and public expenditure; what they're concerned about is borrowing [by government].

Tony Blair has suggested that tax rates should be 'internationally competitive' in order to keep and attract 'highly skilled labour'. Yet while Britain's top tax rates have long been significantly lower than those of nearly all its main competitors, it still has skill shortages.[5] In the developed world only a handful of employees are likely to move to a strange country in order to pay a little less tax. It would be more economical for nations to train their own skilled labour rather than damage society by keeping taxes low to try and attract overseas workers. Skilled workers are scarce in only a minority of occupations. A study of fourteen advanced nations shows that levying the taxes needed for high quality training and a strong welfare state can go hand in hand with a growing economy and low unemployment; in fact this level of public investment helps moderate the disruptions of the economic cycle.[6] Low-tax policies will increase inequality and crime, which is leading the wealthy to retreat into top-security enclaves. Some highly skilled workers will choose to emigrate if their governments fail to cut crime.

Although countries with relatively high taxes are just as likely as others to have successful economies, over the last fifteen years or so the range of tax levels chosen by Western governments has narrowed. As it has become much easier to move capital from one country to another in recent years, governments have become concerned that unless they keep company taxes low, money will be invested abroad. In fact while many countries have cut personal taxes, the level of tax paid by companies in the developed world as a whole has risen as a proportion of those countries' income. And contrary to the concern about globalisation, international evidence shows that a country's openness to international trade has no consistent impact on its economic performance, whether its tax levels are high or low. It is whether the government keeps inflation, investment and its borrowing at acceptable levels which is critical.

However, governments should reduce the possibility that financial markets might decide to penalise a country whose taxes were not considered low enough. Rules need to be agreed across the European Union (EU), or more widely if possible, so that regions and nations do not continue to neglect public investment by competing with tax concessions and other incentives to try and attract company investment.[7] If no such agreement is reached, it may become more and more difficult to attain civilised standards in health and other public services.

In fact company taxation levels are only a small factor in investment decisions. The overall prospects for business, and the quality of transport, communications, the labour force, and government, in the countries under consideration are much more important. Nor should governments weaken trade unions and drive wages down for fear that companies will relocate in poor countries otherwise. A growing share of investment across national boundaries is invested in wealthy rather than poor countries.[8] Provided we educate our citizens well, maintain a good infrastructure of transport and fuel supply, etc., and prevent crime getting out of hand, companies will invest in North America and Western Europe in order to retain access to the world's biggest markets.

Once rules on minimum tax levels have been fixed, it would be wise for the EU, and similar blocs such as NAFTA, to bring in policies on limited investment subsidies to boost employment in their poorer regions. Governments should also locate as many of their own offices as possible there. These policies should aim only to reduce inequality *within* developed nations. They must not be a means of gaining an unfair advantage over the products of developing nations.

Governments' attempts to win votes by keeping taxes low have also involved joint ventures in which the private sector provides what had been public services. This often ends with the taxpayer paying much more in the long run.[9] Such schemes have often foundered when the private sector has failed to take full commercial responsibility, believing that the government would compensate for any losses since for political reasons it could not afford to let the programme fail. EU and British surveys show that the public overwhelmingly reject these schemes, with only around one in twenty of those questioned believing the private sector should provide health or education services. Those who believe that governments spend too much on public services should note that since such criticisms became common in the 1970s, Western Europe has become much wealthier at the same time as welfare spending has grown significantly.

Maintaining employment, protecting the environment

The pressure on governments and regions to cut business taxes and regulation causes environmental damage. As I describe in Chapter Two, unless we take radical measures to reduce global warming, our children and grandchildren will suffer severely. Governments are reluctant to curb greenhouse gas emissions by imposing energy conservation measures, because industries from countries with weaker environmental standards would gain a competitive advantage. At present most governments charge employers too much tax for each worker they employ, while polluting industries have little incentive to clean up their act. Taxes on goods which cause pollution, during their manufacture or their use, are either non-existent, or far too low. Researchers have calculated that if Britain taxed companies' fuel use, and cut tax on employment by a corresponding amount, this would create an astounding 717,000 jobs within ten years.[10] These would include energy conservation work, and recycling industrial waste. The British government is taking some limited steps in this direction by introducing its climate change levy.

Nearly three-quarters of Americans would support an energy tax of this kind.[11] What has stopped governments bringing in such sensible measures? George Bush has opted out of the Kyoto agreement to reduce emissions of the gases which cause global warming. Although the European Commission has proposed an energy tax in order to cut these emissions, European governments have failed to agree. As I write they are trying to finalise an "emissions trading" scheme. This might give industry strong incentives to conserve fuel, but may turn out to be grossly inadequate.

An energy tax need not increase the overall tax burden on industry, as the tax on employment could be cut correspondingly. However industry has opposed any such tax. But if citizens pressed their governments to agree a Europe-wide policy to promote employment by taxing pollution rather than jobs, the industries of each country would not be disadvantaged in relation to their European competitors. All would have to pay a realistic price for fuel, giving them an incentive to find ways of using less. Such a tax could be phased in, so that customers of energy-intensive products had time to adapt to using less polluting substitutes. It would be perfectly practicable; all the Scandinavian countries have had such taxes since 1993.[12]

Ideally a measure of this kind would be introduced in tandem with the major industrial countries outside the EU, so that their exports were unable to undercut European products by being made either with cheaper fuel, or without observing equivalent environmental standards. However the leaders of most non-EU industrial countries are unlikely to agree to a realistic energy tax in the foreseeable future. In that case the EU ought to impose levies on the imports of those countries in line with the competitive advantage they enjoyed by using undertaxed fuel. It may seem unlikely that the EU would take such a stand. However European citizens would have an incentive to reduce not only the economic loss entailed by European products being undercut by these imports, but also the disastrous future consequences of unchecked global warming. Therefore if they asserted themselves to demand an anti-pollution policy of this kind, maybe by boycotting the goods of the most polluting multinationals, politicians prepared to take the lead could rise to power. Any such move should be part of a deal helping the poorer countries to conserve fuel and cut pollution, in return for increased development aid.

Many commentators believe that the rules of the World Trade Organisation (WTO) could allow such levies provided they were genuinely based on environmental standards, and not a bogus means of protecting domestic industries. The WTO has actually admitted the need for international rules to safeguard the environment, though up to now its decisions have put the interests of huge corporations first.[13] If the WTO tries to bar such import levies, the EU should continue with them anyway. Nearly nine tenths of EU trade is between member nations, and it does not have a trade deficit with the rest of the world. Therefore any attempts by countries whose exports were hit by such a levy to retaliate by imposing levies on EU exports would have little overall impact. The EU would lose some export orders, but would gain a similar volume of business by substituting its own products for the items it imported before the introduction of the levy. The benefits in terms of protecting the environment and increasing employment easily justify such steps. Provided the EU stood firm on the issue, it would eventually be able to negotiate an agreement with the countries concerned. It could stress that other nations have defied the WTO, but out of self-interest, for instance the United States by giving large tax breaks to exporters. It should also be inspired by the life-saving campaign which won the backing of the South African courts for the use of generic anti-AIDS drugs, in defiance of the drug multinationals and the WTO.

In fact, tough environmental measures have been of benefit to industry. As such standards rise in various countries, firms which have been stimulated by their own government's high standards to find efficient and cleaner production processes have a competitive advantage over companies elsewhere. Regulation has compelled companies to invest in cleaner processes which actually save them money in due course, in some cases remarkably quickly. One study found that two-thirds of waste reduction schemes either cost the companies involved nothing, or repaid the investment within less than one year.

Taxes on fuel do not need to hit the poor. State benefits should be increased by rather more than the extra costs these taxes cause. This would ensure that poor people were no worse off, but still, like everyone else, had an increased incentive to save energy. Governments should help poor people to make their homes fuel-efficient.

Rich nations should know that their hypocrisy over 'free trade' could stimulate further terror attacks on them, and undermine the international co-operation needed to prevent terrorism. Agricultural subsidies for Western farmers are worth more than the total income of Black Africa, and a massive seven times more than aid for the developing world. At the same time tariffs on poor nations' imports to the West rob them of nearly $2 billion every single day.[14] We will not gain the co-operation of the developing world to preserve the environment if we deny them a fair share of the world's wealth. While WTO rulings in 2004 suggest that wealthy nations may start to cut some of their subsidies, they will probably be slow to do so unless they face continuing political pressure.

As well as scrapping its farm subsidies, and allowing poor countries free access to its markets, the EU should penalise nations whose workers are subject to severe oppression. At the same time it should increase development aid to poor countries considerably provided they guarantee workers' rights. Through these actions the EU could embolden weaker countries who have felt pushed into accepting the commands of the United States government. The latter is trying to form a 'Free Trade Area of the Americas' in which huge corporations would ride roughshod over other countries' attempts to maintain living wage levels, and environmental and safety standards.

George Monbiot has proposed various apt measures to rectify the harmful effects of globalisation, including replacement of the World Trade Organisation with a 'Fair Trade Organisation' to give the poor nations a fair deal. However his ambitious proposals need a much clearer political strategy to gain the power to achieve them. An international citizens' campaign needs to be developed with intermediate goals which could be achieved sooner, to encourage people to take part. Such a campaign would promote Fairtrade products,which give farmers a decent price, rather than the pittance they get on international markets. Politicians who care only for their own careers would try to ignore the campaign. However it could influence them indirectly, and gain publicity, by boycotting the most outrageously subsidised products. These include clothing made of American cotton, which enriches large companies at the expense of poor African farmers.[15] Such a boycott would not need mass support to make a significant dent in a firm's profits. This would be an effective way of reminding politicians to heed public concerns, or suffer the consequences.

Despite the desperate poverty of the developing world, this book focuses chiefly on the developed nations. This is because any significant improvement in the condition of the developing world depends on political will in the developed nations. Their policies perpetuate the misery of the poor nations. But there are many developed world citizens who want their governments to give justice to the developing nations. This chapter outlines how these people can be encouraged to realise their potential power, and show their governments that they will lose many votes unless they take radical steps to enable poor nations to achieve a decent standard of living.

Curb the gamblers

Continued prosperity also depends on inter-governmental action to promote stability in the world economy. Short-term financial speculation has grown enormously in recent years. The West could have been seriously harmed by the South-east Asian crisis in 1997. Speculators suddenly lost confidence in the region, and withdrew $105 billion from the five worst affected countries, causing wide-scale unemployment and bankruptcies there. These nations had to cut their imports from the West, but the global effect could easily have been much greater if investors' fears had weakened other currencies. Such crises could be reduced or averted by governments penalising investors who keep money in their country for less than a minimum period, or seek to remove it during an economic crisis. Chile and Malaysia have successfully used such policies.[16]

When foreign investors have judged that there are large profits to be made in a certain country, their eagerness to do so has often led to a surge in prices of certain key commodities such as real estate. After a while these investors begin to realise that the country's economy will probably not continue to expand. They start to sell their investments. Other investors realise that unless they rapidly follow suit, the price of their assets in the country will fall, and the profits they were expecting will be lost. The resulting panic leads to a complete loss of confidence in the country's economy and a slump in the value of its currency. The country is close to being unable to service its foreign debts.

The International Monetary Fund (IMF) could help national governments resolve such problems in a way which would enable the world economy to expand steadily. But in fact it has prevented countries in this position from taking measures to stem the downturn in their economy. Instead it has insisted on steps which have prioritised shoring up the value of the currency in the short term. These have included interest rate rises, complete repayment of all foreign loans, and cutbacks in essential government programmes which would have helped sustain the economy during the crisis period. By prioritising support of the currency, the IMF protects the value foreign investors can get by selling their assets and taking the money out of the country.

The major flaw in the IMF's approach to these situations is its protection of incautious investors from the severe losses they would otherwise have suffered. Knowing that the IMF has followed such policies, many of those considering an investment in a promising emerging economy fail to give due weight to the risks they are taking. They thus saturate the market, bidding up asset prices to levels which later prove unsustainable. If there was no history of IMF action, these investors would have been more cautious. Instead of a boom-bust disaster, a more moderate level of investment would have enabled the economy to continue steady expansion.

Other government bodies also protect speculators. In 1998 Long-Term Capital Management, a misleadingly named speculative investment fund, nearly crashed with debts fifty times greater than the capital investors had put in it. Alan Greenspan, chair of the US Federal Reserve, said its collapse threatened the stability of the whole world economy. The New York State financial authorities co-ordinated a bail-out of the fund. Once again speculators learned that they could rely on their friends in government to protect them from the full effects of their risk-taking. Controls should be placed on short-term and reckless lending by such funds. Governments should give tax incentives to long-term investments in productive enterprises. And an international mechanism is needed to give temporary support to economies in crisis to enable them to maintain trade and production, and thus prevent a recession becoming a slump.

Many of those who wish to curb currency speculation support the tax on commercial foreign currency transactions proposed by the Nobel-Prize-winning economist James Tobin. While the intentions of this idea are good, nowadays most foreign currency transactions are not speculative, but are undertaken by companies needing to offset the risks which currency fluctuations pose to legitimate trading.[17]

It would be more feasible to campaign for inter-governmental agreement to help weaker countries protect their economies from excessive exposure to the international financial markets, as described above. If the IMF and World Bank will not bring in such measures, countries should cease subscribing to them, and set up alternative bodies. This is another area in which campaigns could put pressure on the EU to act in line with its citizens' wish to help poor countries.

Such measures would give governments more control over their economies. However it is possible *under the present circumstances* for Western governments to invest in their economies much more confidently than they do. Because of the excessive faith placed in markets, most governments make only modest attempts to boost employment. Many welfare-to-work schemes generate additional jobs for only about a third of those who take part in then. When people leave such limited schemes and find work, it is chiefly because of growth in the economy; the schemes have little real effect. Some schemes offer employers subsidies for taking on unemployed people. But the main drawback is that firms will take the subsidies, yet do so for employing people they would have hired anyway, or by laying off their present temporary workers, and later substituting people who qualify for the subsidy. The fate of existing temporary workers is a good guide to what those involved in such schemes can expect. Only one in eight Britons who start temporary jobs are still with the same employer nine months later, while over half are once more unemployed. Two-thirds of those on British government training schemes become unemployed again within nine months.

Welfare-to-work programmes have limited success partly because governments are scared of a more long-term increase in public spending. If instead of dubious subsidies to employers, they were to invest larger sums in improved infrastructure and public services, enabling councils and government agencies to train unemployed people for jobs that are actually needed, none of the money would be wasted. Short-term training schemes will boost private sector employment slightly if the training is of high quality.[18] But private sector investment will expand significantly only when business is confident that the overall level of demand is set to grow on a sustained basis. As most economies have rarely reached this point, once demand begins to grow supply lags behind, as industry has invested too little. Hence interest rates have to be increased in order to prevent inflation, and the recovery is aborted before it can get going. The only way out of this hopeless circle is for government to invest at the phase of the economic cycle when business confidence is too low. But if governments fail to do so because they keep taxes low in their anxiety to buy votes, we will have more unemployment and social unrest in future.

At other points of the economic cycle, companies invest too much when prospects for profit appear good. Hence after a while supply exceeds demand. Prices and then profits fall, and workers are laid off. Provided government has raised sufficient tax during the expansionary phase, it can afford to invest appropriately and help the economy begin to grow again.

Can we have honest politicians?

I have described how politicians could provide what most people want without damaging the economy. But will they do so, and how can we decide which, if any, are worth voting for? International surveys show that the quality valued most in a politician is integrity. In comparison charisma, or the politician's perceived personality strength, is considered much less important. There is increasing evidence that voters are put off by the 'negative campaigning' to which politicians appear addicted. Most of them seem reluctant to explain their policies frankly. They thereby reveal their lack of integrity. Politicians' defensiveness is partly due to their fear that the media will misrepresent them, but unfortunately it merely leads to them being seen as devious.

Politicians have a particularly poor reputation in countries such as America and Britain which use the 'first past the post' electoral system. There a party can gain total power with less than four-tenths of the vote. This great prize encourages politicians to ditch their principles. Small parties become irrelevant as any vote for them is effectively wasted. The two major parties need only compete with each other, and therefore propose middle of the road policies aimed at the undecided voters. Power-hungry leaders over-emphasise the electoral benefits of party unity in order to deter members from arguing for more honest policies.[19] The public have little choice. Whichever politician has the integrity to offer them a real choice, by giving them Proportional Representation, should stand to gain substantial support.

But most politicians' craving for power is too strong for them to trust that integrity will be rewarded. Under 'first past the post' each party becomes stuck in the habit of exaggerating its opponents' failings, and pretending that its policies are the best available for all strata of society. It does not run the risk of being exposed by an honest opponent. As honesty is not on offer in the two-party marketplace, citizens' desire for it can safely be ignored. I discuss electoral reform further below.

Citizens feel powerless

It is not surprising, therefore, that both Americans and Britons are very cynical towards politics. Only two-fifths of Americans are satisfied with their government, which nearly three quarters believe is 'pretty much run by a few big interests'. Four Britons out of five believe that 'most politicians will promise anything to win votes'. Only about half of Americans bother to vote, almost the lowest turnout of any democracy. Even the record 60% turnout in the 2004 presidential election only just exceeded Britain's record *lowest* turnout in 2001. America's relatively low turnouts are not due to indifference; over four-fifths think the public should have more say over government and the Congress. Three-quarters have more confidence in the judgment of the public than that of politicians. Turnout is higher in Europe, but is falling.[20]

Turnout is particularly low among young people. Young people are less likely to take any interest in politics than ever before, with nearly two-thirds of young Britons saying they have no interest in party politics. The explanation for this is not that young people are apathetic; three-quarters want more say over the decisions that affect them. But few consider mainstream politics a viable option to achieve this.

There are several factors underlying this scepticism towards politics. Class-based party loyalty has declined, as the traditional working class has shrunk. Awareness of how business buys political influence has grown. In the United States both Republicans and Democrats reward their donors, with George W. Bush having allowed power plants to emit more pollutants. In preparation for his presidential bid in 2000, Al Gore coerced the South African government into buying expensive American drugs for its AIDS epidemic. The US National Rifle Association spends more than $20 million each year to try and prevent effective gun control. Many politicians are given lucrative business jobs soon after leaving office, possibly as a reward for favours performed in government. They should be forbidden from taking jobs linked to their role in government for at least ten years after leaving government.

Most important of all, national governments *appear* to have given away much of their power to the global financial markets. Public sector power has become more remote, either transferred to regional blocs like the EU, or removed from local councils by national government. These developments have led most mainstream parties to try and appease global business, thus sapping their ability to promote their citizens' welfare.

Believing that any government they may form can do little to mitigate the inequity of the market, left of centre parties have concentrated on competing for the middle-class vote, neglecting the hopes of millions of poor people. The latter, therefore, wrongly but understandably believe that voting will achieve little. But this pessimism goes beyond voting, and also affects most people from all social classes; as many as five Britons out of six believe that between elections ordinary citizens have only a little power over government policies, or none at all.

Although both voting and party activism have declined, other types of political participation have grown. For most participants this involves occasionally signing petitions, boycotting unethical goods, and similar actions.[21]

As many as one-sixth of Britons say they are likely one day to take part in some kind of political protest, for instance by going on a demonstration. In February 2003 an amazing 30 million people throughout the world demonstrated against war on Iraq, showing their rulers that they would pay a heavy electoral price if they backed the war. While young people are the group most alienated with conventional politics, they are slightly more likely to protest than their elders. One survey found that nearly three quarters of British teenagers had signed petitions on social or moral issues. However young people's willingness to serve society by doing voluntary work seems to be in decline, both in America, and in Britain, where a lower proportion of under-25s had done voluntary work in the previous year than among all other age groups except the over-55s.[22] The proportion of young people who give regularly to charity has fallen a lot since 1974.

Certain protestors do not respect democratic decisions that run counter to their demands. Over two thirds of Britons now believe that there are times when protestors are justified in breaking the law, compared to just over half in 1984. In September 2000 lorry drivers and farmers caused huge disruption in several European countries, protesting about the price of petrol. While we should welcome the increased willingness to oppose vested interests, some protestors are merely protecting their own privileges. Unless politicians take steps to regain public confidence, respect for democracy and the rule of law is likely to fall, with some protests being infiltrated by anti-democratic elements. This minority of violent protestors not only lose public support for their cause, but also promote a climate in which all kinds of political violence, such as attacks on abortion clinics, will become more common. This is more likely to lead to restrictions on the right to protest than to any progressive advances.

Unless citizens' groups promote a clear strategy for making society more just, voters' confusion will deliver us into the hands of unrepresentative celebrities. More people like the film actor Arnold Schwarzenegger will gain power unchecked by any truly democratic party membership. This occurred in Italy, where media magnate Silvio Berlusconi filled the void left when voters finally deserted the corrupt parties.

The value of citizen action

In order for public opinion to influence government, or party members to influence their leaders, individuals need to combine and campaign for a candidate whom they can hold accountable. We need to understand what enables party members to co-operate in deciding a political programme, and explaining it honestly to the voters. Political parties continue to exist only because members recognise the long-term value of their internal democracy. Bowing to the will of the majority when one is in a minority on a certain issue is acceptable because one needs the support of the rest of the party on the remaining agreed issues. If, however, the leadership ignored or downplayed certain aims which the party had agreed democratically, many members would feel alienated and leave the party. Parties may be riven by internal conflict, or devious leaders may dominate loyal followers, unless enough ordinary members can co-operate to insist that leaders honour the agreed aims. Leaders cannot afford to ignore an assertive and united membership; they need both the legitimacy that campaigning local members provide, and their donations. Research clearly shows that canvassing *in person* can increase turnout by nearly 10 percentage points, which is much more than either direct mail or phone canvassing.[23]

Parties should be prevented from receiving income apart from limited donations from individuals; otherwise the leadership gains excessive power. It then tries to win elections through expensive propaganda, believing it does not need its members to campaign, and can disregard their wishes. In America's Congressional elections of 2004, candidates spent a remarkable $2.7 billion. Strict limits should be placed on the amounts parties and candidates can spend in election campaigns. Polls have consistently shown that Americans want true campaign finance reform. Despite some technical changes to the campaign finance laws, American candidates still spend vast amounts. This makes them dependent on wealthy donors, and obliged to vote in line with their donors' wishes in order to gain re-election. Having been rewarded with further donations, existing Congress members have an unfair advantage, and nearly always win subsequent elections. Many countries now give parties taxpayers' money, usually in proportion to their vote in the last election. However this makes it much harder for new parties to emerge and become serious competitors, and thus weakens the people's ability to influence the existing parties.[24]

Scholars rarely focus on the important issue of the variations in citizens' ability and inclination to take part in politics. Rather they stress large-scale social trends, such as the decline of traditional industries, or the increased mobility of international capital. These are highly significant, but our response to them depends on our overall political culture, which is the outcome of political discourse among ordinary citizens as well as activists and elites. As I mention in the Introduction, differences between otherwise similar nations in government expenditure choices and social inequality are due partly to the influence of public opinion and campaigns on political decisions. One example is the much better public health services of European nations compared to the

United States. Some strands of opinion neglect the role of party members by being fixated on what they see as repeated betrayal by leaders of rank and file wishes. They fail to consider why party members were unable to sustain sufficient unity either to prevent their leaders obstructing their wishes, or to replace those leaders with others who *would* enact the will of the majority.

Society does not need citizen action only in the field of politics. Countries with strong trade unions have less inequality and insecurity. The effort and initiative of many people in charities and community groups also helps improve society and the quality of life. Voluntary organisations pioneered most of our existing social services, thus revealing previously overlooked need and stimulating more comprehensive state provision. They continue to respond innovatively to such needs, as witnessed by the recent growth of victim support schemes, credit unions, helplines for children, and support groups for survivors of child abuse. As both political and charitable activists give up their free time for similar stated aims, I will analyse the characteristics of both.

We need more activists

The level of need in our society is so great that not only political parties, but also charities and pressure groups of all kinds, need more volunteers.[25] Even if funding for public services were to be increased substantially, volunteers would still be essential. Their commitment, warmth, and example boosts social cohesion in a way which paid employees could not replace. Improved state funding for certain voluntary bodies could enable them to involve more volunteers in vital work, which would actually save public money in the longer term.

The need for volunteers may have increased for various reasons, including the rise in crime, the growth in the number of elderly people, and the increasing divorce rate. In Chapters Three and Five I discussed various organisations which use volunteers to support parents under stress, and befriend delinquents, steering them away from crime. Most districts have no such groups, as there are too few volunteers. While calls to suicide prevention helpline the Samaritans have increased, the number of volunteers for this vital service has declined. If society cannot meet these needs, they tend to increase. For example, if someone who cannot get through to the Samaritans then commits suicide, the effect on their relations and friends is devastating.

Surveys of various advanced countries show that between a sixth and a half of the population had undertaken some form of voluntary work in the previous year. However the regular volunteers on whom organisations really depend are few. Only one in about ten Britons spends an average of four or more hours weekly on voluntary work. Less than one-tenth of the population undertake at least two-thirds of all voluntary work.[26] Politics appeals to a tiny minority; only one person in fifty undertook any unpaid political work in the previous twelve months.

Why people volunteer

Some people believe that a person's social class is the main influence on whether they become involved in voluntary service or politics. But the evidence shows that while this is important, it is only one factor among many. The poorer half of the population performs about a quarter of all voluntary work. Regular volunteers differ from other people of the same social class; *within* each educational level a very small proportion of people undertake about three-quarters of the voluntary work.[27]

Some scholars have suggested that a major reason why many people get involved in voluntary work, whether in charities or politics, is that they happen both to have few other commitments, and to have been asked to take part. But the evidence shows that in fact volunteers on average have more commitments than non-volunteers; they are more likely to be married or cohabiting, have dependent children, and have more opportunities than other employed people to do additional paid work if they wish.[28]

While a great many activists begin after having been asked, this is not a major reason why they take part whereas others do not. People who have already shown an interest in serving the community in some way are more likely to be asked to do so. Evidence suggests that those who start voluntary work through a link with an existing participant, and continue on a regular or intensive basis, have a strong pre-existing affinity with that person or organisation. This makes them far more likely to agree to take part than a mere acquaintance who was asked to do so. A study which tracked a large sample of people over 17 years found that individuals' long-standing social attitudes had a much stronger impact on the amount they volunteered than did the extent of any previous volunteering.

Activists' values

An affinity of this kind is likely to be based on shared values. For some years researchers in several advanced countries have compared individuals with 'materialist' and 'post-materialist' value priorities. The former consider keeping prices down, and 'maintaining order in the nation' to be more important than protecting freedom of speech, and giving people more say in government decisions. Those who regard the latter two aims as being more important are said to have 'postmaterialist' value priorities. Researchers selected these four indicators of a person's values after studying responses to a range of such questions in several large surveys. The two materialism indicators have been shown usually to go together, as have the two indicators of post-materialism. Postmaterialists have been found to be more likely to do voluntary work in politics, especially beyond the strictly electoral sphere, for instance by signing petitions or going on demonstrations. A large survey found that participants in all types of voluntary work are more likely to believe that society places too much emphasis on money and possessions, and that income level is not an important influence on the success of a marriage.[29]

The initiator of the research on value priorities suggests that materialists are less likely to undertake community service because they are more preoccupied with securing the satisfaction of their physical needs, and therefore have less mental energy to apply to wider concerns. By contrast, postmaterialists feel more confident about meeting their basic needs.[30] Long-term studies show that while younger people are more likely to be postmaterialists, people do not become more materialist as they grow older. The evidence strongly suggests that those who grow up in times of material insecurity tend to be materialists, while those who grew up in the secure first few decades after World War Two are more likely to become postmaterialists. As I have outlined in Chapter One, what people perceive to be an adequate standard of living depends on their comparison of their own status with that of others. The less equal our society, the more people will grow up to consider their income inadequate, and will be preoccupied with their material desires. Such people will develop materialist value priorities, and will be less likely to strengthen society by performing voluntary work. This fits in with Robert Putnam's findings about what is called 'social capital', namely the trust and shared norms which is built up in relationships and social networks, and facilitates collective action. It is stronger in countries or regions, and eras, with less inequality.[31]

Activists need to believe in their power

Some may say that those who consider their income too small might become active in politics or trade unions in order to seek a larger share of society's resources. However such people are unlikely to do this unless they believe that the authorities are amenable to influence, and that a campaigning group could cooperate in furthering its members' aims. Many people believe neither of these is possible, which may be one reason why only a third of workers in companies which recognise trade unions are union members. Even in the face of disaster, few people help campaigning groups. In the two and a half years after the Three Mile Island nuclear accident, only one local person in every fourteen gave either money or time to help groups campaigning on the issue. This was despite the fact that over half the local residents had been so concerned as to evacuate their homes after the accident, and only one in twenty were undecided about whether the nuclear plant should close. Many researchers have found that having a sense of competence in being potentially able to influence political decisions makes people more likely to take part in politics or community action. This factor, called 'political efficacy', is not due solely to education; it distinguishes participants from non-participants of the same social class.[32] Most researchers have recognised that political efficacy has two elements: the sense of one's personal competence, and belief in the potential responsiveness of political institutions.

Activists need confidence in other people

Because these bodies are much more likely to respond to many people than to a few, political efficacy depends on confidence in the potential co-operation of sufficient people who share similar political goals. This is illustrated by research which found that opponents of nuclear energy were more likely to express willingness to take part in anti-nuclear protests if they believed there were many other opponents of nuclear energy in their neighbourhood, and if they had a sense of affinity or strong links with some of their neighbours. People who feel there is a sense of community in their neighbourhood, and consider this sense of community to be important, are more likely to be members of community improvement organisations than other people in the same neighbourhood. Conversely, it was found that many working-class Americans had developed a self-reliant outlook as they had felt let down by others who had similar problems. This damaged any belief they may have had in the possibility of mutual aid beyond the family.[33]

It is important to consider why people in similar situations often perceive different degrees of potential support from others for their grievances, and attempt accordingly either individual or collective solutions. These decisions have a powerful influence on the political climate. Between 1989 and 1994 spending on private education, medicine, pensions, and life insurance increased considerably. Having placed their trust in the private sector, people are much less likely to take any political action in support of state services.

There is a great deal of largely overlooked evidence that people are more likely to take part in voluntary work with charities or political groups if they have a positive image of people in general. This is probably because voluntary work of any kind requires cooperation with other people if is not to be deeply frustrating. This positive view of others is the foundation of social capital. Several surveys, including one covering 34,000 people in 33 countries, show that volunteers are more likely than non-volunteers of the same social class to believe that most people can be trusted.[34] This relates to the evidence I presented in Chapter Three showing how children whose parents respond promptly to their needs become emotionally secure, and form a generally positive view of themselves and others. As they learned that they could trust their parents to be loving, so they learned to trust that most people are capable of caring and decent behaviour. As their parents' caring behaviour gave them positive feelings, so they believe it likely that any caring they undertake themselves will promote a positive response in others. Because dispositions which arise from childhood experience generally persist through adulthood, parenting quality thus has a strong effect on the health of society.[35]

Studies comparing many different cultures show that the more parents in a certain culture accept children's needs, rather than trying to train them inappropriately to become independent as soon as possible, the more adults in that society 'spontaneously give sympathy, comfort and support' to people in need. Having grown up in an environment in which love and concern are not scarce, they are willing to devote it to others. Similarly, American research on 5-year-olds found that the more their mother tolerated their dependency, the more sympathetic they were to other people when they were reassessed at age 31.[36]

Research on people who have shown unusual commitment to helping others confirms this picture. Dedicated Civil Rights activists, American Vietnam War resisters, and people who sheltered Jews in Nazi-occupied Europe were much more likely than their uninvolved contemporaries to have had as children warm, positive relationships with their parents, from whom they learned values concerned with caring for others. As I show in Chapter Three, children with responsive parents to whom they can become securely attached are more likely to grow up able to make secure intimate relationships. Research also shows that they are more empathic towards people in need. It is not surprising, therefore, that people who were found to have a happy marriage are more likely to undertake community service.[37] In my own research I found that volunteer workers were more likely than non-volunteers to have a high level of emotional support from a partner or close friend. For example, an environmental activist described his partner as 'the ultimate best friend', and spoke of how she comforted and encouraged him if he became disheartened by any campaigning setback. Having such support and emotional security enables a person to undertake certain kinds of voluntary work which do not fit in with the norms of most people around them; their sense of personal identity is too strong to be undermined by opposition. This could be work with serious criminals or others society views as contemptible or hopeless.

The social context in which parents bring up their children also has a strong impact on whether children develop confidence in other people. In 1959 Americans and Britons had much higher trust in people in general than did Germans and Italians, in whose communities relationships had presumably been damaged under fascism and war. By 1990, after 45 years of democratic normality, this difference was much less. The liberal nations of Denmark and the Netherlands have higher levels of social trust than the other four countries.

Certain studies have investigated the influence of a few personality factors on whether people take part in community service or politics, and found that these factors have relatively little impact. The characteristics they have assessed have included feelings of social responsibility, and the extent of personal influence an individual feels they have over events. However overall little research has studied psychological influences on participation, and such studies have not focused directly on emotional security. I will proceed by reviewing what is known in this area.

Emotional security promotes resilience

The overall picture is that activists are more likely to have had warm relationships with their parents, which have given them a sufficiently positive view of others to be able to sustain good adult relationships, and care for others outside their family. This is in keeping with evidence that on average volunteers enjoy more positive moods, higher self-esteem, and a higher level both of satisfaction with life, and psychological well-being.[38] Research has found that negative moods promote a focus on oneself, and make one feel vulnerable. Therefore they detract from the need intrinsic to voluntary work to focus on others. Securely attached adults have been shown to have optimism, high self-esteem, psychological well-being, and less preoccupation with themselves,[39] showing that these positive qualities give them spare mental energy for matters beyond their personal concerns. I asked a young woman who does voluntary work befriending prisoners why she wanted to bother with people others would consider hopeless. She replied that it was because she had had

> such a happy childhood and a happy upbringing and supportive parents . . . it basically . . . helps you to be more optimistic, positive, cheerful.

Participants in most types of volunteer work need greater resilience than most people possess. Tolerance, including for 'delay and ambiguity', has been shown to promote active participation in community service. Volunteers show more willingness than non-volunteers to act collaboratively, and to change their opinion in the light of group discussion.[40] In doing so they show the ability to tolerate the uncertainty of not knowing whether their own view, or that of other group members, is correct. This resilience was evident in a trade-unionist I interviewed. He went out of his way to invite criticism from the workers about whether he was representing them well.

Clearly not all activists are emotionally secure people able to co-operate and heed others' opinions. Many have other motives, as I outline below. I interviewed a Conservative Party activist who was intolerant of conflicting views. He criticised the committee structure of local councils as being a needless 'means by which the opposition can keep digging away at the programme that has been decided'. He avoided any doubts about whether his own views could be wrong by believing that his political opponents, both in other parties and his own, were motivated by egocentric or destructive motives. His intolerance stemmed from what he called his cynicism 'about public life, and the people who are in it', stressing that 'the failings of human beings are quite considerable'. Unfortunately he was not able to apply this belief to consideration of any possible problems in his own political behaviour. There are many such people in political groups. Their negative view of others makes them unwilling to respect the majority view, and therefore to compromise. Instead they indulge in factional plotting, or try to browbeat their opponents into submission.[41] This conflict drives away many reasonable members, who otherwise could have helped the group present itself as fair-minded and thus gain public support.

Research shows that adults who are securely attached in their intimate relationships, as described in Chapter Four, are more resilient and less anxious than others. They tend to approach conflict with the aim of finding an agreement which can suit all parties, rather than in a argumentative or devious manner. They also have more positive views of human nature and rationality.[42] This no doubt gives them the confidence that people can resolve disagreements sensibly. It also shows how important it is for society to help parents bring up their children to be securely attached, so they may make a positive contribution in the vital sphere of voluntary and political groups.

Many types of voluntary work expose participants to people in distress, whether directly, or by hearing about them in the course of fundraising or campaigning. Research shows that many people would not consider taking part in distress-arousing volunteering, and would find it too upsetting if they did. Volunteers in such activity need both sympathy, and exceptional emotional resilience. Adults who are not securely attached tend to react with distress, or divert their attention from, a plight which arouses empathy in the securely attached.[43]

Some activists are a liability

Some volunteers, however, do not have a particularly positive view of other people, and have egocentric reasons for volunteering, including an apparent need to boost their self-esteem, a desire for friendship or a sense of belonging, or to make business or social contacts. As stated above, negative moods cause a person to focus on him- or herself rather than on other matters. In view of the difficult nature of the work, volunteers motivated by a need to boost self-esteem or a wish for friendship or business contacts might well not attain these aims in their volunteering, and might experience a negative mood as a result. This would increase the extent to which their thoughts were focused on themselves, and therefore reduce their ability to concentrate on the needs of the people or group with whom they were working.

If voluntary organisations are to maximize their potential to meet their goals, they vitally need people who do not volunteer with unrealistic aims. If these people have the emotional security which promotes positive moods, they will be able to bear the inevitable setbacks voluntary groups face, and sustain a clear focus on the group's goals and on those it exists to serve. Some people who lack emotional security avoid the need to face disappointment by joining groups with an ideology which gives them total certainty about all issues of concern. They then follow the party line, sacrificing their individual ability to judge how the group can progress towards its aims.[44]

Due to the shortage of volunteers, many organisations rely heavily on a few key individuals. Some of these volunteers need to maintain a positive self-image by believing in the correctness of established methods of operation and past decisions with which they were closely involved. Such volunteer leaders' resistance to change contributes to organisations continuing with practices which have outlived their usefulness, and to potential new volunteers being unwelcome as they might challenge the prevailing power structure. The goals the organisation was intended to pursue can become subtly displaced by observance of procedures followed through habit, or adapted to suit certain egocentric members' wishes.

Leisure choices

Having a sufficiently positive outlook to devote time to difficult issues beyond one's personal concerns is relevant to understanding the motivation for volunteering. As a spare time pursuit, volunteering has to face the competition of what has been called 'the extraordinary pull of the home in leisure activities'.[45] Robert Putnam shows how our increasing dependence on television parallels the decline in civic participation of all kinds that began soon after most homes had obtained television. The more a person watches TV, the less they take part in civic life, in all social classes. This does not merely show that heavy TV watchers have less time for activism. In all social classes they have lower levels of emotional well-being, and find social interaction less easy. Curiously, people report most other activities as being more enjoyable than watching TV; yet, like a drug, the more one watches, the harder it is to cut down. It appears that TV's attraction is probably due to its predictability and lack of challenge, the very qualities that those with the confidence in human co-operation needed for activism would find its limitations.[46]

Experts on leisure point out that most spare-time companions are family members. They say that in contrast to work, leisure gives one the chance to choose activities in which one's chosen companions affirm one's individuality, and one can live out an image of the self which boosts self-esteem.[47] Clearly this is more valuable to those whose self-esteem needs to be bolstered, who are less likely to have secure intimate attachments. A high proportion of people spend most of their spare time either with family or close friends, or alone. In general the quality of their spare time is predictable. They have considerable prior experience of the people and situations their leisure involves. Unforseen events likely to cause them serious disappointment with their leisure activities are rare. By contrast nearly all types of activism involve mixing and collaborating with a number of people who do not have family or friendship commitments towards the volunteer. Therefore they are unlikely to treat the volunteer with special consideration. The volunteering situation is much more likely than ordinary leisure to involve unpredictable hassles. This is difficult for people with insufficient self-esteem, as it is related to a lack of co-operativeness. By contrast those whose secure intimate attachments have given them emotional security are more willing and able to spend part of their spare time outside the family in more unpredictable and potentially frustrating activities.[48]

As I have shown in the Introduction, research shows that individuals' feelings about their family life have the strongest relationship to their overall satisfaction with life. Those whose family life has not given them sufficient self-esteem remain in need of some kind of ego boost by way of compensation. Leisure is a major opportunity to seek this. Such people are likely to get involved in an activity over which they have enough control to ensure that it gives them substitute emotional satisfaction, such as the recognition referred to above. For instance a young woman who has very little self-confidence despite having done well at school finds reading and writing stories for children her most absorbing pastime. Doing voluntary work with handicapped children has crossed her mind, but she has not done so as she fears she might be 'repulsed' by aspects of the work.

Another non-volunteer whom I interviewed associates groups with conflict:

> My experience is, in a group, that the situation is negative, because you won't get anybody who's honest, or actually cares about what you have to say.

Her negative view of other people originates in her childhood experience. She was 'terrified' of certain 'brutal' school teachers, but feels her parents were not concerned about her. She says that with people beyond her close friends, because of this and other similar experiences, she imagines

> negatives even more than what's actually there, because you're so afraid that they're there, . . . and then, you get kind of paranoid about things.

These psychological consequences have clearly undermined her ability to collaborate with others.

People who were asked why they did not undertake voluntary work mentioned the time required, the need to take part in meetings, and 'to give up personal and family matters' as major reasons. They perceived 'the effort of being a neighbourhood activist', and the conflict they thought it entailed, as being more onerous than actual volunteer workers felt them to be.[49] Tolerance of disagreement and conflict vary. For many people disagreement creates psychological tension, and research shows that those who are more anxious about conflict than most are unlikely to take part in politics.[50] By contrast most voluntary workers, having a more positive view of people, have less fear that disagreement will lead to upsetting conflict.

Promoting open-minded organisations

Organisations whose leadership fails to stimulate vigorous grass-roots participation begin to lose touch with the views of ordinary and potential members. This may be due partly to key volunteers doubting that new recruits could actually be useful; a trade unionist I interviewed, while regretting his group's shortage of voluntary help, said 'it's a lot easier to run things' with fewer people involved in decision-making. But in fact this depends on the amount of goodwill the group can generate in order to resolve potential conflict. A generally positive view of people, fostering confidence that constructive discussion and co-operation is possible, is a crucial asset for leaders to maintain the vitality of their groups. If such organisations' leadership included sufficient members with the resilience which emotional security promotes, the latter might stimulate the new ideas and wider participation which could help revitalize the group. Otherwise decision-making can become distorted by a shared inability to question any of the beliefs members have held dear over the years, no matter how obsolete they have become.

On the other hand, certain voluntary organisations thrive through the example of dedicated leaders who 'embody' the values of the group. These leaders attract new volunteers and inspire their loyalty. Their close attention to both volunteers and beneficiaries gives them a clear understanding of the group's aims and the goals it is feasible to pursue.

If voluntary organisations are aware of the ways in which certain leaders' lack of emotional resilience, or need to boost self-esteem, can divert decisions away from the group's true needs, they can establish procedures to prevent this. These could include activities designed to increase mutual emotional support within the group. The more an organisation creates mechanisms to show appreciation for each volunteer's efforts, the less certain volunteers will need to try and maintain self-esteem by avoiding critical evaluation of the group's performance, or their role in it. Their reluctance to face the possibility that they may have contributed to certain misconceived decisions would be reduced. A climate of confidence and openess would replace one of complacency and defensiveness. Volunteers would be able to have more realistic expectations of their work, and hence would be less stressed by setbacks. They would experience less negative emotion, and consequently be more able to focus on group goals rather than be distracted by their individual emotions.

Volunteers would find individual evaluation of their work more acceptable if the organisation had demonstrated its commitment to support them in undertaking whichever role most suited their abilities. Such evaluation should be a two-way process; volunteers should also be encouraged to consider how well the organisation was enabling them to make a positive contribution.

A few voluntary groups have succeeded in creating a strong ethos of mutual support which can restore the emotional security even of those who have experienced severe psychological problems. One member of Alcoholics Anonymous has a very close relationship with four fellow members to whom she feels she can always turn for help, confident that they will never judge her. She feels they give her unconditional love. As an indication of the emotional security and resilience she has gained from the group, she has become able to help new members, withstanding her frustration when some have tried to take advantage of her good nature. She also has developed the determination to work in support of certain local politicians whom she trusts.

Particular attention should be paid to making new volunteers feel welcome and supported. Many organisations fail to do so, with the result that more new recruits drop out than would do otherwise. Only a minority of volunteers are paid any expenses. If organisations were careful to offer travel expenses to all, they could attract and retain more low-income volunteers.

The decline of community

It is important to consider the causes of the serious decline in recent decades of 'social capital', that is participation in community organisations, and other forms of positive social relations. Robert Putnam's thorough research on the topic shows that in the United States participation in community organisations, and other forms of social connectedness, increased from 1947 to 1965, and have declined since. The American generations that grew up before or during the Second World War are now more likely than younger people to take part in most forms of community action or politics. This is probably because having to fight a common enemy united people, engendering a lasting sense of solidarity. Studies over several decades show that these generations are also more inclined to trust others, which is probably why they consider it worthwhile to collaborate in common endeavours. By contrast, generations that grew up after the war, especially those born since 1968, are less trusting and more individualistic in their outlook.[51] In comparing the states of the USA, Putnam found that a state's average level of trust in others had the strongest relationship to its overall level of social capital.[52]

Putnam's research shows that this difference between the generations is by far the biggest reason for the fall in social capital. In the 1940s and 1950s younger adults were happier than older people, which is what we might expect given that strength and health declines with age. However this age difference in happiness has steadily reversed since then, and by the late 1990s happiness levels were lower in each generation going down the age range, and psychological distress greater. This echoes the link between psychological well-being and participation in community action and politics described above.

The other reasons Putnam found for the decline of social capital are, firstly, the growth of TV watching, and of lesser importance, the decline in community and large rise in commuting time associated with the expansion of suburban areas, and the increase in people feeling both short of time and under financial pressure.[53]

Active communities have a better life

It is possible even in large cities to improve the quality of life significantly by enhancing the sense of community, as shown by Robert Putnam's well-known book *Making Democracy Work*. His research in Italy over many years shows that the more members of voluntary organisations there are in a district, the higher the proportion of people who read newspapers, and who vote in local referendums there. Putnam constructed an index of the degree of 'Civic Community' in a district by combining these three factors with a measure of the extent to which voters' choices in local government elections were free from the influence of corruption. This measure was very strongly related to the other three factors. In surveys over a period of 15 years, the Civic Community index for each region had an extremely strong relationship to the degree of satisfaction with life reported by individuals in that region. When the statistics were analysed so that the influence of Civic Community on satisfaction with life could be assessed separately from that of other factors, its impact was practically as strong as that of the individual's income.[54]

As I explain in the Introduction, these inter-regional differences in community participation are far from being simply a reflection of the wealth or poverty of the region. A century ago most of the regions of northern Italy had more cohesive communities than those in the south, as is still the case today, but at that time economic differences between north and south were much less. The north has become more prosperous than the south largely because its active citizens' organisations have promoted social capital and better government.

When people join community organisations, they get to know others on a personal basis. Once they have come to trust certain other members, they can more easily place their trust in the friends of those members even though at first they do not know them personally. This process sets up the conditions for long-term reciprocal relationships within a network of people who are trusted because of their relationship with the network as a whole, although they are known personally only to some network members. In such a network people develop a willingness to help others, partly because subconsciously they trust that certain network members would feel under an obligation to help them in future if required. In order to promote stable communities governments should boost employment in poorer regions, so that people do not need to move to find work. Those who expect to move within the next five years are less likely to undertake voluntary work. Districts in which a high proportion of residents move have much weaker community ties.[55]

Immigration anxiety

Racism is a major obstacle to the building of strong communities. In Western Europe there has been a huge increase in the vote of racist parties over the past decade. This has accompanied a large rise in the number of asylum seekers, and considerable controversy on this topic. A major EU survey found that a seventh of the population have strong negative attitudes towards ethnic minorities. One in every five actually thinks that all immigrants from outside the EU, whether legal or illegal, should be deported. Only about one in eight is in favour of immigration from outside the Union. However four out of five favour accepting those who have suffered human rights violations in their country of origin.[56]

The origins of these attitudes are complex. The research which best explains them measured how much people considered immigration an economic threat, and their reluctance to interact with an immigrant at various degrees of closeness. The research found that there was no relationship between these two attitudes. However both were related to feeling that illegal immigrants should not get favourable treatment. American research shows that there is much greater opposition to illegal than to legal immigration. Being pessimistic about the future performance of the economy is related to opposition towards legal immigration, but makes no difference to views on illegal immigration, to which most people are opposed.[57] Attitudes towards asylum seekers are on balance accepting, provided they are seen to be at genuine risk of persecution in their own country; otherwise they are perceived as illegal immigrants.

Research has consistently shown that it is people who are suffering, or feel threatened by, economic hardship who are most likely to be hostile to minorities.[58] Therefore in order that asylum seekers and others do not continue to suffer racist violence, radical steps must be taken to empower and improve the lives of our poorest communities, where most minority citizens live. This is even more important now that most wealthy nations plan to encourage more immigration to fill skill shortages, and offset the ageing of the population.

We can understand why many poor people, whose ranks include most members of ethnic minorities, have some anxiety about immigration. Most immigrants will be competing for low-skilled work, and their presence therefore tends to keep low-skilled wages down. Certain firms choose to employ illegal immigrants as they can neither get the minimum wage, nor resist various infringements of the laws which protect workers. Moreover, poor people have most difficulty finding decent accommodation, the supply of which is clearly reduced by immigration in the short term at least. While migrant workers benefit the economy, most poor people perceive a negative impact. The media aggravate the position, running headlines such as 'Homes Crisis Blamed on Asylum Seekers'.But it is a misconception for politicians to blame the media for provoking racism like this, when it is their own policies which create the deprivation in which racism thrives. A German study of polls over nine years showed that the number of recent press articles on asylum seekers had no connection to the tendency of people to nominate asylum as a major problem.[59] Politicians need to bring in the measures I have discussed above to boost the economy when it begins to slow down and thus reduce both the rate and the duration of unemployment They also need to provide first-class training so people can gain the skills they need to find a job again.

Fear and racism

It is also important to note that belief in a strong law and order policy has consistently been a major reason given by French people for supporting the National Front.[60] Crime has a more serious effect on poor people, as it is most prevalent in poor areas. Nearly three out of five West Europeans believe that 'immigrants' are more often involved in criminality than average. Clearly racism is an important factor in this belief. However if crime were lower, people's fears would be less, and would not need to be directed towards a scapegoat. If mainstream parties take more effective action to cut crime, this will reduce racism, which arises largely from fear.

An important indication of racism is voting for parties of the far Right. However, the motivation of such voting is complex. The largest study undertaken on this topic used interviews with nearly 50,000 people from sixteen West European nations during the period 1994–97. It compared the separate influence of a range of factors on whether people voted for the far Right. The strongest influence was holding anti-immigrant attitudes; being unemployed had slightly less impact. Another very important factor was being dissatisfied with how democracy was working in that country. Four other studies have also found that general dissatisfaction with or distrust of government has a strong independent impact on voting for the far Right, or against immigration.[61] If people feel that politicians are not trying to tackle their concerns, many will become susceptible to far Right rhetoric scapegoating 'outsiders'.

Overall public attitudes show that most people could accept a predictable level of immigration provided it was managed in a way which prevented it causing them significant disadvantage. Most people's reservations about immigration are not due to racism. The race of Americans makes little difference to their attitude towards immigration. Almost half of ethnic-minority Britons believe there are too many immigrants in the country. Europeans from ethnic minorities actually expressed *more* negative attitudes towards members of ethnic minorities.[62] These differences still applied with other relevant factors such as education taken into account.

We can shed further light on this area by noting that only one in six EU citizens would be willing to accept Muslim immigrants from outside the EU, and one in five would accept East European immigrants, *without restriction*. However about three times as many people would accept such immigrants *with* restrictions. The survey did not ask about specific types of restrictions. However responses to various surveys suggest what people probably had in mind. In January 2003 five out of six Britons agreed with the proposal that asylum seekers should 'be held in special camps' until their application had been decided. A year earlier the same proportion had felt that the investigation of applications should be speeded up so that those refused asylum could be 'expelled more quickly'. When Europeans were asked if they had certain fears, over half expressed fear of 'ethnic conflict in Europe', which was the fifth strongest fear.[63] In January 2003, soon after the discovery of a group which included asylum seekers trying to make a deadly poison, over a third of Britons endorsed the alarmist view that 'a significant proportion of asylum seekers are terrorists'. Many Australians share this view.

It is when the public have lost confidence in politicians that such fears grow. In 2003 three-quarters of Britons felt that the government was not honest about the scale of immigration, while no fewer than six out of seven felt that immigration was out of control. Politicians need to respond to these concerns about immigration by explaining why a certain amount is helpful to fill labour shortages, and how they can manage it to avoid disadvantage to citizens. A key priority is to build more housing, as dissatisfaction in this fundamental area is likely to lead to racism. Politicians can also respond to fears that immigrants drain public finances by explaining that they nearly all work, few are elderly, and therefore they contribute much more in tax than they receive in benefits. Above all, politicians must not heighten fears by wrongly giving the impression that immigration is unmanageable. To do so would enable the far Right to stir up racism, and thereby increase their vote.

Alleviating racism and racial tension

Hostility towards ethnic minorities is far from being confined to poor people. The American government's Equal Opportunity

Employment Commission reports widespread employer discrimination against non-English speakers. British research shows that because of discrimination it is much harder for Asians and blacks to get a job interview than for whites with identical qualifications. Anti-discrimination laws clearly need to be strengthened. Racist political parties have had success in wealthy nations such as Austria and Holland. In addition, much of the antipathy towards ethnic minorities is not for economic reasons. Over a fifth of Europeans think that minorities must give up their own culture in order to be fully accepted into a nation. Americans' resistance to the use of the Spanish language was the strongest of all factors, apart from respondents' education level, as to whether or not they opposed immigration.[64]

It is hard to understand the basis for this opposition to cultural diversity. However, a researcher who discussed the issue with many white French people felt it could best be summed up by the phrase 'we are no longer at home here because *they* [ethnic minorities] feel at home here'.[65] This is probably due to fear of the potential loss of a familiar and therefore reassuring way of life. This underlines the importance of helping different ethnic groups to get to know each other. Having previously lived in a racially mixed neighbourhood or attended a racially mixed school has a strong influence on having friends of another race thereafter.

A large body of research on situations in which people of different races have regular contact shows clearly that such contact reduces prejudice. This effect is much stronger under various conditions, including people of different races having equal status, and common goals, in that situation. This can be achieved best in schools, especially when the school creates an ethos of co-operation between pupils. Research has also shown that co-operative learning promotes not only inter-racial friendship and understanding, but also higher achievement and creativity. This underlines the importance of schools catering for pupils/ students of all races. Schools for a certain religious faith nearly always lead to a dearth of inter-racial contact between people in that area. In addition, governments should aim to ensure that the racial composition of each school's teachers broadly reflects that of the region. This would increase the extent to which ethnic minority pupils/students felt they had equal status in the school, and thus help to reduce racial prejudice.

Meeting people of other races in everyday life ensures that they are known as individuals; some will be liked, thus weakening the tendency to identify with one's own group and regard other groups as alien or inferior in certain ways. Research shows that race riots are much more likely to take place before an indigenous population has had time to get used to recent immigrants, and before local officials have gained experience of resolving conflicts between the two groups.[66]

If racism is not tackled vigorously, ethnic groups will segregate themselves more and more. This reinforces the suspicions of other groups. Minor incidents can then ignite serious conflict. Politicians need to ensure that all neighbourhoods and schools have positive features, and welcome people from all ethnic/ religious groups. This will gradually encourage people to live in mixed neighbourhoods and use mixed schools, rather than segregate themselves for want of a viable alternative.

It is important that ethnic minorities gain the political influence they deserve. Throughout America and Britain black people are severely under-represented in the legislatures. Britain has a mere fifteen black or Asian MPs. Hence it is not surprising that in Britain a quarter of black and Asian citizens do not even register to vote. However, in a London district which enabled its citizens to have a greater say through Neighbourhood Forums, the forums' ethnic minority membership was in line with the ethnic minority proportion of the overall district population. The more that people of all races feel that they can influence local decision-making in a legitimate way, the less likely they are to feel powerless and become infected by racism. In the early 1980s the American city of Chattanooga was described as 'the armpit of the south', suffering from high unemployment, and severe urban and civic decay. Encouraged by a consultant and foundation funding, a small band of citizens studied how to regenerate the city. Through their determination they involved as many as 1,700 local people in planning city renewal. Residents of a housing estate once plagued by drugs and violence obtained support to improve its physical condition and establish adult education programmes.

The estate's murder rate fell from nearly one per week to only two per year. A racially divisive school reorganisation plan was shelved and a sensible compromise substituted.

Empowering the excluded

In disadvantaged areas community development workers can help residents who would be unlikely to do so otherwise to join together to improve their neighbourhoods. One project found that each hour of professional community work gave rise to fifteen hours of voluntary work by local people.[67] Community workers identify suitable people and, by putting them in touch with others of like mind, enable them to support each other in working on issues of common concern. This has led to the emergence of broad-based community campaigns uniting people of different races and backgrounds.

Disadvantaged areas contain fewer people with the self-confidence which education promotes. They are therefore less able to obtain a fair deal through the democratic process, for instance in arguing for funds for local services, or resisting a new road which would blight the community. Funding for community development depends partly on bids made for central government funds by local authorities, with whom local communities are sometimes in conflict. Many councils do not want to secure funds for a potential opponent, while community groups are often inhibited from arguing their case strongly for fear of losing the goodwill of the local authority on which they depend. This situation should be rectified by giving all areas below a certain level of deprivation a statutory right to a certain level of unconditional central government funding for properly constituted democratic community groups.

Skilled community workers can empower potential working-class activists by fostering

the first revolution – the internal one that comes from an awareness of self and self-worth. [68]

One community activist described the difference it made to

herself and her colleagues once they had been encouraged to help manage a neighbourhood centre:

> We were housewives with kids to fetch up and that was it
> ... We are not timid now; we can deal with professionals
> ... We will talk to anybody now, even influential people.

Community workers need to be independent of local politicians so they can respond to the needs of poor communities without any conflict of interest. In order to help build vibrant and representative organisations they need to devote time to getting to know potential activists on a personal basis, helping them both to explore their own values, and learn how to collaborate with others in working for these values through local politics. This type of community work can build resilient organisations, with many capable leaders, able to focus on a range of issues which embody local people's shared values. Mary-Beth Rogers' inspiring book *Cold Anger* describes democracy at its best, with volunteers representing their impoverished communities' interests, recognising the legitimate needs of other groups, and at the same time growing in humanity and personal fulfilment.[69]

Making politicians accountable

Both democracy and community cohesion are likely to weaken if political leaders have the chance to become complacent. Under the 'first past the post' electoral system, in which two strong parties dominate politics, they inevitably try to win votes by attracting floating voters in the centre. They can take for granted all voters whose political position is further from the centre than their own, as these electors have no other credible party worth voting for. In nations or districts where one party feels firmly entrenched in power, leaders have no need to do their best for people in order to win their votes, and corruption is more likely.

Election turnout is lower in such areas than in marginal constituencies. In the future, under first past the post, more voters will inevitably become alienated with democracy, believing it can make no practical difference to their lives. In view of the growing cynicism towards politics described earlier, and the fact that in most Congressional and parliamentary seats the result is predictable,[70] the trend towards lower turnouts will continue. Even in Britain's 1997 Labour landslide nearly three-quarters of seats proved to be safe seats. It is extremely rare under 'first past the post' for a third party to become a serious challenger. This is chiefly because such parties struggle to build support as they appear to have no chance of winning in most seats. A British poll showed that the number intending to vote for the Liberal Democrats would rise nearly three-fold, to the same level as Labour, if they actually had a chance of winning in that district. Many people would vote for a Green party if it could have real influence. In 1989 the Greens obtained nearly a sixth of the vote in Britain's elections to the European Parliament, but gained no seats. This shows why the credibility of democracy, and therefore the peace of society, requires the introduction of Proportional Representation (PR). Countries which use PR have an average election turnout as much as 9 percentage points higher than those which use first past the post.

Unlike first past the post, PR is a truly democratic system. Rather than giving total power to a party gaining about two-fifths of the vote, it ensures that parliamentary decisions need to be made by a majority of MPs elected by a majority of voters. This means that as no one party can be confident of gaining more than half the votes, each party realises it will need to compromise with other parties in order to get any of its proposals passed. As gaining about 40 per cent of the vote by appealing to electors in the centre no longer secures victory, parties need to attract the support of those non-centre voters whose wishes they could ignore under 'first past the post'. These non-centre views thus have an influence on whichever coalition is formed to secure a majority of MPs, ensuring that government policy reflects the wishes of the majority to a greater degree than at present. Opponents of PR suggest that such bargaining between parties denies the electorate the chance provided by first past the post, to make a clear choice for the programme of one party. But this choice is in fact very limited, because the programmes of the two leading parties are relatively similar, and exclude policies many voters would support. Under PR there are several parties, which between them represent all major points of view. The government programme which emerges is much more likely to reflect these points of view in relation to the support each commands throughout the electorate.

Under first past the post, only the votes of fewer than two people in every thousand need to switch for one party to gain the key marginal seats and win total power.[71] This explains the excessive reliance of major parties in first past the post countries on focus groups. These are small panels of undecided electors with whom the parties hold regular discussions in order to tailor their election campaign to the capture of floating votes. The parties make election pledges in line with the focus group members' views, disregarding public opinion as a whole, thus limiting their ability when in government to respond to the needs of the country.

Stable and fair government

Supporters of first past the post sidestep criticisms of its unfairness by portraying it as a system enabling strong governments to make clear decisions. However research comparing different countries' levels of economic growth, inflation, and unemployment shows that first past the post does not deliver better economic performance.[72] The view is also put forward that the coalition government which is usual under PR is always weak and ineffective. In fact coalition government in politically stable countries is *more* likely to be effective than unrepresentative one-party rule. Proposed legislation is considered and amended carefully in order to win a majority in parliament, rather than being the outcome of covert bargaining, or pressure by party whips. The largest party is not inhibited from negotiating for the votes of various allies, which would undermine the party discipline on which 'first past the post' depends. Research shows that coalition governments are much less likely to manipulate the economy for electoral advantage.[73]

Politicians often repeat the myth that PR gives too much power to small parties. This tends to be based on examples such as Israel, which is far from typical. There coalitions are hard to form because a relatively large party which is trying to secure a majority needs to win the support of several small parties to do so. In exchange for its support each demands certain policies, which may be unacceptable to other prospective coalition partners. Even after a coalition is formed, any of the small parties may threaten to withhold its support over a new issue. Then a new coalition has to be negotiated. By contrast, nearly all West European countries have a better system of PR. Very few small parties gain representation. Coalition negotiations are much more manageable, and there are stable coalition governments. Unlike Israel, most countries with PR require that a party must gain about one-twentieth of the national vote in order to be represented in parliament. In most countries this ensures that anti-democratic or racist parties have very few or no MPs, and thus cannot exert any influence on the government. It is of course regrettable when racist parties gain *any* representation in the legislature. However, evidence shows that countries with proportional representation have less racial conflict, probably because minorities of all kinds feel that their concerns can be raised in the legislature; they are therefore less likely to turn to violence. And as the success of the French National Front shows, it is possible for racist parties to get many representatives under a non-proportional system.[74]

Certain small parties clearly have very little influence under PR if their views are too extreme for any larger party to strike a deal with them. In most countries using PR large parties can choose with which smaller party they wish to make an alliance. For instance in Germany the Social Democrats could have formed a coalition with the centrist Free Democrats rather than the Greens if they had considered the Greens' demands too radical. This would have given them a strong bargaining position in relation to the Greens, who would have had to moderate their demands in order to strike a coalition agreement. If the Social Democrats had formed a coalition with the Free Democrats, the latter would not have succeeded in diluting many of the Social Democrats' policies. They would have known that if their policy demands had been rejected, the Social Democrats would have turned to the Greens instead to obtain a majority on those issues. Bargaining of this nature is democratic because on each issue the most likely compromise is that which reflects the views of the average voter.

Certain strategically placed small parties merely appear to exercise disproportionate power because their views are closer to those of a key governing party than are the views of their larger opponents. We are familiar with democracy working in this way in everyday life. Imagine that four members of a family of nine wanted the family to take its holiday in Spain, while two wanted to go to Morocco, and three to Norway. The four favouring Spain would be able to form a majority alliance with the two wanting to visit Morocco, on the basis of their shared love of Mediterranean heat. This compromise would be in line with the wishes of the average family member, whose position in this example is found not on on a Left–Right political spectrum, but on a North–South holiday spectrum, somewhere in Southern Spain. Perhaps the family would agree to go to Spain the first year, and to Morocco the next.

Italy is an exceptional nation whose political instability before the 1990s reforms was sometimes wrongly attributed to PR. But at that time a party needed less than 1 per cent of the national vote in order to gain an MP. Before public opinion destroyed most of its major parties in 1993–4, the weakness of Italy's political system was largely due to the polarisation between the Christian Democrats and the Communists. While the Communists had a significant loyal vote, they were distrusted by so many other people that they were unable to create a large enough alliance with other parties to form an electable alternative to the Christian Democrats. Therefore the Christian Democrats knew that they would always dominate whatever ruling coalition was formed, and became effectively unaccountable to public opinion. They and their coalition partners took advantage of their electoral strength by indulging in corruption. It was not the system that was chiefly to blame, but the weakness of Italian political culture for failing to generate a strong, uncorrupt left of centre party.

PR would help to rectify women's under-representation. All the European countries with a third or more woman MPs have PR. Four out of every ten MPs in both Sweden and Norway are women. Women constitute less than a fifth of British MPs, and a seventh of members of the US Congress. America actually has fewer women legislators than Pakistan.[75] A 1997 poll found that nearly three quarters of British women felt that the parties neglected issues of concern to women. Women particularly dislike politicians' tendency to attack their opponents rather than outline their own policies. If we are to rise above the confrontations which obscure the issues and repel most people, we need more women in politics to set a constructive example.

Government by the people

A more democratic and collaborative style of politics would limit the excessive influence of charismatic politicians, who trade on their parties' mistaken belief that the leader's personality is the key to re-election. In fact evidence shows that in most nations with parliamentary systems, electors' perceptions of the party leaders have a fairly modest impact on the votes. In a 2003 poll Britons were asked to rate the importance of various attributes of political parties. Having good policies for the long-term was rated top, whereas an impressive leader was near the bottom of the list.[76]

It is also essential that all areas of government are made truly accountable. Governments devolve too many of their functions to unelected bodies which take decisions in private.

The current trend is for a few top politicians to grow ever stronger while backbench MPs, ordinary Members of Congress, party members, and voters become even weaker. Instead what we need are reforms to give ordinary citizens more say. Tony Blair said

The people are the masters. We are the servants of the people. We will never forget that.

Bearing this in mind, Mr Blair should note that in the above poll, listening to what voters think was one of the most valued attributes of a party. As governments do not listen enough, the people want a direct say: three quarters of Britons believe that a referendum should be held on any issue endorsed by a million citizens. National polls show that a majority of Americans want referendums of this kind, known as 'citizens' initiatives', introduced throughout the country.[77] Citizens' initiatives have made a positive contribution to social harmony and the extension of democracy in various countries, most notably Switzerland, Italy, and the United States. Other nations which use them are New Zealand, Denmark, and certain of the German regions.

Some people fear that citizens' initiatives provide an opportunity for backward-looking proposals, and for the majority to oppress minorities. This occurred in the USA when 11 states banned same-sex marriage in 2004. But in other Western democracies there is little evidence to support these fears. Switzerland is a conservative country in many ways, and it is well known that it was late in giving women the vote. However, since then it has approved citizens' initiatives to legalise abortion and homosexuality, and to raise petrol tax by one fifth in order to protect the environment. An initiative aiming to restrict immigration was defeated. Citizens' initiatives have enabled the Italians to combat corruption, and restrict the use of nuclear energy, and the Californians to improve environmental protection.[78]

Even in the United States, where many intolerant initiatives have been proposed, most have been defeated. While three states have passed initiatives banning public funding of abortions, all four initiatives threatening the legal right to abortion have been defeated. Oregon defeated an initiative requiring local councils to discourage homosexuality, while California voted not to dismiss lesbian and gay school teachers. Nearly all civilised countries have nothing to fear from citizens' initiatives, as any initiative which attacked fundamental human rights would be unconstitutional. Overall the benefits of initiatives clearly outweigh the risks. Western countries have advanced enormously in overcoming various prejudices over the past 40 years. The occasional initiative has slowed this advance. However extensions of democracy give citizens more control over their lives, and hence the fears which generate intolerance recede. The history of democratisation shows that it has gradually increased respect for others' differences. The availability of initiatives in the United States has not increased anti-gay prejudice; six out of ten Americans favour official recognition of lesbian/gay partnerships.

Another ground on which some people have opposed citizens' initiatives is that they have been used in America to limit the taxes state governments can raise. But in nearly every such case, the tax reductions passed have been modest, while other states have voted to raise certain taxes.[79] In view of this, and the considerable evidence presented in Chapter One that in the past few years most Americans and Britons have been willing to pay higher taxes to improve key public services, the introduction of such initiatives could enable citizens' wishes to be realised in this respect.

The fact that voters could challenge politicians' decisions in this way could force the government to justify the amount it raises by taxes, and spends on the various services, rather than voters feeling that their taxes are taken for granted and may be spent carelessly. The effect could be to strengthen public support for better public services, and to encourage politicians to propose whichever level of tax their country actually needs.

Referendums for vital issues

Another important benefit of citizens' initiatives is that they can tackle issues which governing parties tend to avoid, either because they are too controversial, such as drug use, or because their consequences are too long-term. Such issues are thought to be worth too few votes at the next election for a sitting government to devote significant resources or attention to them. This is why irresponsible politicians are neglecting the environment. We need to demand citizens' initiatives on such issues, and demonstrate that most people will accept sacrifices to protect the welfare of their children and grandchildren.

In countries using 'first past the post', party leaders are protected from the results of public dissatisfaction since general elections take place only every four or five years; in any case, voters have little choice, because the two main parties usually appear so similar. Therefore ministers feel that their efforts to tackle key social problems need not be radical. But there are many commited party supporters who will protest vehemently if their party neglects its aspirations. The consequent divisions will damage that party's re-election prospects. In Switzerland the ability to achieve a citizens' initiative referendum helps members remain loyal to their parties. The fact that they disagree with certain policies need not lead to feuding which harms the party's public support, as the issue can be resolved by a referendum.

Referendums improve government

The long-standing dissatisfaction with political parties is shown by a 1996 British poll which found that three-quarters of people believe that Parliament does not have enough control over the government. As a former minister suggested, this may be because at any time one-third of the governing party's MPs are ministers or aides, while a further third aim to become ministers and do not want to fall out with the party leadership. Hence they often fail to challenge government measures, even in the committees which are supposed to scrutinise proposed laws carefully. In America Congress fails to enact public wishes because most representatives vote in line with the wishes of their corporate backers or party leaders, whereas in Britain most follow the orders of their party whips. They are inhibited even from constructive criticism, which would be misrepresented as a snub to the party leader.

In Switzerland the availability of citizens' initiatives has given backbench MPs freedom to express their views. It has also enabled previously weak pressure groups to win public support, as occurred in 1982 when the Women's Consumer Forum's referendum on price control was passed. While business and commercial lobby groups play an important role in Swiss referendums, such bodies could be prevented from exerting undue influence in the media by strict limits on expenditure during referendum campaigns. In 1974 Californians voted to introduce a limit for initiative campaigns, and to prevent one side spending more than half a million dollars in excess of the other. The Supreme Court ruled this unconstitutional. But while money helps to win initiative campaigns in both the USA and Switzerland, it is far from invincible. As stated above, canvassing in person is much more persuasive than phone canvassing by contractors.

In 1988 tobacco companies spent $21 million unsuccessfully opposing a tobacco tax increase in California, and in Maryland the National Rifle Association spent $8 million, but failed to defeat an initiative for the registration of handguns. Freedom of information legislation, democratic control of public service broadcasting, and the prohibition of large media conglomerates, as proposed above, would help ensure balanced coverage of referendum campaigns.

Studies show that powerful groups such as those described above exercise no more power in countries which use referendums than elsewhere.[80] At least the availability of referendums obliges them to argue their case publicly, while limiting the ability of government to grant their wishes with no popular challenge. In Switzerland, for example, the constitution provides that any federal law can be challenged before it comes into effect if 50,000 voters demand a referendum. The possibility of such a citizens' initiative weakens party leaders, and encourages the formation of temporary alliances in support of a particular issue. It therefore reduces politicians' ability to build powerful or corrupt factions on a 'you scratch my back, I'll scratch yours' basis.

The availability of citizens' initiative referendums does not undermine legislators' legitimate role. Only a minority of issues become the subject of an initiative. Even in Switzerland, where initiatives are used most, only about one law in fifteen has been challenged since 1945. Sponsors often withdraw an initiative when the government either adopts all or part of their idea, or puts forward a counter-proposal likely to gain more votes. Of all the federal referendums which have actually gone to a vote in Switzerland since 1848, electors agreed with Parliament's view in over three cases out of every five. Under such a system Parliament is likely to earn more respect, as citizens will know that the laws it does pass have been considered with a view to the possibility of being challenged by an initiative. Before introducing legislation Parliament would be forced to consult those groups who would be affected more carefully.[81]

The example of Switzerland shows that the availability of initiatives promotes government which is responsive to society as a whole. Since 1959 when the present Swiss agreement to share government between the four major parties began, far fewer laws have been sufficiently unpopular to be challenged. Other research has shown that the more the local government system gives citizens a direct say in council decisions, the more they are in line with the views of the average voter. Such a system of government wastes less time on useless conflict, enabling political energy to be focused on the most critical issues.

A political system which includes initiatives would promote adherence to the law and commitment to one's community. Experiments have shown that people are more willing to accept decisions in which they have had a say. For example, in those regions of Switzerland which allow citizens the most direct say over local decisions, there is less tax evasion.[82]

A system permitting initiatives can be designed to prevent inflexibility or delay. For instance, in Switzerland any law which parliament considers urgent comes into effect immediately, and remains in force for a year even if it is challenged by an initiative. Countries which have citizens' initiatives suffer less corruption and discrimination. This is probably because firstly, the availability of initiatives encourages minorities to stand up for their rights, and secondly, officials considering setting up corrupt deals know that if the measure were to be challenged by an initiative, the consequent publicity could bring any corruption to light.

Referendums get people involved

Some people oppose referendums on the ground that they simplify issues into one question requiring a yes or no answer. One author suggests that this entails them promoting the consumption rather than the production of politics. I take this to mean that only those who draft the referendum have taken any part in the production of politics. But when the signature of about one elector in every hundred is needed before an initiative can be put to the vote, many more people play a part in the production of politics than in purely parliamentary government. Any organisation contemplating the effort and expense of seeking what in America would be over a million signatures would need to consult widely in order to choose the right question to win a majority.

Legislatures could make a rule requiring anyone proposing an initiative to hold a public meeting before doing so, and to make a video presenting their case. The TV companies could be given the legal duty to broadcast this film a few weeks before the initiative question was officially registered. They might choose to do so in the middle of the night, but if they were also obliged to make several announcements of the broadcast during peak viewing times, anyone who was interested could video it. During the following few weeks anyone could contact the sponsors of the initiative asking them to amend the question. These arrangements would enable many people to influence the formulation of the initiative question.

Swiss evidence shows that initiatives help to educate the public about politics. Surveys show that more than nine-tenths of electors who vote in a referendum spontaneously remember relevant facts about the topic. As initiative votes can be timed to coincide with parliamentary elections, candidates need to take a clear position on each initiative. This makes political debate more informative, and reduces the extent to which the media focus on irrelevant aspects of candidates' personalities.

Referendums have public support

Citizens' initiatives are not merely a Swiss favourite. Twenty-seven states in America have the initiative or something very similar. They are becoming more popular there, with three times more in the 1990s than in the 1970s. Three-quarters of Californians polled in 1989 approved of the initiative system.[83] Many European citizens are trying to achieve some such system for their country.

Given politicians' poor standing with the public, it would be hard for them to oppose a strong campaign for the introduction of initiatives. Any response along the lines of 'leave government to us; it's too complex for you' would be received with scorn. In particular young people, whose participation in democracy needs to be increased, would be likely to support the call for initiatives.

If citizens feel that their government is not taking strong enough action on key issues, many will be keen to campaign for this restoration of power to the people.

Giving local government responsibility

Governments should also strengthen democracy by making local government more accountable, and giving it greater scope to tackle local problems. If local government's role is merely to manage a meagre budget to fulfil an onerous set of duties laid down by central government, it will attract neither the public support nor the high calibre leadership it needs.

Local politics is a crucial area for the strengthening of community life. People are more likely to be moved to take part in politics by a local issue. As it is easier to feel a part of a smaller district, people are more likely to be politically active, and vote, when local government boundaries cover smaller areas.[84] In areas where many local people take part in the political process, whether entirely on their own initiative or through the decentralisation of council decision-making, local government policies are more in keeping with local wishes. Council decentralisation has helped many people to become better informed politically, gain political skills, and move beyond neighbourhood politics to make a wider contribution. It can also lead to a substantial increase in local election turnout.[85]

In the past some local authorities have been able to act irresponsibly. This is why it is vital to introduce Proportional Representation for local government to end the absurdity of permanent one-party rule in many councils. Under PR each council will have a credible opposition which *could* gain control at the next election, and councillors will be motivated to address citizens' needs carefully. It is also important to devolve certain powers from central government. In over-centralised countries, councils lack the comprehensive control over public services which they need in order to plan integrated solutions to local problems. This increased control is best exercised by regional councils. Local councils whose services are superior, or taxes lower, than neighbouring councils, can have great problems if people move into their area seeking to benefit. But as population movements take place largely within regions, this problem would not be significant at regional level.

Regional councils would take over some functions already performed by existing bodies, some of which are not democratically accountable. They would not be a needless additional level of bureaucracy, but would provide solutions informed by the specific needs of their region's economy and population.

As regional councils would be spending large amounts of money, they should bear a corresponding level of responsibility, for instance for certain social security and penal system costs incurred by regional citizens. If regional councils ran the police and the health service in their area, and thus had more room for manoeuvre in dividing their total budget among their various duties, they would no longer neglect the needs of children clearly heading for delinquency. At the moment if British children excluded from school commit crimes, as described in Chapter Five, the council does not bear the cost of their misdeeds. If sex education is inadequate, the council does not pick up the bill for teenage pregnancy. Once regional councils knew they would have to pay for the imprisonment of their criminal citizens, the psychiatric care needed by children whose learning difficulties they had neglected, and the unemployment benefits paid to their poorly educated citizens, they would improve preventive policies to reduce these problems. Citizens would have a strong incentive to try and influence these policies. Research shows that when councils have significant powers, electors are more likely to be politically active.[86]

Regions will rise to these new challenges only if their grant from central government reflects their needs as compared to those of other regions. Disadvantaged regions have more children who need extra help at school, higher crime rates, and more illness. But they should not be penalised for the success of any improvements they make. If through enhancing its services a region succeeds in reducing its costs, its grant should not be reduced unless a later assessment of its needs indicates this is justified.

Giving regions this extra responsibility would stimulate creativity. Innovative schemes would emerge which other councils could then copy.

Citizens' rights and responsibilities

It is important that councils promote citizens' commitment to the community. This fosters good social relationships, reduces crime, and provides a pool of people to take leadership roles and stimulate community service. To help build this commitment, local authorities should give certain rights to citizens who have lived in their area for more than a minimum period. Councils (and those to whom they award contracts) should be obliged to employ only local people, unless none of their own citizens are suitable for a certain job. As this would cut the distance people travel to work, pollution and congestion would fall.

Another fundamental human right is housing. The need to move away from one's town in order to find an affordable home damages crucial family relationships, as the British government has recognised. Therefore each citizen, apart from those with sufficient income to buy a home, or those who wilfully refuse suitable employment, should have the right to rent an affordable council home. This right would apply only to those who had lived in the council area since childhood or settling in Britain. Otherwise councils which offered this right would attract an influx of people from other areas which did not. Having the right to rent a home at age 27 could gradually influence young people not to become parents at a younger age. The consequent increase in the supply of rented housing would reduce the demand to purchase homes, thus cutting prices for first-time buyers. The additional public sector homes should be in socially mixed areas.

This policy would be problematic for certain densely populated districts. Governments' regional policies should reduce the economic disparities which cause population concentrations in certain areas.

While this policy would require substantial investment, it would promote social cohesion by removing the stigma attached to public sector housing. Estates with a preponderance of deprived people, and consequent high crime rates, would no longer be the norm for public sector housing. Most citizens would be willing to pay the extra tax required, realising it would help their children or grandchildren. In addition, tax on larger properties should be increased. At present, their owners pay little tax in relation to the value of their home.

Certain people entitled to rent a council home might not have a strong wish to do so, but might do so for casual motives, thus adding to the public investment needed. To discourage this, property taxes should be increased significantly while income tax is reduced a corresponding amount.

Rights of this kind need to be matched by responsibilities. Very few societies before the late 20th century have failed to penalise men who father children for whom they are unable to provide. Yet half of American, and a remarkable three-quarters of British fathers who do not live with their child are not paying the amounts assessed by law for the child's support.[87] In order that the law-abiding do not subsidise the irresponsible, payments of child support should be enforced through the social security and tax systems. Councils which aim to promote a sense of belonging in their citizens should foster awareness in boys of the responsibilities of fathering a child. Meeting men who have to pay towards the care of a child they have fathered through lack of foresight could be an important part of sex education, reminding boys to use a condom. This policy should in due course help to ensure that there are fewer children born without a father willing to share in their care. However sex education for boys must be much wider than this; a recent report found that boys consider its present message to be 'almost entirely negative.' The report recommended that 'boys must be actively involved in developing sex education programmes'.

In keeping with the principle underlying these proposals, the right to vote should be extended to those aged 16 and 17. Workers of this age pay tax, if they earn enough. While most young people feel alienated from politics, partly because of its present confrontational and petty style, there is plenty of evidence that with encouragement many could become involved. When asked what change they would propose to connect them more to the political process, a focus group of ordinary young people said democracy and politics should be taught in school.

Overwork, stress, and disconnection

Excessive working hours, which have increased particularly among the middle classes, are reducing people's ability to care about political issues. As the time they can spend with their families becomes scarcer, they tend to cut themselves off from society. Well over half of those in the highest social class see the home as 'a retreat' from the stress of life outside. Another major factor in this stress is the fear of crime, which afflicts people across all social classes. In Britain nearly two-thirds of women feel at least somewhat unsafe walking alone at night in their area. Over half of men, and two thirds of women, feel either 'fairly' or 'very' worried about the risk of being burgled. These fears deter some people from going out to take part in community organisations. In order to arrest community decline, it is vital to cut crime, as suggested in Chapter Five, and reduce working hours.

Workers are adjusting to the fact that cutting their hours may be the best way to safeguard their jobs. French workers with the multinational Philips agreed a deal under which they work 32 hours weekly (or 24 hours for weekend workers), for the same pay they received when working 35 hours. The company was able to afford this by opening the factory round the clock. They now employ nearly double the workforce. The French law limiting hours to 35 for most companies has probably created an extra 300,000 jobs. Four-fifths of French workers whose hours have been cut say this has improved their lives.[88]

Governments can help cut unemployment by providing incentives to reduce working hours and thus increase the number of jobs available. They should also improve retraining opportunities, provide an earnings-related supplement to unemployed benefit, and help certain people who can no longer afford their mortgage to become tenants of their home. By helping people adjust to the shock of unemployment, these measures would reduce the fear of redundancy which causes such widespread stress.

Cutting working hours by as little as half of one per cent every year would create 10 million new jobs throughout the EU within eight years.[89] Once workers see that other activities can give them greater fulfilment, they will gradually begin to value their free time more. A Danish scheme allowing extended parental or training leave has proved very popular. These changes would reduce inequality and crime by providing more jobs, and encourage some people to use part of their free time to help strengthen their communities.

Citizen co-operation

We cannot rely on politicians to protect our planet, or to build a better society. We need large numbers of confident and co-operative people to put pressure on politicians to make the correct decisions. Such activists can build mature organisations with the resilience needed to win long-term struggles. We can all help, by giving time or money to campaigns to protect the environment, promote racial equality, improve public education, or many others.

The American community groups described by Mary-Beth Rogers' book *Cold Anger* always thoroughly and supportively evaluate the strengths and weaknesses of any action they undertake. Rogers contrasts this with her experience in the American Democratic Party, in which

> we rarely made any kind of thoughtful analysis of our failures, and certainly never worked through with our leaders any kind of understanding of how things might have been handled differently . . . If you challenged the leadership's ability to run the meeting, you had a blood bath. If you admitted any kind of weakness, your cohorts would sprout vulture wings and circle in for the kill.

This atmosphere of conflict and suspicion is common to most political parties. In contrast, the groups Rogers describes create unity, and concern for others' needs. One organiser tells how

Over the years, I've seen people mellow. In the early years it was 'Hey, I want my street fixed first!' Now people wait for communities that need it more.[90]

This organiser seeks as potential activists balanced people 'who like their families', and have a sense of humour. In emphasizing these qualities, he recognises the value of emotional security which underlies the confidence in human co-operation activists need.

As well as developing in the children of families with responsive parents, this confidence is fostered by schools which help children to learn together co-operatively. One researcher analysed over 600 studies showing that this approach promotes social competence, psychological health, and more positive relationships among the children, including between those of different races.[91] A teacher of 8- to 9-year-olds illustrates how the introduction of a daily class meeting helped create a better learning environment. The children and teacher discussed how to penalise those who called out in class without waiting for their turn to speak. Having agreed on two punishments which they later felt caused too much embarrassment, after some weeks the meeting decided to abolish them. Having done so, the problem disappeared. The teacher attributed the improvement in this aspect of the children's behaviour to their increased 'sense of loyalty and concern for each other', arising from the daily discussions.

Involving secondary school students in decision-making also has many benefits. A well-established New York state school involves its students in democratic bodies governing school life, including a weekly meeting of all staff and students. Far from using their input to lower their workload, the students have voted both to increase the minimum number of credits needed for graduation, and to add a requirement for each student to undertake community service. Every time someone has proposed replacing the weekly All School Meeting with a representative forum, the students have voted the proposal down overwhelmingly. Students also run the school's disciplinary board, with staff support. Parents have often commented on how their child's attitude to education improved enormously after moving to the school, which is now heavily over-subscribed. The children also learn how to resolve conflicts with sensitivity to minority views. All schools should provide these opportunities, which by giving students the relevant skills will make them more likely to take part in civic life as adults.[92]

Education focused on co-operation can succeed even in the most difficult circumstances. The School for Peace workshops run by the remarkable bicultural village of Neve Shalom/Wahat Al-Salam have fostered understanding and friendship between Palestinian and Jewish adolescents from all over Israel. Having seen the peace and co-operation among the villagers, a young Palestinian man believed that peace could be possible between the Palestinians and the Jews. A Palestinian girl said that despite 'having been taught all my life' that Jews were intolerant opressors, she realised having seen the Jewish and Palestinian facilitators working together respectfully that her previous view of the Jews was a stereotype based on unfamiliarity.[93] The lessons of this unique programme should be applied in other areas of ethnic conflict.

Governments should encourage democratic structures in schools, to help nurture citizens who can work for the common good. We need such people to form inclusive organisations, which as well as fighting injustice build the relationships and sense of belonging which are the essence of community. Even in the poor American neighbourhoods Rogers describes, such groups have established among their members 'a powerful bond to one another because they share a common commitment to something larger than self'. This bond is based on confidence in the potential of human co-operation, which as I have described is the key to improving our society. Without this confidence, countless projects, large and small, would never have been started, let alone attained their aims.

As I have described, this confidence in human co-operation is most likely to be developed through receiving warm, sensitive parental care. However it can also be gained through having a supportive partner or close friend in adulthood.

The positive view of other people such activists possess fosters a love of life's simple pleasures. A young environmental volunteer speaks of the many people 'who have helped me love myself . . . and spent time helping me'. These relationships have given her a precious contentment. She is satisfied with her low income, and loves painting, singing, dancing and walking. Hence she has spare energy to devote to the welfare of humanity. Asked to name her main hopes for the future, she wishes

> that people wake up, take responsibility for their lives and the planet, stop destroying each other and the planet, and start loving and respecting life and themselves.

By supporting parents, cutting inequality, and extending democracy, our society can bring up many other young people with the faith and determination to join her in building a better world.

Society is becoming more and more competitive and individualistic. Globalisation is eroding the limited security for which citizens in industrial nations have fought. Hostility towards Western dominance, and resistance to the rise in migration, are leading to increased social conflict and violence. These developments may entrench the power of a wealthy elite. But if we can encourage more citizens to join groups promoting human welfare, we can advance social harmony and equality. Trust, understanding, and respect can defeat greed and hatred. We can *all* help humanity to win.

References

INTRODUCTION

1 John Burnett (ed.), Destiny Obscure: Autobiographies of Childhood, Education, and Family from the 1820s to the 1920s (Allen Lane, 1982), 16–17; Michael Young and Peter Willmott, Family and Kinship in East London (Penguin, 1957), 50, 68, 123, 142–54, 161

2 Spencer Kagan and Helena Carlson, 'Development of adaptive assertiveness in Mexican and United States children', Developmental Psychology 11, 1975, 71–8, esp. 76–7; Millard C. Madsen, 'Developmental and cross-cultural differences in the cooperative and competitive behavior of young children', Journal of Cross-Cultural Psychology 2, 1971, 365–71, esp. 368; Anthony G. Miller and Ron Thomas, 'Cooperation and competition among Blackfoot Indian and urban Canadian children', Child Development 43, 1972, 1104–10, esp. 1107–10

3 William Julius Wilson, 'Rising inequality and the case for coalition politics', Annals of the American Academy of Political and Social Science 568, 2000, 78–99, esp. 86; Kevin Doogan, 'Insecurity and long-term employment', Work, Employment and Society 15, 2001, 419–41, esp. 421, 435, 438

4 Employee Satisfaction: Tracking European Trends (International Survey Research, 1995), 12, 14, 17, 19; Shiv Malik, 'A Very British Sickness', New Statesman, 10 January 2005, 27–9.

5 Peter Sunley, Ron Martin and Corrine Nativel, 'Mapping the New Deal: local disparities in the performance of welfare-to-work', Transactions of the Institute of British Geographers 26, 2001, 484–512; Jamie Peck 'Getting real with welfare-to-work: hard lessons from America', Renewal 7, 1999, 39–49, esp. 42–3; Heather Stewart, 'New deal has boosted economy', Guardian, 4 August 2001, 23

6 Ichiro Kawachi and Bruce P. Kennedy, The Health of Nations: Why Inequality is Harmful to Your Health (The New Press, 2002), 35; see also Wilson, 'Rising Inequality'

7 Richard G. Wilkinson, Unfair Shares: the Effects of Widening Income Differences on the Welfare of the Young (Barnardo's, 1994), 59; Kristina Orth-Gomer, Annika Rosengren, and Lars Wilhelmsen, 'Lack of social support and coronary heart disease in middle-aged Swedish men', Psychosomatic Medicine 55, 1993, 37, 39, 41; Michael Argyle, The Psychology of Happiness (Methuen, 1987), 181, 183; John Mordechai Gottmann, What Predicts Divorce? The Relationship between Marital Processes and Marital Outcomes (Erlbaum, 1994), 2–3

8 Ruut Veenhoven, *Conditions of Happiness* (Erasmus University, Rotterdam, 1984), p. 349; Robert Wuthnow, *Acts of Compassion: Caring for Others and Helping Ourselves* (Princeton University Press, 1991), 97, 317; Alex C. Michalos, 'Job Satisfaction, Marital Satisfaction, and the Quality of Life: a Review and a Preview', In Frank M. Andrews (ed), *Research on the Quality of Life* (Survey Research Centre, Institute of Social Research, University of Michigan, 1986), 57–83, esp. 62; Robert D. Putnam, *Bowling Alone: The Collapse and Revival of American Community* (Simon and Schuster, 2000), 333

9 Washington Post poll of October 2003, and Pew Research Centre poll of July-August 2003: 'Health Care Delivery', www.pollingreport.com/ health1.htm; Associated Press-Ipsos poll of March 2004, and Los Angeles Times Poll of April 2003: 'Federal Budget and Taxes' www.pollingreport. com/budget.htm; Coleen McMurray, 'Medicare Changes Fall Short with Seniors', 27 January 2004: www.gallup.com/content/default. aspx?ci=10414&pg=1; see also www.gallup.com/poll/releases/pr010124. asp; Martin Kettle, 'Bush Stakes All on Promise to Halve Tax Bills', *Guardian*, 22 January 2000, 19

10 Lydia Saad, 'Environment Not a Pressing Concern', 19 April 2004: www. gallup.com/content/?ci=11380; Frank Newport, 'Americans Clear that Economy is Most Important Problem Facing Country', 12 May 2003: www.gallup.com/content/default.aspx?ci=8368

11 Jeffrey M. Jones, 'More Positive View of Taxes Persists', 14 April 2004: www.gallup.com/content/?ci=11329; 'Federal Budget and Taxes' (see note 9; Commission on Taxation and Citizenship, *Paying for Progress: A New Politics of Tax for Public Spending* (Fabian Society, 2000), p. 3; John Callaghan, *The Retreat of Social Democracy* (Manchester University Press, 2000), p. 221

12 Torben Iversen and Anne Wren, 'Equality, Employment, and Budgetary Restraint: The Trilemma of the Service Economy', *World Politics* 50, 1998, 507–46, esp. 534

13 Mary-Beth Rogers, *Cold Anger: a Story of Faith and Power Politics* (University of North Texas Press, 1990), 106–24. The successes of similar groups to COPS are outlined in Francesca Polletta, *Freedom is an Endless Meeting: Democracy in American Social Movements* (University of Chicago Press, 2002), 177, 180.

14 Robert D. Putnam, with Robert Leonardi and Raffaella Y. Nanetti, *Making Democracy Work: Civic Traditions in Modern Italy* (Princeton University Press, 1993), 98, 102–05, 106, 111, 114, 143, 148–58, 163, 223, 226; Matt Frei, *Italy: The Unfinished Revolution* (Sinclair Stevenson, 1996), 174–8; Salvatore Lupo, 'The changing Mezzogiorno: between representations and reality', in Stephen Gundle and Simon Parker (eds) *The New Italian Republic: from the Fall of the Berlin Wall to Berlusconi* (Routledge, 1996), 247–262, esp. 249; Tom W. Rice and Alexander F. Sunberg, 'Civic culture and government performance in the American states', *Publius: The Journal of Federalism* 27, 1997, 99–114, esp. 106–14; Putnam, *Bowling Alone*, 296

15 Michael Rutter and David J. Smith, 'Towards causal explanations of time trends in psychosocial disorders of young people', in Michael Rutter and David J. Smith (eds), *Psychosocial Disorders in Young People:*

Time Trends and their Causes (Wiley, 1995), 782–808, esp. 783; Patricia Hersch, *A Tribe Apart: A Journey into the Heart of American Adolescence* (Ballantine, 1999), 12, 366

16 Stevi Bloomfield, 'Something for the Weekend', *Guardian*, 29 May 1999, 24

17 Robert J. Stevens and Robert E. Slavin, 'The cooperative elementary school: effects on students' achievement, attitudes and social relations', *American Educational Research Journal* 32, 1995, 321–51, esp. 323, 324, 335, 336, 339, 342, 344; *Others Study Democracy, We Do It* [Interview with Dave Lehman, Principal of the Alternative Community School, Ithaca, New York], Centre for Living Democracy, Brattleboro, Vermont (n.d.)

18 Kim Quaile Hill, 'The policy agendas of the president and the mass public: a research validation and extension', *American Journal of Political Science* 42, 1998, 1328–34, esp. 1331–2; Tim Tilton, *The Political Theory of Swedish Social Democracy: through the Welfare State to Socialism* (Clarendon Press, 1991), 9, 15, 23, 38, 126, 144, 192, 200, 207, 259, 278; Shirley Zimmerman, *Family Policies and Family Well-being: the Role of Political Culture* (Sage, 1992), 111, 132; Commission on Social Justice, *Social Justice: Strategies for National Renewal* (Vintage, 1994), 199; Geoffrey Garrett, 'The politics of structural change: Swedish social democracy and Thatcherism in comparative perspective', *Comparative Political Studies* 25, 1993, 521–47, esp. 534; E. Stina Lyon, 'Between a rock and a hard place: the Swedish Social Democratic Party into Europe', *Contemporary Politics* 2, 1996, 101–25, esp. 118.

19 Stephen Zunes, *Tinderbox: US Middle East Policy and the Roots of Terrorism* (Zed Press, 2003), 233; David Niven, 'The mobilization calendar: the time-dependent effects of personal contact on turnout', *American Politics Research* 30, 2002, 307–22, esp. 309, 315–7; Alan S. Gerber and Donald P. Green, 'The effects of canvassing, telephone calls and direct mail on voter turnout: a field experiment', *American Political Science Review* 94, 2000, 653–63, esp. 653, 654, 658, 660, 661

20 Bob Purdie, *Politics in the Streets: the Origins of the Civil Rights Movement in Northern Ireland* (Blackstaff, 1990), 166; L. Martin Overby and Sarah J. Ritchie, 'Mobilized masses and strategic opponents: a resource mobilization analysis of the clean air and nuclear freeze movements', *Western Political Quarterly* 44, 1991, 329–51, esp. 347.

21 Overseas Aid figures from *Annual Abstract of Statistics* (HMSO, 1995), 233–4; charity income figures from Susan Saxon-Harrold and Jeremy Kendall, *Dimensions of the Voluntary Sector 1* (Charities Aid Foundation, 1995), 114; Joseph E. Stiglitz, *Globalization and its Discontents* (Allen Lane, 2002), 244.

1 Leah Z. Ziskin, 'Time for change: mental illness in public health', *New Jersey Medicine*, 96, November 1999, 37–9, esp. 37

2 Robert D. Putnam, *Bowling Alone: The Collapse and Revival of American Community* (Simon and Schuster, 2000), 331

3   1999 Gallup poll; information originally obtained at www.gallup.com/
     poll/releases/pr990903.asp; *British Public Opinion*, Spring 2003, 24
4   John Nicholson, 'Men and Sex in Britain', *Esquire*, April 1992, 44–56,
     esp. 47; see also Robin W. Simon, 'Gender, multiple roles, role meaning,
     and mental health', *Journal of Health and Social Behavior* 36, 1995, 182–
     94, esp. 185–186; Viktor Gecas and Monica A. Seff, 'Social class and self-
     esteem: psychological centrality, compensation, and the relative effects
     of work and home', *Social Psychology Quarterly* 53, 1990, 165–73, esp.
     169
5   Danny Danziger, *All in a Day's Work* (Fontana, 1987), 224
6   Rebecca J. Erickson, 'Reconceptualizing family work: the effects of
     emotion work on perceptions of marital quality', *Journal of Marriage and
     the Family* 55, 1993, 888–900, esp. 895–7
7   Cited in Arlie Hochschild, with Anne Machung, *Second Shift: Working
     Parents and the Revolution at Home* (Piatkus, 1989), 214–5
8   Sheena Ashford and Noel Timms, *What Europe Thinks: a Study of Western
     European Values: Unity, Diversity and Change* (Dartmouth, 1992), 134;
     Stephen Harding, David Phillips, and Michael Fogarty, *Contrasting Values
     in Western Europe*, (Macmillan, 1986), Question No. 308
9   William Julius Wilson, 'Rising inequality and the case for coalition
     politics', *Annals of the American Academy of Political and Social Science*
     568, 2000, 78–99, esp.84; Will Hutton, *The World We're In* (Little, Brown,
     2002), 25
10   Paul Lunt and Sonia Livingstone, *Mass Consumption and Personal
     Identity: Everyday Economic Experience* (Open University Press, 1992),
     38, 44
11   Robert N. Bellah, Richard Madsen, William M. Sullivan, Ann Swidler, and
     Steven M. Tipton, *Habits of the Heart: Individualism and Commitment in
     American Life* (University of California Press, 1985), 294
12   Putnam, *Bowling Alone*, 260; Alexander W. Astin, William S. Korn, and
     Ellyne R. Berg, *The American Freshman: National Norms for Fall 1990*,
     (Higher Education Research Institute, University of California, 1990), 5
13   Min-Sun Kim and John E. Hunter, 'Relationships among attitudes,
     behavioral intentions, and behavior: a meta-analysis of past research, pt.
     2', *Communication Research* 20, 1993, 331–64, esp. 331, 336, 348, 355
14   Lunt and Livingstone, *Mass Consumption*, 27
15   Ichiro Kawachi and Bruce P. Kennedy, *The Health of Nations: Why
     Inequality is Harmful to Your Health* (The New Press, 2002), 34
16   Alex C. Michalos, 'Job satisfaction, marital satisfaction, and the quality
     of life: a review and a preview', In Frank M. Andrews (ed.), *Research on
     the Quality of Life* (Survey Research Centre, Institute of Social Research,
     University of Michigan, 1986), 57–83, esp. 75; Earl Hopper, *Social Mobility:
     a Study of Social Control and Insatiability* (Basil Blackwell, 1981), 117;
     Michael A. Argyle and Maryanne Martin, 'The psychological causes of
     happiness', in Fritz Strack, Michael Argyle, and Norbert Schwarz (eds),
     Subjective Well-being: an Interdisciplinary Perspective (Pergamon, 1991),
     77–100, esp. 81; Robert E. Lane, *The Market Experience* (Cambridge
     University Press, 1991), 472
17   Lunt and Livingstone, *Mass Consumption*, 45; Steven Miles, 'Towards an
     Understanding of the Relationship Between Youth Identities and Consumer

Culture', *Youth and Policy* 51, 35–45; Susan B. Kaiser, *The Social Psychology of Clothing and Personal Adornment* (Macmillan, 1985), 119, 166, 167; Jennifer Yurchisin and Kim K.P. Johnson, 'Compulsive Buying Behavior and its Relationship to Perceived Social Status Associated with Buying, Materialism, Self-Esteem, and Apparel-Product Involvement', *Family and Consumer Sciences Research Journal* 32, 2004, 291–314, esp. 296, 304, 306, 308

18 Studs Terkel, *Working People Talk About What They Do All Day And How They Feel About What They Do* (Penguin, 1985), 222; Danziger, *Day's Work*, 216; Rosalind Coward, *Our Treacherous Hearts: Why Women Let Men Get Their Way* (Faber, 1992), 76

19 Nicholas Emler, *Self-Esteem: the Costs and Causes of Low Self-Worth* (Joseph Rowntree Foundation, 2001), 42; Naomi Wolf, *The Beauty Myth* (Chatto & Windus, 1990), 1; Jill Dawson, *How Do I Look?* (Virago, 1990), cited in Coward, *Our Treacherous Hearts*, 155, 157

20 Ruut Veenhoven, *Conditions of Happiness* (Erasmus University, Rotterdam, 1984), 177, 192, 281, 343; Antonia Abbey and Frank M. Andrews, 'Modelling the psychological determinants of life quality', In Frank M. Andrews (ed), *Research on the Quality of Life* (Survey Research Centre, Institute of Social Research, University of Michigan, 1986), 85–116, esp. 109; Melvin L. Kohn, Atsushi Naoi, Carrie Schoenbach, Carmi Schooler, and Kazimierz M. Slomczynski, 'Position in the class structure and psychological functioning in the United States, Japan, and Poland', *American Journal of Sociology* 95, 1990, 964–1008, esp. 984, 989; Ed Diener and Marissa Diener, 'Cross-cultural correlates of life satisfaction and self-esteem', *Journal of Personality and Social Psychology* 68, 1995, 653–63, esp. 654, 657, 661

21 Veenhoven, *Conditions*, 349; Robert Wuthnow, *Acts of Compassion: Caring for Others and Helping Ourselves* (Princeton University Press, 1991), 97, 317; Michalos, 'Job satisfaction', 57–83, esp. 62; Andrew Oswald, 'Happiness and Economic Performance', *Economic Journal* 107, 1997, 1815–31, esp. 1815

22 Luo Lu and Michael Argyle, 'Happiness and cooperation', *Personality and Individual Differences* 12, 1991, 1019–30, esp. 1024; Diener and Diener, 'Cross-Cultural Correlates', 653, 655; Jeffry A. Simpson, 'Influence of attachment styles on adult romantic relationships', *Journal of Personality and Social Psychology* 59, 1990, 971–80, esp. 976; M. Carole Pistole, 'Attachment in adult romantic relationships: style of conflict resolution and relationship satisfaction', *Journal of Social and Personal Relationships* 6, 1989, 505–10, esp. 508; Kim Bartholomew and Leonard M. Horowitz, 'Attachment styles among young adults: a test of a four-category model', *Journal of Personality and Social Psychology* 61, 1991, 226–44, esp. 231;

23 Marc Levy and Keith Davis, 'Love styles and attachment styles compared: their relations to each Other and to various relationship characteristics', *Journal of Social and Personal Relationships* 5, 1988, 439–71, esp. 457; Pistole, 'Attachment', 505–10, esp. 508; R. Rogers Kobak and Cindy Hazan, 'Attachment in marriage: effects of security and accuracy of working models', *Journal of Personality and Social Psychology* 60, 1990, 861–9, esp. 864–5; Cindy Hazan and Philip R. Shaver, 'Love and work:

an attachment-theoretical perspective', *Journal of Personality and Social Psychology* 59, 1990, 270–80, esp. 275–6; R. Rogers Kobak and Amy Sceery, 'Attachment in late adolescence: working models, affect regulation, and representations of self and others', *Child Development* 59, 1988,135–46, esp. 140, 143; M. Mikulincer, V. Florian, and R. Tolmacz, 'Attachment styles and fear of personal death: a case study of affect regulation, *Journal of Personality and Social Psychology* 58, 1990, 273–80, esp. 279

24 Kim K. R. McKeage, Marsha L. Richins, and Kathleen Debevec, 'Self-gifts and the manifestation of material values', *Advances in Consumer Research* 20, 1993, 359–64, esp. 359

25 Susan Fournier and Michael Guiry, ' "An emerald-green Jaguar, a house on Nantucket, and an African safari:" wish lists and consumption dreams in materialist society', *Advances in Consumer Research* 20, 1993, 352–8, esp. 356

26 Shere Hite, *Women and Love: A Cultural Revolution in Progress* (Viking 1988), 279

27 Colin Campbell, *The Romantic Ethic and the Spirit of Modern Consumerism* (Basil Blackwell, 1987), 39, 73, 74; Marshall Sahlins, *Stone Age Economics* (Aldine, 1972), 37, also quoted in Mihaly Csikszentmihalyi and Eugene Rochberg-Halton, *The Meaning of Things: Domestic Symbols and the Self* (Cambridge University Press, 1981), 230

28 Lita Furby, 'Possessions: toward a theory of their meaning and function throughout the life cycle', in Paul B. Baltes (ed.), *Life-span Development and Behavior, vol. 1* (Academic Press, 1978), 297–336, esp. 324

29 David G. Blanchflower and Andrew J. Oswald, 'Well-being over time in Britain and the USA' (paper submitted to the NBER Summer Institute Presentation, 2000; accessed at www.oswald.co.uk), 5, 8

30 Michael Marmot and Richard G. Wilkinson, 'Psychosocial and material pathways in the relation between income and health: a response to Lynch et al', *British Medical Journal* 322, 2001, 1233–6; Alberto Alesina, Rafael Di Tella, and Robert MacCulloch, *Inequality and Happiness: Are Europeans and Americans Different?* (Centre for Economic Policy Research, 2001, Discussion Paper No. 2877), accessed at www.cepr.org/pubs/new-dps/dplist.asp?authorid=104125]

31 Michael Marmot, 'The influence of income on health: the views of an epidemiologist', *Health Affairs*, March/April 2002, 31–46, esp. 37; Richard S. Cooper, Joan F. Kennelly, Ramon Durazo-Arvizu, Hyun-Joo Oh, George Kaplan, and John Lynch, 'Relationship between premature mortality and socioeconomic factors in black and white populations of US metropolitan areas', *Public Health Reports* 116, 2001, 464–73, esp. 468; Nancy A. Ross, Michael C. Wolfson, James R. Dunn, Jean-Marie Berthelot, George A. Kaplan, and John W. Lynch, 'Relation between income inequality and mortality in Canada and in the United States: cross-sectional assessment using census data and vital statistics', *British Medical Journal* 320, 2000, 898–902

32 Marmot, 'Influence', 36, 38, 39; Kawachi and Kennedy, *Health of Nations*, 57–60

33 Mikko Laaksonen et al., 'Do health behaviour and psychosocial risk factors explain the European East–West gap in health status?', *European Journal of Public Health* 11, 2001, 65–73; Kawachi and Kennedy, *Health*

of Nations, 59–60; Leiyu Shi, James Macinko, Barbara Starfield, John Wulu, Jerri Regan, and Robert Politzer, 'The relationship between primary care, income inequality, and mortality in US states, 1980–1995', *Journal of the American Board of Family Practice* 16, 2003, 412–22, tables 2, 3, 4

34 Eric Brunner, 'Socioeconomic determinants of health: stress and the biology of inequality', *British Medical Journal* 314, 1997, 1472ff. (accessed at http://bmj.com); Marmot and Wilkinson, 'Psychosocial and material pathways' (*passim*)

35 Margie E. Lachman and Suzanne L. Weaver, 'The sense of control as a moderator of social class differences in health and well-being', *Journal of Personality and Social Psychology* 74, 1998, 763–73, esp. 766, 771, 772; Martin Bobak, Hynek Pikhart, Richard Rose, Clyde Hertzman, and Michael Marmot, 'Socioeconomic factors, material inequalities, and perceived control in self-rated health: cross-sectional data from seven post-communist countries', *Social Science and Medicine* 51, 2000, 1343–50, esp. 1346, 1347, 1349

36 Bruce P. Kennedy, Ichiro Kawachi, Kimberley Lochner, Camara Jones, and Deborah Prothrow-Stith, '(Dis)respect and black mortality', *Ethnicity and Disease* 7, 1997, 207–14, esp. 210–1

37 Gerald Mikula, Klaus R. Scherer, and Ursula Athenstaedt, 'The role of injustice in the elicitation of differential emotional reactions', *Personality and Social Psychology Bulletin* 24, 1998, 769–83, esp. 770, 777, 778

38 Steven Allan and Paul Gilbert, 'Anger and anger expression in relation to perceptions of social rank, entrapment and depressive symptoms', *Personality and Individual Differences* 32, 2002, 551, 552, 558–60 565

39 Tony Parker, *The People of Providence:A Housing Estate and Some of its Inhabitants* (Hutchinson, 1983), 288–9; Michael Young and Peter Willmott, *Family and Kinship in East London* (Penguin, 1957), 152, 154, 161–4

40 Michael Argyle, *The Psychology of Social Class* (Routledge, 1994), 215, 279; *see also* Theo Nichols and Peter Armstrong, *Workers Divided* (Fontana, 1976), 204; Andrew Oswald, 'Happiness and economic performance', *Economic Journal* 107, 1997, 1815–31, esp. 1820

41 Timothy W. Smith, 'Hostility and health: current status of a psychosomatic hypothesis', *Health Psychology* 11, 1992, 139–50, esp. 143–7

42 I. Kawachi et al., 'Social capital, income inequality and mortality', *American Journal of Public Health*, 87, 1997, 1491–8, cited in Richard Wilkinson, 'Income Inequality, Social Cohesion, and Health', *International Journal of Health Services* 29, 1999, 525–43, esp. 526

43 Ellen E. Pinderhughes, Robert Nix, E. Michael Foster, Damon Jones, and the Conduct Problems Prevention Research Group, 'Parenting in context: impact of neighbourhood poverty, residential stability, public services, social networks, and danger on parental behaviors', *Journal of Marriage and the Family*, 63, 2001, 941–53, esp. 942–3

44 Frances E. Kuo, 'Coping with poverty: impacts of environment and attention in the inner city', *Environment and Behavior* 33, 2001, 5–34, esp. 22–4, 28, 29,31; George Galster and Anne Zobel, 'Will dispersed housing programmes reduce social problems in the U.S.?', *Housing Studies* 13, 1998, 605–22, esp. 612–3

45   Rather than analysing the effect of individual income, what actually helps clarify the causes of regions' variations in illness is to compare the contribution made by average income with that of level of inequality: Johan P. Mackenbach, 'Income inequality and population health', *British Medical Journal* 324, 2002, 1–2; Richard Wilkinson, 'Income inequality and population health', *British Medical Journal* 324, 2004, 978; Ichiro Kawachi, S. V. Subramanian, and N. Almeida-Filho, 'A glossary for health inequalities', *Journal of Epidemiology and Community Health* 56, 2002, 647–52, esp. 650; S.V Subramanian and Ichiro Kawachi, 'Response: In Defence of the Income Inequality Hypothesis', *International Journal of Epidemiology* 32, 2003, 1037–40, esp. 1038; Regarding race, see Angus Deaton and Darren Lubotsky, 'Mortality, Inequality, and Race in American Cities and States', *Social Science and Medicine* 56, 2003, 1139–53, esp. 1144, 1145, 1150, 1152; S.V Subramanian and Ichiro Kawachi, 'The Association between State Income Inequality and Worse Health is not Confounded by Race', *International Journal of Epidemiology* 32, 2003, 1022–8, esp. 1023, 1025, 1026; Timothy Brezina and Kenisha Winder, 'Economic Disadvantage, Status Generalization, and Negative Racial Stereotyping by White Americans', *Social Psychology Quarterly* 66, 2003, 402–18, esp. 402, 406, 407, 409, 411, 412, 414

46   Andreas Muller, 'Education income inequality, and mortality: a multiple regression analysis', *British Medical Journal* 324, 2002, 23ff, accessed at www.bmj.com

47   Richard Wilkinson, 'Health, redistribution, and growth', in Andrew Glyn and David Miliband (eds.), *Paying for Inequality: the Economic Cost of Social Injustice* (Rivers Oram, 1994), 24–43, esp. 36; Lawrence S. Wrightsman, 'Measurement of philosophies of human nature', *Psychological Reports* 14, 1964, 743–51, esp. 749

48   Morris Rosenberg and Leonard I. Pearlin 'Social class and self-esteem among chldren and adults', *American Journal of Sociology* 84, 1978, 53–77, esp. 55–7; Viktor Gecas and Monica A. Seff, 'Social class and self-esteem: psychological centrality, compensation, and the relative effects of work and home', *Social Psychology Quarterly* 53, 1990, 165–73, esp. 169; Les B. Whitbeck, Ronald L. Simons, Rand D. Conger, Frederick O. Lorenz, Shirley Huck, and Glen H. Elder Jr., 'Family economic hardship, parental support, and adolescent self-esteem', *Social Psychology Quarterly* 54, 1991, 353–63, esp. 359

49   Adewale Maja-Pearce, *How Many Miles to Babylon?* (Heinemann, 1990), 7, 13

50   Argyle, *Social Class*, 260

51   C. R. Leslie, *Memoirs of the Life of John Constable* (J. M. Dent, 1911), 246, 248

52   Michael Argyle, *The Psychology of Happiness* (Methuen, 1987), 3, 113–5, 124; Peter M. Lewinsohn, Julie E. Redner, and John R. Seeley, 'The relationship between life satisfaction and psychosocial variables: new perspectives', in Strack, Argyle, and Schwarz (eds.), *Subjective Well-being*, 141–69, esp. 155

53   Ching-Chi Hsieh and M.D. Pugh, 'Poverty, inequality, and violent crime: a meta-analysis of recent aggregate data studies', *Criminal Justice Review* 18, 1993, 182–202, esp. 192; Miles D. Harer and Darrell Steffensmeier,

'The differing effects of economic inequality on black and white rates of violence', *Social Forces* 70, 1992, 1035–54, esp. 1041

54 Susan E. Mayer, 'How did the increase in economic inequality between 1970 and 1990 affect children's educational attainment?', *American Journal of Sociology* 107, 2001, 1–32, esp. 2, 15–7, 19–21; S. Demack, D. Drew, and M. Grimsley, 'Minding the gap: ethnic, gender, and social class differences in attainment at 16 1988–1995', *Race, Ethnicity, and Education* 3, 2000, 117–43

55 Jean Anyon, *Ghetto Schooling: A Political Economy of Urban Educational Reform* (Teachers College Press, 1997), 182

56 Samuel R. Lucas, 'Effectively maintained inequality: education transitions, track mobility, and social background effects', *American Journal of Sociology* 106, 2001, 1642–90, esp. 1643, 1646, 1671–4, 1678; Kathryn Wilson, 'The determinants of educational attainment: modeling and estimating the human capital model and education production functions', *Southern Economic Journal* 67, 2001, 518–51, esp. 522, 539; M. Reza Nakhaie, 'Social origins and educational attainment in Canada: 1985 and 1994', *Review of Radical Political Economics* 32, 2000, 577–609, esp. 587–600, 603; Anyon, *Ghetto Schooling*, 164

57 Robert Erikson and Jan O. Jonsson, 'Explaining class inequality in education: the Swedish test case', in Robert Erikson and Jan O. Jonsson (eds.), *Can Education Be Equalized: The Swedish Case in Comparative Perspective* (Westview, 1996) 1–64, esp. 10; Robert Erikson, 'Explaining change in educational inequality: economic security and school reforms', in *ibid.*, 95–112, esp. 105

58 Galster and Zobel, 'Dispersed housing programmes', 605–22, esp. 614, 617, 618

59 Hutton, *World We're In*, 172

60 Eric Thorbecke and Chutatong Charumilind, 'Economic inequality and its socio-economic impact', *World Development* 30, 2002, 1477–95, esp. 1480, 1482, 1483, 1487; John Mills, *Managing the World Economy* (Macmillan, 2000), 177, 220; Dan Corry and Andrew Glyn, 'The macroeconomics of equality, stability, and growth', in Glyn and Miliband, *Paying for Inequality*, 208, 210, 212–215, esp. 214; W. Henry Chiu, 'Income inequality, human capital accumulation, and economic performance', *Economic Journal* 108, 1998, 44–59, esp. 45

61 Harvey Cole, 'Statistics watch', *Prospect*, January 2003, 7; Edward Chancellor, 'Perverse incentives', *Prospect*, June 2002, 28–33, esp. 30; John Plender, *Going off the Rails: Global Capital and the Crisis of Legitimacy* (Wiley, 2003), 6

62 Peter Birch Sorensen, 'The case for international tax co-ordination reconsidered', *Economic Policy,* October 2000, 429–72, esp. 457; World Economic Forum, *Global Competitiveness Report 2002–2003* (at www.weforum.org/site/homepublic.nsf/Content/Global+Competitveness+Programme%5CGlobal+Competitiveness+Report); David Smith, 'Taxing questions of growth', *Sunday Times (Business News)*, March 2, 2002, 4

63 Timothy Tilton, *The Political Theory of Swedish Social Democracy* (Clarendon, 1991), 189–92, 261

64 Hutton, *The World We're In*, 238, 244, 245, 264, 265, 268

65 *Ibid.*, 20, 133, 136; Plender, *Going off the Rails*, 10, 16, 18, 21; Chancellor,

'Perverse incentives', 31; Richard Sennett, *The Corrosion of Character: The Personal Consequences of Work in the New Capitalism* (Norton, 1998), 22

66 David W. Johnson and Roger T. Johnson, 'Constructive conflict in the schools', *Journal of Social Issues* 50, 1994, 117–37, esp. 130–1; Cathie McNamara, ' "Say no to bullying!" a message from your peers', *Pastoral Care* 14(2), 1996, 1996, 16–20, esp. 17; Hilary Stacey, 'Mediation into schools does go: an outline of the mediation process and how it can be used to promote positive relationships and effective conflict resolution in schools', *Pastoral Care* 14 (2), 1996, 7–9, esp. 9; Kathy Bickmore, 'Student conflict resolution, power "sharing" in schools, and citizenship education', *Curriculum Inquiry* 31, 2001, 137–62, esp. 152, 156

67 See the chapter by Robert McKechnie in Anna Coote (ed.), *Families, Children, and Crime* (Institute for Public Policy Research, 1994), 143–5; Bickmore, 'Student conflict resolution', 144

CHAPTER 2

1   Paul Webster, 'Europe's storms kill more than 100 people', *Guardian*, 28 December 1999, 10; Paul Brown, 'The dilemma that confronts the world', *Guardian*, 16 September 1999, 3

2   Stephen Timms, 'Global warming: sue the US now', *Guardian*, 25 July 2001, 17; *see also* Andrew Simms, 'High cost of climate disasters waiting to happen', *Guardian Weekly*, 18–24 July 2002, 26

3   Tim Radford and Paul Brown, 'Warming could be worst in 10,000 years', *Guardian*, 23 January 2001, 1

4   'Green growth', *Guardian Weekly* (editorial), 22–28 August 2002, 12

5   Information originally obtained at www.gallup.com/poll/indicators/indenvironment.asp (July 2001)

6   Paul Brown, 'Danes put faith in wind power at sea', *Guardian*, 10 May 1999, 13 ; Simon Jones, 'Rays of hope', *Guardian (Society)*, 18 February 1998, 4; Ashok Sinha and John Vidal, 'Solar's day dawning', *Guardian (Society)*, 23 June 1999, 4; Britons can choose a green electricity supplier by visiting www.foe.org.uk/campaigns/climate/press_for_change/choose_green_energy/

7   Jonathon Porritt, *Save the Earth* (Dorling Kindersley, 1991), 34

8   Linda Saad, 'Americans mostly "green" in the energy versus environment debate', www.gallup.com/poll/releases/pr010316.asp (March 2001); Commission on Taxation and Citizenship, Michael Jacobs, *Paying for Progress: A New Politics of Tax for Public Spending* (Fabian Society, 2000), 371; Walter H. Corson, 'Recognising hidden environmental and social costs and reducing ecological and societal damage through tax, price, and subsidy reform', *The Environmentalist* 22, 2002, 67–82, esp. 75

9   'The day the oceans boiled' *Equinox*, Channel 4 TV, June 2001; *see also* speech by Jan Pronk, Dutch Environment Minister, to the conference on Innovative Policy Solutions to Global Climate Change, Washington DC, 25 April 2000, information originally obtained at http://208.211.164.177/media/transcript_jpronk2.cfm

10 Rob Geuterbock, 'Greenpeace Campaign Case Study – StopEsso', *Journal*

of Consumer Behaviour 3, 2004, 265–71, esp. 266, 269–71; 'Drivers Decide on Petrol', www.mori.com/polls/2002/greenpeace-esso.shtml; 'Stop Exxon Mobil campaign information', www.pacificenvironment.org/ stopexxonmobil/campaign_info.html; 'How to sabotage a summit', www. stopesso.com/press/00000034.php; 'Campaign news', www.stopesso. com/campaign/00000066.php

11   Tom Robbins, 'Traffic fumes may cause babies to be born with heart defects', *Sunday Times*, 30 December 2001, 2

12   Corson, 'Hidden environmental and social costs', 67–82, esp. 68

13   Robert D. Putnam, *Bowling Alone: The Collapse and Revival of American Community* (Simon and Schuster, 2000), 212–13

14   Gallup, Jeffrey M. Jones, 'High gas prices affecting many Americans' driving and travel', 4, information originally obtained at www.gallup.com/ poll/releases/pr000620.asp; Adair Turner, 'Kyoto is good for business' *New Statesman*, 7 May 2001, 23; Chris Hewett, 'Drivers should pay', *Guardian*, 14 September 2000, 21

15   'The Hard Numbers on Climate Change' (press release of the Worldwatch Institute, 16 July 2001: www.worldwatch.org/alerts/010716.html); Andrew Simms, 'Would you buy a car that looked like this?', *New Statesman*, 29 November 2004, 10–11

CHAPTER 3

1   Paul Ritter and Jean Ritter, *Free Family and Feedback, 1949–1974: a Creative Experiment in Self-Regulation for Children* (Gollancz, 1975), 186, 341, 348

2   Sue Gerhardt, *Why Love Matters: How Affection Shapes a Baby's Brain* (Brunner-Routledge, 2004), 48, 62–7, 74–9, 101–2, 117, 118, 139–46; Rolf Loeber and Magda Stouthamer-Loeber, 'Family factors as correlates and predictors of juvenile conduct problems and delinquency', in Michael Tonry and Norval Morris (eds.), *Crime and Justice: an Annual Review of Research*, vol. 7 (University of Chicago Press, 1986), 29–150, esp. 124

3   Rebecca J. Erickson, 'Reconceptualizing family work: the effect of emotional work on perceptions of marital quality', *Journal of Marriage and the Family* 55, 888–900, esp. 893–4; Shirley L. Zimmerman, *Family Policies and Family Well-Being: the Role of Political Culture* (Sage, 1992, 28); Alex C. Michalos, 'Job satisfaction, marital satisfaction, and the quality of life: a review and preview', in Frank M. Andrews (ed.), *Research on the Quality of Life* (Survey Research Centre, Institute for Social Research, University of Michigan, 1986), 57–83, esp. 63; Rosalind Miles, 'Give children time, not television', *Sunday Times*, 2 June 1996, 13

4   Penelope Leach, *The First Six Months: Getting Together with Your Baby* (Fontana Collins, 1986), 66.

5   Benjamin Spock and Michael B. Rothenberg, *Dr Spock's Baby and Child Care* (Simon & Schuster, 1992), 16; Miriam Stoppard, *The New Baby Care Book* (Dorling Kindersley, 1993), 12

6   Deborah Jackson, *Three in a Bed: Why You Should Sleep with your Baby* (Bloomsbury, 1989), 157

7   Ronald P. Rohner, *They Love Me, They Love Me Not: a Worldwide Study of*

the Effects of Parental Acceptance and Rejection (Human Relations Area Files, 1975), 100–03

8   E. Richard Sorenson, 'Cooperation and freedom among the Fore of New Guinea', in Ashley Montagu (ed.) *Learning Non-Aggression: the Experience of Pre-Literate Societies* (Oxford University Press, 1978), 15, 25; Annette Hamilton, *Nature and Nurture: Aboriginal Child-Rearing in North Central Arnhemland* (Australian Institute for Anthropological Studies, 1981), 76; Melvin Konner, 'Aspects of the developmental ethology of a foraging people', in N. Blurton Jones (ed.) *Ethnological Studies of Child Behaviour* (Cambridge University Press, 1972), p. 301; Beatrice Blyth Whiting and Carolyn Pope Edwards, *Children of Different Worlds: the Formation of Social Behaviour* (Harvard University Press, 1992), 144; Helena Norberg-Hodge, *Ancient Futures: Learning from Ladakh* (Rider, 1991), 63–6; Rohner, *They Love Me*, 120

9   Boston Women's Health Book Collective, *Ourselves and Our Children: A Book by and for Parents* (Penguin, 1978), 31, 101, 132; W. Robert Beavers and Robert B. Hampson, *Successful Families: Assessment and Intervention* (Norton, 1990), 186; Ivan Sokolov and Deborah Hutton, *The Parents' Book: Getting on Well with our Children* (Thorsons, 1988), 22, 109

10   Deborah Finkel and Adam P. Matheny Jr, 'Genetic and environmental influences on a measure of infant attachment security', *Twin Research* 2000 (3), 242–50, esp. 245, 247, 248; Marianne S. De Wolff and Marinus van IJzendoorn, 'Sensitivity and attachment: a meta-analysis on parental antecedents of infant attachment', *Child Development* 68, 1997, 571–91, esp. 586; Gerhardt, *Why Love Matters*, esp. 68, 169–72

11   Ann Oakley, *Becoming a Mother* (Martin Robertson, 1979), 6, 161; Dana Breen, *Talking with Mothers* (Free Association Books, 1989), 114

12   Rohner, *They Love Me*, 98

13   Norbert-Hodge, *Ancient Futures*, 187; Lawrence O. Clayton 'The impact upon child-rearing attitudes of parental views of the nature of humankind', *Journal of Psychology and Christianity* 4, 1985, 50–2

14   John Newson and Elizabeth Newson, *The Extent of Parental Physical Punishment in the UK* (Approach, 1989), 1

15   Hugh Lytton, 'Disciplinary encounters between young boys and their mothers and fathers: is there a contingency system?', *Developmental Psychology* 15, 1979, 261–5; Cheryl Minton, Jerome Kagan and Janet A. Levine 'Maternal control and obedience in the two year old', *Child Development* 42, 1971, 1873–94, esp. 1876, 1892

16   Pope Edwards, *Children of Different Worlds*, 153

17   Sheila Kitzinger and Celia Kitzinger, *Talking with Children about Things that Matter* (Pandora, 1989), 63; Ritter and Ritter, *Free Family*, 145

18   Anthony Storr, *Human Aggression* (Pelican, 1992), 64–5, cited in Deborah Jackson, *Do Not Disturb: Giving Our Children Room to Grow* (Bloomsbury, 1993), 151, esp. 4, 47

19   Lucy Adams, 'Crimes against children drop', *Sunday Times*, 11 June 2000, 5

20   *Parenting* (LWT Action, 1993), 21

21   Penelope Leach, *Children First: What We Must Do – and Are Not Doing – for Our Children Today* (Michael Joseph, 1994), 247

22 'More than a quarter of children have no one in whom they feel able to confide', NSPCC Press release, 7 December 1994, 1

23 Adele Faber and Elaine Mazlish, *Liberated Parents, Liberated Children* (Avon, 1974), 56, 63

24 *Ibid.*, 19–20; Steve Biddulph, *The Secret of Happy Children: a New Guide for Parents* (Bay Books, 1984), 48; Hutton, *The Parents Book*, 117

25 Herbert Barry and Leonora Paxson, 'Infancy and early childhood: cross-cultural codes 2, *Ethnology*, 1971 vol. 10, 466–508

26 Mary G. Boulton, *On Being a Mother* (Tavistock, 1983), 122, 129; Anne Oakley, *Women Confined: Towards a Sociology of Childbirth* (Martin Robertson, 1980), 120, 130

27 John W. M. Whiting and Beatrice Blyth Whiting, 'Altruistic and egoistic behavior in six cultures', in Laura Nader and Thomas W. Maretzki (eds.), *Cultural Illness and Health: Essays in Human Adaptation* (American Anthropological Association, 1973), 61

28 Margaret K. Bacon, Irvin L. Child, and Herbert Barry, 'A cross-cultural study of the correlates of crime', *Journal of Abnormal and Social Psychology* 66, 1963, 291–300, esp. 294, 298

29 Patricia Hewitt and Penelope Leach, *Social Justice, Children, and Families* (Institute for Public Policy Research, 1993), 15

30 Monica Cockett and John Tripp, *The Exeter Family Study: Family Breakdown and its Impact on Children* (University of Exeter Press, 1995), 14, 57

31 Diane Ehrensaft, *Parenting Together: Men and Women Sharing the Care of Their Children* (Free Press, 1987), 191, 201, 237, 235, 236; Myriam Miedzian, *Boys Will Be Boys: Breaking the Link Between Masculinity and Violence* (Virago, 1992), 97

32 Robert D. Putnam, *Bowling Alone: The Collapse and Revival of American Community* (Simon and Schuster, 2000), 200

33 Olga Craig and Cherry Norton, 'Women cast aside feminism to take to future like a man', *Sunday Times*, 2 March 1997, 10; Catherine Hakim, *Models of the Family in Modern Societies: Ideals and Realities* (Ashgate, 2003), 78, 124

34 Hakim, *Models of the Family*, 106, 234; Rosemary Crompton, Michaela Brockmann and Richard D. Wiggins, 'A Woman's Place . . . Employment and Family Life for Men and Women', in Alison Park, John Curtice, Katrina Thomson, Lindsey Jarvis and Catherine Bromley (eds) *British Social Attitudes, the 20th Report* (Sage 2003), 161–87, esp. 164, 167, 179, 187; see also Catherine Hakim, 'Five feminist myths about women's employment', *British Journal of Sociology*, 46, 1995, 429–55

35 Zoe Brennan, 'Mothers spurn chance of full-time childcare', *Sunday Times*, 9 November 1997, 5; Maureen Freely, 'Lies, damned lies, and working mothers', *Guardian* (2), 11 November 1997, 4

36 Hakim, *Models of the Family*, 124, 125, 131; see also Sharon Witherspoon and Gillian Prior, 'Working mothers: free to choose?', in Roger Jowell, Lindsay Brook, and Bridget Taylor, with Gillian Prior (eds.), *British Social Attitudes: the Eighth Report* (Dartmouth, 1991), 151

37 Patricia Morgan, *Farewell to the Family? Public Policy and Family Breakdown in Britain and the USA* (Institute for Economic Affairs, 1995), 58

38 Linda Haas, *Equal Parenthood and Social Policy: A Study of Parental Leave in Sweden* (State University of New York Press, 1992), 76, 77, 130, 131

39 *Ibid.*, 138, 147; Margaret O'Brien and Deborah Jones, 'The Responsibilities of Fatherhood: Young People's Perspectives', paper presented to the International Sociological Association, Committee on Family Research, London, 1994.

40 Sheila Kitzinger, *Ourselves as Mothers* (Doubleday, 1992), 193; Ann Oakley, *Becoming a Mother* (Martin Robertson, 1979), 141; Leach, *First Six Months*, 11

41 Alice Miller, *The Drama of Being a Child: The Search for the True Self* (Virago, 1995), 72–3

42 Boston Women, *Ourselves and our Children*, 365

43 Sheila Kitzinger, *The Crying Baby*, 144, (Viking 1989); Dana Breen, *Talking with Mothers* (Free Association Books, 1989), 113, 142–145

44 Rosalind Coward, *Our Treacherous Hearts: How Women Let Men Get Their Way* (Faber, 1992), 77; Breen, *Talking with Mothers*, 115, 162

45 A. Scher, 'Facilitators and regulators: maternal orientation as an antecedent of attachment security', *Journal of Reproductive and Infant Psychology* 19, 2001, 325–33, esp. 327; Mary Main, Nancy Kaplan, and Jude Cassidy, 'Security in infancy, adulthood, and childhood: a move to the level of representation', in Inge Bretherton and Everett Waters, *Growing Points of Attachment Theory and Research*, 1985, serial no. 209, vol. 50, 1–2, (Monographs of the Society for Research in Child Development, 1985), 66–106, esp. 90–93; Marinus H. Van IJzendoorn and Marianne S. De Wolff, 'In search of the absent father – meta-analyses of infant–father attachment: a rejoinder to our discussants', *Child Development* 68, 1997, 604–09, esp. 607; Mary Main, 'Introduction to the special section on attachment and psychopathology: 2. overview of the field of attachment', *Journal of Consulting and Clinical Psychology* 64, 1996, 237–43; Deborah A. Cohn, Philip A. Cowan, Carolyn P. Cowan and Jane Pearson, 'Mothers' and fathers' working models of childhood attachment relationships, parenting styles, and child behavior', *Development and Psychopathology* 4, 1992, 417–31; Peter Fonagy, Howard Steele and Miriam Steele, 'Maternal representations of attachment during pregnancy predict the organization of infant–mother attachment at one year of age', *Child Development* 62, 1991, 891–905

46 Fonagy, Steele and Steele, 'Maternal Representations', 897; Karin Grossmann, Elisabeth Fremmer-Bombik, Josef Rudolph, and Klaus E. Grossmann, 'Maternal Attachment Representations as related to Patterns of Infant-Mother Attachment and Maternal Care During the First Year', in Robert Hinde & Joan Stevenson-Hinde, *Relationships within Families: Mutual Influences* (Oxford University Press, 1988, 241–60; Cowan, Cowan and Pearson, 'Working Models', 422; Charles H. Zeanah, Diane Benoit, Marianne Barton, Cara Regan, Laurence M. Hirshberg & Lewis P. Lipsitt, 'Representations of Attachment in Mothers and Their One Year Old Infants', *Journal of the American Academy of Child and Adolescent Psychiatry* 32, 1993, 278–86; Main, Kaplan and Cassidy, 'Security in Infancy', 97

47 Avshalom Caspi and Glen H. Elder Jr, 'Emergent family patterns: the

intergenerational construction of problem behaviour and relationships', in Robert Hinde and Joan Stevenson-Hinde, *Relationships within Families: Mutual Influences* (Oxford University Press, 1988), 219–40, esp. 229, 230, 234; Jay Belsky, Lise Youngblade and Emily Pensky, 'Child-rearing history, marital quality, and maternal affect: intergenerational transmission in a low risk sample', *Development and Psychopathology* 1, 1989, 291–304, esp. 293, 298–9

48 Beavers and Hampson, *Successful Families*, 16

49 Paul Howes and Howard J. Markman, 'Marital quality and child functioning: a longitudinal investigation', *Child Development* 60, 1989, 1044–51, esp. 1044, 1048; Caspi and Elder 'Emergent family patterns', 233

50 Oakley, *Becoming a Mother*, 227–9; Neil S. Jacobson and Michael E. Addis, 'Research on couples and couples therapy: what do we know? where are we going?', *Journal of Consulting & Clinical Psychology* 61, 1993, 85–93, esp. 90

51 Tirril O. Harris, George W. Brown, and Antonia T. Bifulco, 'Depression and situational helplessness/mastery in a sample selected to study childhood parental loss', *Journal of Affective Disorders*, 1990, vol. 20, 27–41, esp. 34; George W. Brown and Tirril O. Harris, *Social Origins of Depression: a Study of Psychiatric Disorder in Women* (Tavistock, 1978), 181; Steven R. H. Beach and K. Daniel O'Leary, 'Marital discord and dysphoria: for whom does the marital relationship predict depressive symptomatology?', *Journal of Social and Personal Relationships* 10, 1993, 405–20, esp. 405, 411, 418

52 Leach, *Children First*, 50

53 Marianne Grabrucker, (transl. Wendy Philipson), *There's a Good Girl: Gender Stereotyping in the First Three Years of Life: a Diary* (Women's Press, 1988), 15

54 Spock and Rothenberg, *Baby and Child Care*, 18

55 *The New Baby Care Book* (see note 5 above), p. 17, 283, 262

56 Coward, *Our Treacherous Hearts*, 77

57 *Parents Together* information is at www.parentlineplus.org.uk/index. php?id.=7

58 N. Richman, J. E. Stevenson and P. J. Graham, *Pre-School to School: a Behavioural Study* (Academic Press, 1982), cited in Pam Pritchard, 'Behavioural work with pre-school children in the community', *Health Visitor* 67, 54–6, esp. 54

59 Susan A. Beebe, Rosemary Casey, Jennifer Pinto-Martin, 'Association of reported infant crying and maternal parenting stress', *Clinical Pediatrics* 32, 1993, 15–19, esp. 15, 18

60 Jennifer Somerville, *Feminism and the Family: Politics and Society in the United Kingdom and the USA* (Macmillan, 2000), 7

61 John Bowlby, *Attachment and Loss, vol. 3: Loss, Sadness, and Depression* (Penguin, 1984), 242

62 Van IJzendoorn and De Wolff, 'In search of the absent father', 605; Elizabeth Anisfeld, Virginia Casper, Molly Nozyce and Nicholas Cunningham, 'Does infant carrying promote attachment? An experimental study of the effects of increased physical contact on the development of attachment', *Child Development* 61, 1990, 1617–27, esp. 1624; A.

Scher, 'Facilitators', 326, 328; Heidi Neufeld Bailey, Carey Anne Waters, David R. Pederson, and Greg Moran, 'Ainsworth revisited: an empirical analysis of interactive behaviour in the home', *Attachment and Human Development* 2, 2000, 191–216; Marinus H. van IJzendoorn and Frans O. A. Hubbard, 'Are infant crying and maternal responsiveness during the first year related to infant–mother attachment at 15 months?', *Attachment and Human Development* 2, 371–91; Urs A. Hunziker and Ronald G. Barr, 'Increased carrying reduces infant crying: a randomized controlled trial', *Pediatrics* 77 (5), 1986, 641–8, esp. 644

63 Mary D. Salter Ainsworth, Mary C. Blehar, Everett Waters and Sally Wall, *Patterns of Attachment: a Psychological Study of the Strange Situation* (Erlbaum, 1978)

64 De Wolff and van IJzendoorn, 'Sensitivity and attachment', 571–91, esp. 584; Sandra J. Weiss, Peggy Wilson, Matthew J. Hertenstein, and Rosemary Campos, 'The tactile context of a mother's caregiving: implications for low birth weight infants', *Infant Behavior and Development* 23, 2000, 91–111, esp. 93, 93, 102–03; Van IJzendoorn and Hubbard, 'Infant crying and maternal responsiveness', 374, 376; Bailey, Waters, Pederson and Moran, 'Ainsworth revisited', 192, 198, 203; Scher, 'Facilitators and regulators', 326; Van IJzendoorn and De Wolff, 'In search of the absent father'; Peter Fonagy, Miriam Steele, Howard Steele, Anna Higgitt, and Mary Target, 'The theory and practice of resilience', *Journal of Child Psychology and Psychiatry and Allied Disciplines* 35, 1994, 231–57, esp. 246, 235, 236; Ainsworth, Blehar, Waters and Wall, 'Patterns of attachment', 121

65 Anisfeld et al, 'Does infant carrying promote attachment?', 1622–4

66 Van IJzendoorn and De Woolf, 'In search of the absent father', 607

67 Main, Kaplan and Cassidy, 'Security in infancy, childhood, and adulthood', 83–8; Mary Main and Jude Cassidy, 'Categories of response to reunion with the parent at age six: predictable from infant attachment classifications and stable over a 1-month period', *Developmental Psychology* 24, 1988, 415–26; Jude Cassidy, 'Truth, lies, and intimacy: an attachment perspective', *Attachment and Human Development* 3, 2001, 121–55, esp. 131; Roberta Kestenbaum, Ellen A. Farber and L. Alan Sroufe, 'Individual differences in empathy among preschoolers: relation to attachment history', in Nancy Eisenberg (ed.), *Empathy and Related Emotional Responses: New Directions for Child Development,* No. 44, 1989, 51–64; Joan Urban, Elizabeth Carlson, Byron Egeland and L. Alan Sroufe, 'Patterns of individual adaptation across childhood', *Development and Psychopathology* 3, 1991, 445–60, esp. 453; Everett Waters, Susan Merrick, Dominique Treboux, Judith Crowell and Leah Albersheim, 'Attachment security in infancy and early adulthood: a twenty year longitudinal study', *Child Development* 71, 2000, 684–9, esp. 686; Everett Waters, Nancy S. Weinfeld and Claire E. Hamilton, 'The stability of attachment security from infancy to adolescence and early adulthood: general discussion', *Child Development* 71, 2001, 703–06, esp. 703–04; L. Alan Sroufe, Elizabeth Carlson, and Shmuel Shulman, 'Individuals in relationships: development from infancy through adolescence', in D. Funder, R. Parke, C. Tomlinson-Keesey and K. Widaman (eds.), *Studying Lives Through Time: Approaches to Personality and Development* (American Psychological Association, 1993, 315–42, esp. 333; Klaus E. Grossmann and Karin Grossmann, 'Co-operation

versus anxiety and aggression as an outcome of quality of attachment representation', *Aggressive Behavior* 19, 1993, 19

68 Anna Beth Doyle, Dorothy Markiewicz, Mara Brendgen Melissa Lieberman and Kirsten Voss, 'Child attachment security and self-concept: associations with mother and father attachment style and marital auality', *Merrill-Palmer Quarterly* 46, 2000, 514–39, esp. 516, 520, 530; Glenn I. Roisman, Stephanie D. Madsen Katherine H. Hennighausen, L. Alan Sroufe, and W. Andrew Collins, 'The coherence of dyadic behavior across parent–child and romantic relationships as mediated by the internalized representation of experience', *Attachment and Human Development* 3, 2001, 156–72, esp. 158, 159, 165, 167

69 Waters, Weinfeld and Hamilton, 'The stability of attachment security'; Waters, Merrick, Treboux, et al, 'Attachment security in infancy and early adulthood', 686–8;

70 Gregory S. Pettit and John E. Bates, 'Family interaction patterns and children's behavior problems from infancy to 4 years', *Developmental Psychology* 25, 1989, 413–20, esp. 418; Carolyn Zahn-Waxler, Marian Radke-Yarrow, and Robert A. King, 'Child rearing and children's prosocial initiations toward victims of distress', *Child Development* 50, 1979, 319–30, esp. 327

71 Miriam Steele, Howard Steele, and Martin Johansson, 'Maternal predictors of children's social cognition: an attachment perspective', *Journal of Child Psychology and Psychiatry* 43, 2002, 861–72, esp. 868

72 Mark T. Greenberg, Matthew L. Speltz, and Michelle DeKlyen, 'The role of attachment in the early development of disruptive behavior problems', *Development and Psychopathology* 5, 1993, 191–213, esp. 196; Hugh Lytton, 'Correlates of compliance and the rudiments of conscience in two-year-old boys', *Canadian Journal of Behavioral Science* 9 (3), 242–51, esp. 248; Richard Koestner, Carol Franz, and Joel Weinberger, 'The family origins of empathic concern: a 26 year longitudinal study', *Journal of Personality and Social Psychology* 58, 1990, 709–17, esp. 712

73 Helena Norberg-Hodge, *Ancient Futures*, 21, 29, 35, 46, 63–66, 68, 86

74 Michael Rutter and Marjorie Rutter, *Developing Minds: Challenge and Continuity Across the Life Span* (Penguin, 1992), 210

75 Peggy Estrada, William F. Arsenio, Robert D. Hess, and Susan D. Holloway, 'Affective quality of the mother–child relationship: longitudinal consequences for children's school-relevant cognitive functioning', *Developmental Psychology*, 23, 1987, 210–15; C. Philip Hwang, Anders Broberg, and Michael E. Lamb, 'Swedish childcare research', in Edward Melhuish and Peter Moss (eds.), *Day Care for Young Children* (Routledge, 1991), 102–20; Ellen A. Skinner, 'The origins of young children's perceived control: mother contingent and sensitive behavior', *International Journal of Behavioral Development* 9, 1986, 359–82; Teresa Jacobsen, Wolfgang Edelstein, and Volker Hofmann, 'A longitudinal study of the relation between representations of attachment in childhood and cognitive functioning in childhood and adolescence', *Developmental Psychology* 30, 1994, 112–24

76 Marinus H. Van IJzendoorn, Susan Goldberg, Pieter M Kroonenberg, and Oded J. Frenkel, 'The relative effects of maternal and child problems on the quality of attachment: a meta-analysis of attachment in clinical

samples', *Child Development* 63, 1992, 840–58; Jane Washington, Klaus Minde, and Susan Goldberg, 'Temperament in preterm infants: style and stability', *Journal of the American Academy of Child Psychiatry* 25, 1986, 493–502; Scher, 'Facilitators and Regulators', 330; Everett Waters, Brian E. Vaughn, and Byron R. Egeland, 'Individual differences in infant–mother attachment relationships at age one: antecedents in neonatal behavior in an urban, economically disadvantaged sample', *Child Development* 51, 1980, 208–16; Karin Grossmann, Klaus E. Grossmann, Gottfried Spangler, Gerhard Suess, and Lothar Unzer, 'Maternal sensitivity and newborns' orientation responses as related to quality of attachment in Northern Germany', in Inge Bretherton and Everett Waters (eds), *Growing Points of Attachment Theory and Research* (Monographs of the Society for Research in Child Development, 1985, serial No. 209, vol. 50, Nos. 1– 2), 233–56; Mary Main, 'Introduction to the special section on attachment and psychopathology: 2. Overview of the field of attachment', *Journal of Consulting and Clinical Psychology* 64, 1996, 237–43; Pettit and Bates, 'Family interaction patterns', 413–20

77   Main, 'Introduction', 237–43, esp. 240

78   Cockett and Tripp, *Exeter Family Study*, 22, 36, 42, 43, 54, 57, 69, 85

79   Walter H. Corson, 'Recognising hidden environmental and social costs and reducing ecological and societal damage through tax, price, and subsidy reform', *The Environmentalist* 22, 2002, 67– 82, esp. 69

80   Stevan E. Hobfoll, Arie Nadler, and Joseph Leiberman, 'Satisfaction with social support during crisis: intimacy and self-esteem as crucial determinants, *Journal of Personality and Social Psychology*, 1986, vol. 51, no. 2, 299–302

81   Waters, Weinfeld and Hamilton, 'Stability of Attachment', 704

82   Weiss, Wilson, Hertenstein and Campos, 'Tactile Context', 101; Ellen E. Pinderhughes, Robert Nix, E. Michael Foster, Damon Jones, and the Conduct Problems Prevention Research Group, 'Parenting in context: impact of neighbourhood poverty, residential stability, public services, social networks, and danger on parental behaviors', *Journal of Marriage and the Family* 63, 2001, 941–53, esp. 942, 948, 951; Andrew McCulloch and Heather E. Joshi, 'Neighbourhood and family influences on the cognitive ability of children in the British national child development study', *Social Science and Medicine* 53, 2001, 579–591, pp. 586–588

83   Pinderhughes, Nix, Foster, Jones et al., 'Parenting in context', 942, 948; McCulloch and Joshi, 'Neighbourhood and family influences', 579, 580, 588; Leach, *Children First*, 191

84   W. Barker and R. Anderson, *The Child Development Programme: an Evaluation of Process and Outcomes* (Early Childhood Development Unit, University of Bristol, 1988), 61, 64, 108

85   Early Child Development Unit, W. E. Barker, R. M. Anderson, and C. Chalmers, *Child Protection: the Impact of the Child Development Programme* (University of Bristol, 1992), 34

86   Leach, *Children First*, 190; Ronald P. Rohner, *The Warmth Dimension: Foundations of Parental Acceptance – Rejection Theory* (Sage, 1986), 111–13

87   Mark T. Greenberg, Matthew L. Speltz, and Michelle DeKlyen, 'The role of attachment in the early development of disruptive behavior problems',

Development and Psychopathology 5, 1993, 191–213, esp. 192; Leonard D. Eron, L. Rowell Huesmann, Eric Dubow, Richard Romanoff, and Patty Warwick Yarmel, 'Aggression and its correlates over 22 years', in David H. Crowell, Ian M. Evans, and Clifford R. O'Donnell (eds.), *Childhood Aggression and Violence: Sources of Influence, Prevention, and Control* (Plenum, 1987), 249–62, esp. 253–60; Avshalom Caspi, Glen H. Elder Jr., and Ellen S. Herbener, 'Childhood personality and the prediction of life-course patterns', in Lee N. Robins and Michael Rutter (eds), *Straight and Devious Pathways from Childhood to Adulthood* (Cambridge University Press, 1990), 13–35, esp. 19–26; Bryan Rodgers, 'Influences of early life and recent factors on affective disorder in women: an exploration of vulnerability models', in Lee N. Robins and Michael Rutter (eds.), *Straight and Devious Pathways from Childhood to Adulthood* (Cambridge University Press, 1990), 314–27, esp. 324, 325

88   Dorothy Otnow Lewis, 'The development of the symptom of violence', in Melvin Lewis (ed.), *Child and Adolescent Psychiatry: a Comprehensive Textbook* (Williams and Wilkins, 1991), 331–40, esp. 335; Brent Willcock, 'Narcissistic vulnerability in the hyperaggressive child: the disregarded (unloved, uncared-for) self', *Psychoanalytic Psychology* 3,1986, 59–80, esp 64; 72–4; John E. Lochman, 'Cognitive-behavioral intervention with aggressive boys: three-year follow-up and preventive effects', *Journal of Consulting and Clinical Psychology* 60, 1992, 426–32, esp. 426; Brent Willcock, 'The devalued (unloved, repugnant) self – a second facet of narcissistic vulnerability in the aggressive, conduct-disordered child', *Psychoanalytic Psychology* 4, 1987, 219–240, esp. 227

89   David Mark Mantel, *True Americanism: Green Berets and War Resisters: A Study of Commitment* (Teachers' College Press, 1974), 24–37, 86–7

90   John Newson and Elizabeth Newson, *The Extent of Parental Physical Punishment in the U.K.* (Approach, 1989), 4, 21, 25; David Utting, Jon Bright, and Clem Henricson, *Crime and the Family: Improving Child-Rearing and Preventing Delinquency* (Family Policy Studies Centre, 1993), 17; Lytton, 'Correlates of compliance', 247, 250; Paul Light, *The Development of Social Sensitivity: A Study of Social Aspects of Role-Taking in Young Children* (Cambridge University Press, 1979), 90–92; Cherry Norton, 'Smacking "Hits a Child's IQ" ', *Sunday Times*, 2 August 1998, 4; Leach, *Children First*, 117

91   *Survey of Childhood Experiences and Attitudes to Children* (NSPCC, 7 December 1994);

92   David P. Farrington, 'Early precursors of frequent offending', in James 2Q. Wilson and Glenn C. Loury (eds.), *From Children to Citizens: vol. 3, Families, Schools, and Delinquency Prevention* (Springer Verlag, 1987), 27–50, esp. 41; Catherine Stanger, Thomas M. Achenbach, and Stephanie H. McConaughy, 'Three-year course of behavioral/emotional problems in a national sample of 4- to 16-year-olds: 3. predictors of signs of disturbance, *Journal of Consulting and Clinical Psychology* 61, 1993, 839–48, esp. 844–5

93   Michael Lynch and Dante Cicchetti, 'Maltreated children's reports of relatedness to their teachers', in R. C. Pianta (ed.), *Beyond the Parent: the Role of Other Adults in Children's Lives: New Directions for Child Development* 57 (Jossey-Bass, 1992), 81–107

94 Janet Younger, 'A model of parenting stress', *Research in Nursing and Health* 14, 197–204, esp. 198, 201

95 Charles P. Larson, 'Efficacy of prenatal and postpartum home visits on child health and development', *Pediatrics* 66, 1980, 191–7; Ontario Ministry of Community and Social Services, *Better Beginnings, Better Futures: an Integrated Model of Primary Prevention of Emotional and Behavioral Problems* (Queen's Printer for Ontario, 1989), 18; David L. Olds, Charles R. Henderson Jr, and Harriet Kitzman, 'Does prenatal and infancy nurse home visitation have enduring effects on qualities of parental caregiving and child health at 25 to 50 months of life?', *Pediatrics* 93, 89–98

96 Sandra A. Elliott, Marion Sanjack, and Teresa J. Leverton, 'Parents' groups in pregnancy: a preventive intervention or post-natal depression?', in Benjamin H. Gottlieb (ed.), *Marshalling Social Support: Formats, Processes, and Effects* (Sage, 1988), 87–110

97 Early Childhood Development Unit, *Child Protection*, 15, 40–1

98 Health Visitors' Association, *A Cause for Concern: An Analysis of Staffing Levels and Training Plans in Health Visiting and School Nursing* (Health Visitors' Association, 1994), 1

99 *High Quality Preschool Program Found to Improve Adult Status* (High/ Scope Educational Research Foundation, Ypsilanti, Michigan, undated press release ; John R. Berrueta-Clement, Lawrence J. Schweinhart, W. Steven Barnett, Ann S. Epstein, and David P. Weikart, *Changed Lives: the Effects of the Perry Preschool Program on Youths Through Age 19* (High/Scope Press, 1984), 2, 90, 91; Gary Younge, 'Traditional teaching "produces criminals" ', *Guardian*, 7 April 1997, 4; Ontario Ministry of Community and School Services, *Better Beginnings*, 29; Frances A. Campbell and Craig T. Ramey, 'Cognitive and school outcomes for high-risk African-American students at middle adolescence: positive effects of early intervention', *American Educational Research Journal* 32, 1995, 743–72

100 Z. Johnson, F. Howell & B. Molloy, 'Community Mothers Programme: Randomized Controlled Trial of Non-Professional Intervention in Parenting', *British Medical Journal*, 306, 1993, 1449–52; Willem Van Der Eyken, *Home-start: a Four Year Evaluation* (Home-start Consultancy, 1982), 50–4, 77; Ann Oakley, Lynda Rajan, and Helen Turner, 'Evaluating parent support initiatives: lessons from two case studies', *Health and Social Care in the Community* 6, 1998, 318–30, esp. 327

101 Carolyn Webster-Stratton, Terri Hollingsworth, and Mary Kolpacoff, 'The long-term effectiveness and clinical significance of three cost-effective training programs for families with conduct-problem children', *Journal of Consulting and Clinical Psychology* 57, 1989, 550–3, esp. 551, 552; Carolyn Webster-Stratton, Mary Kolpacoff, and Terri Hollingsworth, 'Self-administered videotape therapy for families with conduct-problem children: comparison with two cost-effective treatments and a control group', *Journal of Consulting and Clinical Psychology* 56, 1988, 558–66, esp. 561–3

102 William R. Shadish, Linda M. Montgomery, Paul Wilson, Mary R. Wilson, Ivey Bright, and Theresa Okwumabua, 'Effects of family and marital psychotherapies: a meta-analysis', *Journal of Consulting and Clinical Psychology* 61, 1993, 992–1002, esp. 994

103 S. Bavolek, *Parenting: Theory, Policy, and Practice – Research and Validation Report of the Nurturing Programs* (Family Development Resources, Inc., 1990), quoted in Gillian Pugh, Erica De'Ath, and Celia Smith, *Confident Parents, Confident Children: Policy and Practice in Parent Education and Support* (National Children's Bureau, 1994), 78

104 Selma Fraiberg, Edna Adelson, and Vivian Shapiro, 'Ghosts in the nursery: a psychoanalytic approach to the problems of impaired infant–mother relationships', *Journal of the American Academy of Child Psychiatry* 14, 1975, 387–421, esp. 412, 413

105 Utting, Bright, and Henricson, *Crime and the Family*, 38–9

106 Zimmerman, *Family Policies*, 144; Elise F. Jones, Jacqueline Darroch Forrest, Noreen Goldman, Stanley Henshaw, Richard Lincoln, Jeannie I. Rosoff, Charles F. Westoff and Deirdre Wulf, *Teenage Pregnancy in Industrialized Countries: a Study Sponsored by the Alan Guttmacher Institute* (Yale University Press, 1986), 172

107 Zimmerman, *Family Policies*, 119

108 Family Planning Association, *Teenage Pregnancies, Factsheet 5a* (Family Planning Association, 1994), 6; Leach, *Children First*, 190; Early Childhood Development Unit, *Child Protection*, 14; 134; Department of Health, *Child Protection: Messages from Research* (HMSO, 1995), 14; Patricia L. East, Karen L. Matthews, and Marianne E. Felice, 'Qualities of adolescent mothers' parenting', *Journal of Adolescent Health* 15, 1994, 163–8, esp. 163; Cynthia T. Garcia Coll, 'Developmental outcomes of minority infants: a process-oriented look into our beginnings', *Child Development* 61, 1990, 270–89, esp. 278

109 Jones et al., *Teenage Pregnancy*, 161, 162, 213; Alexander McKay, 'Research supports broadly based sex education', *Canadian Journal of Human Sexuality* 2 (2), 1993, 89–98, esp. 89, 90; Alison Hadley, 'How to cut teenage pregnancies', *New Statesman*, 3 July 1998, esp. 24–5.

110 Miedzian, *Boys Will Be Boys*, 113–30

CHAPTER 4

1 Ruut Veenhoven, *Conditions of Happiness* (Erasmus University, Rotterdam, 1984), 349; Robert Wuthnow, *Acts of Compassion: Caring for Others and Helping Ourselves* (Princeton University Press, 1991), 97, 317; Alex C. Michalos, 'Job satisfaction, marital satisfaction, and the quality of life: a review and a preview', in Frank M. Andrews (ed.), *Research on the Quality of Life* (University of Michigan, 1986), 57–83, esp. 62

2 John Mordechai Gottman, *What Predicts Divorce?: the Relationship Between Marital Processes and Marital Outcomes* (Erlbaum, 1994), 2, 3; Michael Argyle, *The Psychology of Happiness* (Methuen, 1987), 183; Lynda Clarke and Fiona McAllister, 'Healthy, wealthy, wise – and married', *Family Policy Studies Centre Bulletin*, July/August 1996, 7

3 Shere Hite, *Women and Love* (Viking, 1988), 531

4 *Ibid.*, 470

5 Philip R. Shaver and Kelly A. Brennan, 'Attachment styles and the "big five" personality traits: their connections with each other and with romantic relationship outcomes', *Personality and Social Psychology Bulletin* 18, 1992, 536–45, esp. 541; Lee A. Kirkpatrick and Keith A.

Davis, 'Attachment style, gender, and relationship stability: a longitudinal analysis', *Journal of Personality and Social Psychology* 66, 1994, 502–12, esp. 508

6   Rolf Loeber and Magda Stouthamer-Loeber, 'Family factors as correlates and predictors of juvenile conduct problems and delinquency', in Michael Tonry and Norval Morris, *Crime and Justice: an Annual Review of Research*, vol. 7 (University of Chicago Press), 29–150, esp. 72

7   *Supporting Families: A Consultation Document* (HMSO, 1998), 30; R. Mincy and A. DuPree, 'Welfare, child support, and family formation', *Children and Youth Services Review* 23, Part 6, 2001, 590

8   Hite, *Women and Love*, 485; Penny Mansfield and Jean Collard, *The Beginning of the Rest of Your Life? A Portrait of Newly-Wed Marriage* (Macmillan, 1988), 173, 191; Maggie Scarf, *Intimate Partners* (Random House, 1987), 16, 205; Janet Finch, 'Kinship and friendship', in Roger Jowell, Sharon Witherspoon and Lindsay Brook, *British Social Attitudes: Special International Report* (Gower, 1989), 87–103, esp. 96

9   Mansfield and Collard, *Beginning*, 173; Gottman, *Divorce?*, 436

10 Philip R. Shaver, David Papalia, Catherine L. Clark Lilah Raynor Koski, Marie C. Tidwell and David Nalbone, 'Androgyny and attachment security: two related models of optimal personality', *Personality and Social Psychology Bulletin* 22, 1996, 582–97, esp. 583, 587; Karin F. Helmers and Andrew Mente, 'Alexithymia and health behaviors in healthy male volunteers', *Journal of Psychosomatic Research* 47, 1999, 635–45, esp. 641

11 Rosalind Coward, *Our Treacherous Hearts: Why Women Let Men Get Their Way* (Faber, 1992), 124, 128

12 Kim Bartholomew and Leonard M. Horowitz, 'Attachment styles among young adults: a test of a four-category model', *Journal of Personality and Social Psychology* 61, 1991, 226–44, esp. 229, 236; Shaver et al., 'Androgyny and Attachment Security', 589

13 R. Rogers Kobak and Amy Sceery, 'Attachment in late adolescence: working models, affect regulation, and representations of the self and others', *Child Development* 59, 1988, 135–46, esp. 139; Nancy L. Collins and Stephen Read, 'Adult attachment, working models, and relationship quality in dating couples', *Journal of Personality and Social Psychology* 58, 1990, 644–63, esp. 654, 657; Judith Feeney and Patricia Noller, 'Attachment style as a predictor of adult romantic relationships', *Journal of Personality and Social Psychology* 58. 1990, 281–91, esp. 283; Peter Fonagy, Howard Steele, and Miriam Steele, 'Maternal representations of attachment during pregnancy predict the organization of infant–mother attachment at one year of age', *Child Development* 62, 1991, 891–905, esp. 900; Deborah A. Cohn, Philip A. Cowan, Carolyn P. Cowan, and Jane Pearson, 'Mothers' and fathers' working models of childhood attachment relationships, parenting styles, and child behavior', *Development and Psychopathology* 4, 1992, 417–31, esp. 424; Bartholomew and Horowitz, 'Attachment Styles', 236; Shaver and Brennan, 'Attachment Styles', 539; Cindy Hazan and Philip R. Shaver, 'Love and work: an attachment theoretical perspective', *Journal of Personality and Social Psychology* 59, 1990, 270–80, esp. 278

14 M. Carole Pistole, 'Attachment in adult romantic relationships: style

of conflict resolution and relationship satisfaction', *Journal of Social and Personal Relationships* 6, 1989, 505–10, esp. 508; Kirkpatrick and Davis, 'Attachment Style', 502–12, esp. 506–08; Katherine B. Carnelley and Ronnie Janoff-Bulman, 'Optimism about love relationships: general Versus Specific Lessons from One's Personal Experiences' *Journal of Social and Personal Relationships* 9, 1992, pp. 5–20, p. 15; Marc Levy and Keith Davis, 'Love Styles and attachment styles compared: their relations to each other and to various relationship characteristics', *Journal of Social and Personal Relationships* 5, 1988, 439–71, esp. 458; Hazan and Shaver, 'Love and Work', 275; Glenn I. Roisman, Stephanie D. Madsen Katherine H. Hennighausen, L. Alan Sroufe, and W. Andrew Collins, 'The coherence of dyadic behavior across parent–child and romantic relationships as mediated by the internalized representation of experience', *Attachment and Human Development* 3, 156–72, esp. 159; Jeffrey A. Simpson, 'Influence of attachment styles on adult romantic relationships', *Journal of Personality and Social Psychology* 59, 1990, 971–80, esp. 975; Feeney and Noller, 'Attachment Style', 287; Shaver et al., 'Androgyny and attachment security', 582

15 Bartholomew and Horowitz, 'Attachment Styles', 227, 228; Kirkpatrick and Davis, 'Attachment Style', 503
16 Bartholomew and Horowitz, 'Attachment Styles', 227, 228
17 *Ibid.*, 228, 240
18 William B. Swann Jr, and Stephen C. Predmore, 'Intimates as agents of social support: sources of consolation or despair', *Journal of Personality and Social Psychology* 49, 1985, 1609–17, esp. 1615; Kirkpatrick and Davis, 'Attachment Style', 506
19 Shaver and Brennan, 'Attachment Styles', 541; Avshalom Caspi and Ellen S. Herbener, 'Continuity and change: assortative marriage and the consistency of personality in adulthood', *Journal of Personality and Social Psychology* 58, 1990, 250–8, esp. 251–3; Paul Howes and Howard J. Markman, 'Marital quality and child functioning: a longitudinal investigation', *Child Development* 60, 1989, 1044–51, esp. 1047
20 Gottman, *Divorce?*, 406; Christopher L. Heavey, Christopher Layne, and Andrew Christensen, 'Gender and conflict structure in marital interaction: a replication and extension', *Journal of Consulting and Clinical Psychology* 61, 1993, 16–27, esp. 20; Howes and Markman, 'Marital quality and child functioning', 1047; Mansfield and Collard, *Beginning*, 26
21 Shaver and Brennan, 'Attachment Styles', 540
22 Tirril O. Harris, George W. Brown, and Antonia T. Bifulco, 'Depression and situational helplessness/mastery in a sample selected to study childhood parental loss', *Journal of Affective Disorders* 20, 1990, 27–41, esp. 34; Antonia Bifulco, 'The first steps on the road to depression', *Medical Research Council News* 63, Summer 1994, 24–7, esp. 26–7
23 Eileen Fairweather, 'From suicide to survival', in Scarlett MccGwrire (ed.), *Transforming Moments* (Virago, 1989), 87–9
24 Stephanie Dowrick, *Intimacy and Solitude: Balancing Closeness and Independence* (Women's Press, 1992), 276–78
25 *Ibid.*, 287
26 Gottman, *Divorce?*, 379
27 Janet Reibstein, 'Attachment, pain, and detachment for the adults in

divorce', *Sexual and Marital Therapy* 13, 1998, 352

28　Mansfield and Collard, *Beginning*, 41, 52, 59, 73

29　Patricia Morgan, *Farewell to the Family? Public Policy and Family Breakdown in Britain and the USA* (Institute for Economic Affairs, 1995 [IEA Health and Welfare Unit, London]), 58; Jack Dominian, *Marriage: the Definitive Guide to What Makes a Marriage Work* (Heinemann, 1995), 210; Martie L. Skinner, Glen H. Elder Jr, and Rand D. Conger, 'Linking economic hardship to adolescent aggression', *Journal of Youth and Adolescence* 21, 259–76, esp. 260, 264, 268; Richard G. Wilkinson, *Unfair Shares: the Effects of Widening Income Differences on the Welfare of the Young* (Barnardo's, 1994), 61

30　Martie L. Skinner, Glen H. Elder Jr., and Rand D. Conger, 'Linking Economic Hardship to Adolescent Aggression', *Journal of Youth and Adolescence* 21, 1992, 259–76, esp. 260, 264, 268

31　Morgan, *Farewell*, 55

32　Jan Pahl, *Money and Marriage* (Macmillan, 1989), 174

33　Howard J. Markman, Mari Jo Renick, Frank J. Floyd, Scott M. Stanley, and Mari Clements, 'Preventing marital distress through communication and conflict management training: a four- and five-year follow-up', *Journal of Consulting and Clinical Psychology* 61, 1993, 70–7, esp.72; Mari Jo Renick, Susan L. Blumberg, and Howard J. Markman, 'The prevention and relationship enhancement program (PREP): an empirically based preventive intervention program for couples', *Family Relations* 41, 1992, 141–7, 144–5

34　Gottman, *Divorce?*, 6, 8

35　Marriage Enrichment events are run by the Association for Couples in Marriage Enrichment (www.bettermarriages.org), and the Association for Marriage Enrichment (www.ame-uk.org.uk).

36　Neil S. Jacobson and Michael E. Addis, 'Research on couples and couples therapy: what do we know? Where are we going?', *Journal of Consulting and Clinical Psychology* 61, 1992, 1993, 85–93, esp. 85–6; Douglas K. Snyder, Laurel F. Mangrum, and Robert M. Wills, 'Predicting couples' response to marital therapy: a comparison of long- and short-term predictors', *Journal of Consulting and Clinical Psychology* 61, 1993, 61–9, esp. 66; Gottman, *Divorce?*, 428

37　Harville Hendrix, *Getting the Love You Want: a Guide for Couples* (Pocket Books, 1993), 218–51

38　Hite, *Women and Love*, 471

CHAPTER 5

1　*International Crime Victim Survey,* accessed at www.unicri.it/icvs/ publications/pdf_files/key2000i/app4.pdf (Additional Tables), 178–9, 181; *see also* David W. Moore, *Crime Victimization About the Same as Last Year* (Gallup Organization, 2003), information originally obtained at www.gallup.com/poll/releases/pr031103.asp; Gallup Organization, *One in Four Households Victimized by Crime During Past Year* (2002) (at www.gallup.com/poll/releases/pr021119.asp?Version=p); Jan J. M. van Dijk and Pat Mayhew, *Criminal Victimization in the Industrialised World; Key*

Findings of the 1989 and 1992 International Crime Surveys (Netherlands Ministry of Justice, 1992), 1; John Benyon, *Law and Order Review 1993* (Centre for the Study of Public Order, University of Leicester, 1994), 13

2 Fran H. Norris and Krzysztof Kaniasty, 'Psychological distress following criminal victimization in the general population: cross-sectional, longitudinal, and prospective analyses', *Journal of Consulting and Clinical Psychology* 62, 1994, 111–23, esp. 111, 114, 117, 118; *see also* Audit Commission, *Misspent Youth: Young People and Crime* (Audit Commission, 1996), 10

3 Jim Shultz, *The Democracy Owner's Manual: A Practical Guide to Changing the World* (Rutgers University Press, 2002), 10; Lydia Saad, *Pessimism about Crime is Up, Despite Declining Crime Rate* (Gallup Organisation, 2003), information originally obtained at www.gallup.com/poll/releases/pr031023.asp; Richard G. Wilkinson, *Unhealthy Societies: the Afflictions of Inequality* (Routledge, 1996), 229

4 Roger Graef, *Living Dangerously: Young Offenders in Their Own Words* (HarperCollins, 1993), 256

5 Daniel Kessler and Steven D. Levitt, 'Using sentence enhancements to distinguish between deterrence and incapacitation', *Journal of Law and Economics* 42, 1999, 343–63, esp. 356–8, 360

6 Adrian Raine, *The Psychopathology of Crime: Criminal Behaviour as a Clinical Disorder* (Academic Press, 1993), p. 61; Tim Radford, 'Scientists identify gene link to violence', *Guardian*, 2 August 2002, 3

7 Anne Moir and David Jessel, *A Mind to Crime: The Controversial Link Between the Mind and Criminal Behaviour* (Michael Joseph, 1995), p. 319

8 Wilkinson, *Unhealthy Societies*, 156; David Halpern, 'Moral values, social trust and inequality: can values explain crime?, *British Journal of Criminology* 41, 2001, 236–51, esp. 242, 244, 245, 247, 249; Ichiro Kawachi, Bruce P. Kennedy, and Richard G. Wilkinson, 'Crime: social disorganization and relative deprivation', *Social Science and Medicine* 48, 1999, 719–31, esp. 726; Erik Thorbecke and Chutatong Charumilind, 'Economic inequality and its socio-economic impact', *World Development* 30, 2002, 1477–95, esp. 1491–2; Johan van Wilsem, 'Criminal Victimization in Cross-National Perspective: An Analysis of Rates of Theft, Violence and Vandalism across 27 Countries', *European Journal of Criminology*, 1, 2004, 89-109, esp. 92, 102, 103

9 J. M. Van Dijk, 'Opportunities for crime: a test of the rational-interactionist model', in *Crime and Economy: Reports Presented to the 11th Criminological Colloquium, 1994* (Council of Europe, Committee on Crime Problems, 1995), 97–145, esp. 114; Clive Wilkinson, *The Drop-Out Society: Young People on the Margin* (Youth Work Press, 1995), 78; *see also* Ann Hagell and Tim Newburn, *Persistent Young Offenders* (Policy Studies Institute, 1994), 89

10 Barbara Schneider and David Stevenson, *The Ambitious Generation: America's Teenagers, Motivated but Directionless* (Yale University Press, 1999), 2, 4, 6

11 Tony Parker, *The People of Providence: A Housing Estate and Some of its Inhabitants* (Hutchinson, 1983), 255–7; Peter Fysh and Jim Wolfreys, *The Politics of Racism in France* (Macmillan, 1998), 151

12 David J. Smith, 'Explaining crime trends', in William Saulsbury, Joy Mott, and Tim Newburn (eds.), *Themes in Contemporary Policing* (Independent Committee of Inquiry into the Role and Responsibilities of the Police, 1996), 1–14, esp. 10; Rod Morgan and Tim Newburn, *The Future of Policing* (Clarendon, 1997), 33, 37

13 Van Dijk, *Opportunities*, 101, 105, 116

14 *Ibid.*, 116

15 Halpern 'Moral Values', 246

16 Hagell and Newburn, *Young Offenders*, 78

17 van Wilsem, 'Criminal Victimization', 98, 107; David H. Bayley, *Forces of Order: Policing Modern Japan* (University of California Press, 1991), 115, 176–8, 179, 186, 187

18 *Ibid.*, 179, 170, 181; Minoru Shikita and Shinichi Tsuchiya (eds.), *Crime and Criminal Policy in Japan from 1926 to 1988: Analysis and Evaluation of the Showa Era* (Japanese Criminal Policy Society, 1990), 331, 368–70

19 Steven D. Levitt, 'Why do increased arrest rates appear to reduce crime: deterrence, incapacitation or measurement error?', *Economic Inquiry* 36, 1998, 353–72, esp. 364; Simon Field, *Trends in Crime and Their Interpretation: A Study of Recorded Crime in Post-War England and Wales* (Home Office Research Study 119, 1990), quoted in Michael Brake and Chris Hale, *Public Order and Private Lives: The Politics of Law and Order* (Routledge, 1992), 114; D. J. Pyle, *Cutting the Costs of Crime: The Economics of Crime and Criminal Justice* (Institute of Economic Affairs, 1995), pp. 28, 29

20 Raine, *Psychopathology*, 280, 281; Hagell and Newburn, *Young Offenders*, 42; Wilkinson, *Drop-Out Society*, 41, 101; David F. Greenberg, 'Delinquency and the age structure of society', in Sheldon L. Messinger and Egon Bittner, *Criminology Review Yearbook*, vol. 1 (Sage, 1979), 586–620, esp. 602; Audit Commission, *Misspent Youth*, 51

21 Michael Argyle, *The Psychology of Social Class* (Routledge, 1994), p. 253); Moir and Jessel, *Mind to Crime*, 144

22 Melvin L. Kohn, Atsushi Naoi, Carrie Schoenbach, Carmi Schooler, and Kazimierz M. Slomczynski, 'Position in the class structure and psychological functioning in the United States, Japan, and Poland', *American Journal of Sociology* 95, 1990, 964–1008, esp. 984–6, 994, 1000, 1005

23 John Graham and Ben Bowling, *Young People and Crime* (Home Office Research Study 145, 1995), 37; Albert F. Osborn, 'Resilient children: a longitudinal study of high achieving socially disadvantaged children', *Early Child Development and Care* 62, 23–47, esp. 37

24 Timothy C. Brock and Carolyn Del Giudice, 'Stealing and temporal orientation', *Journal of Abnormal and Social Psychology* 66, 1963, 91–4, esp. 93

25 John R. Berrueta-Clement, Lawrence J. Schweinhart, W. Steven Barnett, Ann S. Epstein, and David P. Weikart, *Changed Lives: the Effects of the Perry Preschool Program on Youths through Age 19* (The High/Scope Press, 1984), 81

26 Sanders Korenman and Christopher Winship, 'A re-analysis of "The Bell Curve": intelligence, family background, and schooling', in Kenneth Arrow, Samuel Bowles, and Steven Durlauf (eds.), *Meritocracy and*

Economic Inequality (Princeton University Press, 2000), 137–78, esp. 137–65; Frances A. Campbell and Craig T. Ramey, 'Cognitive and school outcomes for high-risk African-American students at middle adolescence: positive effects of early intervention', *American Educational Research Journal* 32 (4), 1995, 743–72, esp. 757–65

27 Roger Graef, *Living Dangerously: Young Offenders in their Own Words* (Harper Collins, 1993), pp. 15, 31, 82, 108, 129, 226, 260, 261; *see also* Christine McCaughey, 'The word on the street', in Anna Coote (ed.), *Families, Children, and Crime* (Institute for Public Policy Research, 1994), 36–43, esp. 39

28 Rolf Loeber and Magda Stouthamer-Loeber, 'Family factors as correlates and predictors of juvenile conduct problems and delinquency', in Michael Tonry and Norval Morris (eds.), *Crime and Justice: an Annual Review of Research*, vol. 7 (University of Chicago Press, 29–150, esp. 41–90; Oliver James, *Juvenile Violence in a Winner–Loser Culture: Socioeconomic and Familial Origins of the Rise in Violence Against the Person* (Free Association Books, 1995), 5; Adrian Raine, Patricia Brennan, and Sarnoff A. Mednick, 'Birth complications combined with early maternal rejection at age 1 year predispose to violent crime at age 18 years', *Archives of General Psychiatry* 51, 1994, 984–8, esp. 986; Moir and Jessel, *Mind to Crime*, 115; Raine, *Psychopathology*, 197

29 James H. Satterfield, 'Childhood diagnostic and neurophysiological predictors of teenage arrest rates: an eight year prospective study', in Sarnoff A. Mednick, Terrie E. Moffitt, and Susan A. Stack (eds.), *The Causes of Crime: New Biological Approaches* (Cambridge University Press, 1987), 146–67, esp. 162 (my calculation from data therein); Joel L. Milner and Thomas R. McCanne, 'Neuropsychological correlates of physical child abuse', in Joel L. Milner (ed.), *Neuropsychology of Aggression* (Kluwer, 1991), 131–46, esp. 136–8; Raine, *Psychopathology*, 187, 193

30 Editorial in *The Magistrate*, December 1990/January 1991, quoted in Penal Affairs Consortium, *Parental Responsibility, Youth Crime, and the Criminal Law* (Penal Affairs Consortium, 1995), 3; NACRO Young Offenders Committee, *Partnership with Parents in Dealing with Young Offenders* (NACRO, Policy Paper 4, 1994), 5

31 Cities in Schools, *Turning Lives Around: Evaluation of Cities in Schools (Westminster) Bridge Courses 1994/5* (Cities in Schools, 1995), 10, 15, 16; Crime Concern, *The Prevention of Criminality* (Crime Concern, Briefing Paper 2, 1995), 4; Audit Commission, *Misspent Youth*, 41; Milton F. Shore and Joseph L. Massimo, 'After ten years: a follow-up study of comprehensive vocationally oriented psychotherapy', *American Journal of Orthopsychiatry* 43, 1973, 128–32, esp. 130, 131; see also Joseph L. Massimo and Milton F. Shore, 'The effectiveness of a comprehensive vocationally oriented psychotherapeutic program for adolescent delinquent boys', *American Journal of Orthopsychiatry* 33, 1963, 634–42

32 Graham and Bowling, *Young People and Crime*, 25, 56; Edward Balls, 'Missing school is hallmark of criminal class', *Guardian*, 16 October 1995, 15

33 Mary McMurran, 'Alcohol, drugs, and criminal behaviour', in Clive R. Hollin (ed.), *Working with Offenders: Psychological Practice in Offender Rehabilitation* (Wiley, 1996), 211–42, esp. 214)

34 Cyril S. Smith, M. R. Farrant and H. J. Marchant, *The Wincroft Youth Project: A Social Work Programme in a Slum Area* (Tavistock, 1972); Ontario Ministry of Community and Social Services, *Better Beginnings, Better Futures: An Integrated Model of Primary Prevention of Emotional and Behavioral Problems* (Queen's Printer for Ontario, 1989), 50; *see also Crime – The Local Solution: Current Practice* (Local Government Association, and Local Government Management Board, 1997), 23, 24

35 Graham and Bowling, *Young People and Crime*, 71, 100; Michael Hough, *Drug Misusers and the Criminal Justice System: A Review of the Literature* (Home Office, 1996), 11; J. M. Otero-Lopez, A. Luengo-Martin, L. Miron-Redondo, M. T. Carrillo de la Pena, and E. Romero-Trinanes, 'An empirical study of the relations between drug abuse and delinquency among adolescents', *British Journal of Criminology* 34, 1994, 459–78, esp. 472; McMurran, 'Alcohol, Drugs', 212, 214; Nicholas Emler, *Self-Esteem: The Costs and Causes of Low Self-Worth* (Joseph Rowntree Foundation, 2001), 23; Robert MacDonald and Jane Marsh, 'Crossing the Rubicon: youth transitions, poverty, drugs, and social exclusion', *International Journal of Drug Policy* 13, 2002, 27–38

36 Duncan Campbell, 'Tsar Wars', *Guardian*, 23 October 1999, 22

37 *Idem*, 'US judges call for legalising of drugs', *Guardian*, 10 June 2000, 22; Lesley Thomas and Julie Cohen, 'Right joins drive to legalise drugs', *Sunday Times*, 14 May 1995; Cherry Norton and Simon Trump, 'Judges shift towards legalising soft drugs', *Sunday Times*, 1 December 1996, 5

38 Frances Rickford, 'The lure of drugs, drink, and sects', *Guardian (Society)*, 25 June 1997, 2, 3, 9; Department of Health, *The National Treatment Outcome Research Study, 2nd Bulletin* (Department of Health, 1997); Owen Bennett Jones, 'Swiss back heroin handout', *Guardian*, 29 September 1997, 10

39 Raine, *Psychopathology*, 95; Moir and Jessel, *A Mind to Crime*, 70–1, 178, 203; W. Wayt Gibbs, 'Seeking the criminal element', *Scientific American*, March 1995, 76–83, esp. 82; 'Equinox', *BBC2* TV, 15 September 1996

40 Charles Pollard, 'Zero tolerance: short-term fix, long-term liability', in Norman Dennis (ed.), *Zero Tolerance: Policing a Free Society* (Institute of Economic Affairs, 1997), 43–60, esp. 44; Ben Bowling, 'Zero tolerance: cracking down on crime in New York city', *Criminal Justice Matters,* 25, 11; Charles Leadbeater, *The Self-Policing Society* (Demos, 1996), 18; Ian Katz, 'New York, new safety', *Guardian*, 2 January 1997, 2

41 Ann Power and Rebecca Tunstall, 'Estates of siege', *Guardian (Society)*, 25 June 1997, 9

42 Alan Travis, 'Jumping to the beat', *Guardian (Society)*, 16 April 1997, 2–3; Morgan and Newburn, *Policing*, 126; Michael Hough, 'The police patrol function: what research can tell us', in Saulsbury, Mott and Newburn (eds.) *Contemporary Policing*, 60–71, esp. 63; Trevor Bennett, 'Problem-solving policing and crime prevention: an assessment of the role of the police in preventing crime', in Trevor Bennett (ed.), *Preventing Crime and Disorder: Targeting, Strategies, and Responsibilities* (University of Cambridge Institute of Criminology, 1996), 253–76, esp. 267–70); Joanna Shapland, 'Targeted crime reduction: the needs of local groups', in Bennett (ed.), *Preventing Crime*, 353–64, esp. 355

43 Alan Trickett, Denise R. Osborn, Julie Seymour, and Ken Pease, 'What

is different about high crime areas?', *British Journal of Criminology* 32, 81–9, esp. 83

44 Thomas L. McNulty, 'More on the costs of racial exclusion: race and violent crime in New York City 1980–1990', *Race and Society* 2, 2000, 51–68, esp. 52, 53, 59

45 NACRO, *Crime, Community, and Change* (NACRO, 1996), cited in 'Estate from Hell', *Probation Journal*, September 1996, 168; Janet Foster, *Villains: Crime and Community in the Inner City* (Routledge, 1990), 164; also *Crime – The Local Solution: Current Practice* (Local Government Association, and Local Government Management Board, 1997), 38, 35; Steve Osborn and Henry Shaftoe, *Safer Neighbourhoods? Successes and Failures in Crime Prevention* (Safe Neighbourhoods Unit, 1995), 10, 14, 21; Morgan and Newburn, *Future of Policing*, 61; Home Office, *Protecting the Public: The Government's Strategy on Crime in England and Wales* (Command No. 3190, HMSO, 1996), 6–7; HM Chief Inspector of Constabulary, *Report for 1995/6* (Stationery Office, 1996), p. 33; Saulsbury, Mott and Newburn (eds.) *Contemporary Policing*, 97

46 Peter Goldblatt, 'Comparative effectiveness of different approaches', in Peter Goldblatt and Chris Lewis (eds.), *Reducing Offending: An Assessment of Research Evidence on Ways of Dealing with Offending Behaviour* (Home Office Research Study 187, 1998), 123–37, esp. 126; Osborn and Shaftoe, *Safer Neighbourhoods*, 25–8

47 'Policing, race, and the Lawrence case', *British Public Opinion*, March 1999, 3; David Robins, *Tarnished Vision: Crime and Conflict in the Inner City* (Oxford University Press, 1992), 121; Police Federation, *The Policing Agenda 1995/6* (Police Federation, 1996), 2; *idem, Where We Stand on Firearms and the Police* (Police Federation briefing paper, September 1996); Alan Travis, 'Survey gives the lie to Howard's boast', *Guardian*, 27 May 1997, 3

48 Amnesty International USA, *United States of America: Race, Rights, and Police Brutality* (Amnesty International, 1999), information originally obtained at www.amnestyusa.org/rightsforall/police/brutality/brutality-4.html ; Inquest, *Racial Discrimination and Deaths in Custody* (Inquest, 1996), 19; M. Pogrebin, M. Dodge, and H. Chatman, 'Reflections of African–American women on their careers in urban policing: their experiences of racial and sexual discrimination', *International Journal of the Sociology of Law* 28, 2000, 311–326; E. Cashmore, 'The experiences of ethnic minority police officers in Britain: under-recruitment and racial profiling in a performance culture', *Ethnic and Racial Studies* 24, 2001, 642–59

49 James Messerschmidt, *Masculinities and Crime: Critique and Reconceptualisation of Theory* (Rowman and Littlefield, 1993), 90

50 Lynn Segal, *Slow Motion: Changing Masculinities, Changing Men* (Rutgers University Press, 1990), 245, quoted in Messerschmidt, *Masculinities*, 114

51 Carolyn Zahn-Waxler, Marian Radke-Yarrow, and Robert A. King, 'Child-rearing and children's prosocial initiations toward victims of distress', *Child Development* 50, 319–30, esp. 325, 327

52 Michael D. Lynch and Dante Cicchetti, 'Maltreated children's reports of relatedness to their teachers', in R. C. Pianta, *Beyond the Parent: The Role*

of Other Adults in Children's Lives, New Directions for Child Development vol. 57 (Jossey-Bass, 1992), 81–107, esp. 99

53 *GQ*, January 1994, 82; Women's Aid Federation of England, *Domestic Violence, Service Provision and Policy Research Findings and Statistics*, briefing paper, August 1996; survey commissioned by the London Borough of Hammersmith and Fulham, cited in 'Bullies Make 'Life Misery' for Inner City Women', *Daily Telegraph*, 12 October 1989

54 J. A. Golde, D. S. Strassberg, C. M. Turner and K. Lowe, 'Attitudinal effects of degrading themes and sexual explicitness in video materials', *Sexual Abuse: A Journal of Research and Treatment* 12, 2000, 223–32; M. C. Seto, A. Maric, and H. E. Barbaree, 'The role of pornography in the etiology of sexual aggression', *Aggression and Violent Behavior* 6, 2001, 35–53; Myriam Miedzian, *Boys Will Be Boys: Breaking the Link Between Masculinity and Violence* (Virago, 1992), 212, 240–1; K. J. Mitchell, D. Finkelhor, and J. Wolak, 'The exposure of youth to unwanted sexual material on the internet: national survey of risk, impact, and prevention', *Youth and Society* 34, 330–58

55 Health Resources and Service Administration, *Domestic and Family Violence Initiatives* (at www.hrsa.gov/WomensHealth/1_15_02 per cent20HRSA per cent20DV per cent20Initiatives.doc, US Department of Justice; *Criminal Victimization in United States, 1999*, US Department of Justice ,Table 43a at www.ojp.usdoj.gov/bjs/pub/pdf/cvus99; C. Mirlees-Black T. Budd, S. Partridge, and P. Mayhew, *British Crime Survey 1998* (Home Office Statistical Bulletin 21/98, 1998), 6, 47

56 *See* http://endabuse.org; this is the website of an American organisation which puts on advertisements about domestic violence.

57 Richard Woods, 'New ways to stop the men who kill children', *Sunday Times (News Review)*, 16 December 2001, 6–7; Alan Travis and Geoffrey Gibbs, 'Vigilantes blamed for wrecking paedophile watch', *Guardian*, 25 April 1998, 1

58 Don Grubin, 'Predictors of risk in serious sex offenders', *British Journal of Psychiatry* 170, supplement 32, 1997, 17–21, esp. 20; Inside Story, 'Megan's law', BBC1 TV, 4 February 1997

59 Grubin, 'Inferring Predictors of Risk', *International Review of Psychiatry* 9, 1997, 225–31, esp. 226, 228

60 *Ibid.*, 227

61 Mark W. Lipsey, 'What do we learn from 400 research studies on the effectiveness of treatment with juvenile delinquents?', in James McGuire (ed.), *What Works – Reducing Reoffending: Guidelines from Research and Practice* (Wiley, 1995), 63–78, esp. 67, 72

62 Robert R. Ross, Elizabeth A. Fabiano, and Cristal Diemer Ewles, 'The Pickering Project for high-risk probationers', in Robert R. Ross and Roslynn D. Ross (eds.), *Thinking Straight: The Reasoning and Rehabilitation Program for Delinquency Prevention and Offender Rehabilitation* (Air Training and Publications, 1995), 145–53, esp. 150; James McGuire, 'Community-based reasoning and rehabiltation programmes in the United Kingdom', in Ross and Ross (eds.), *Thinking Straight*, 261–86, esp. 274–5; Jack Bush, 'Teaching self-risk management to violent offenders', in McGuire (ed.), *What Works*, 139–54, esp. 152–3

63 John C. Gibbs, 'Sociomoral group treatment for young offenders', in Clive

R. Hollin and Kevin Howells, *Clinical Approaches to Working with Young Offenders* (Wiley, 1996), 129–49, 130–2, 138, 145

64 This was shown on Channel 4 TV in April 1994, and is reported in James S. Fishkin, *The Voice of the People: Public Opinion and Democracy* (Yale University Press, 1995), 179

65 Graham and Bowling, *Young People*, 4–5, 23, 27, 29, 30, 58; Daniel H. Antonowicz, Rhena L. Izzo, and Robert R. Ross, 'Characteristics of effective offender rehabilitation programmes', in Ross and Ross (eds.), *Thinking Straight*, 39–61, esp. 52; Frank J. Porporino and David Robinson, 'An evaluation of the reasoning and rehabilitation program with Canadian Federal Offenders', in *idem*, 4–5, 23, 27, 29, 30, 58; Richard Joseph Kownacki, 'The effectiveness of a brief cognitive-behavioral program on the reduction of antisocial behavior in high-risk adult probationers in a Texas community', in *idem*, 249–57, esp, 251; McGuire, 'Community-based reasoning', 261–86, esp. 278; Robert R. Ross and Roslynn D. Ross, 'The reasoning and rehabilitation program', in *idem*, 82–144, esp. 128, 130; Moir and Jessel, *Mind to Crime*, 241–2

66 Don Andrews, 'The psychology of criminal conduct and effective correctional treatment', in McGuire (ed.), *What Works*, 35–62, esp. 48; Mark W. Lipsey, 'What do we learn from 400 research studies on the effectiveness of treatment with juvenile delinquents', in *idem*, 63–78, esp. 73; Alfred Blumstein, Jacqueline Cohen, Jeffrey A. Roth, and Christy A. Visher, *Criminal Careers and "Career Criminals"* (National Academy Press, 1986), 118; Eric Mendelson and Stephen Mason, 'A pilot study into the feasibility of compulsory treatment of opiate-addicted offenders', *Journal of Forensic Psychiatry* 4, 1993, 507–15, esp. 507; Department of Health, *The Task Force to Review Services for Drug Misusers: Report of an Independent Review of Drug Treatment Services in England* (Department of Health, 1996), 13; Friedrich Losel, 'The efficacy of correctional treatment: a review and synthesis of meta-analyses', in McGuire (ed.) *What Works*, 79–111, esp. 94

67 John Braithwaite and Stephen Mugford, 'Conditions of successful reintegration ceremonies: dealing with juvenile offenders', *British Journal of Criminology* 34, 1994, 139–71; John Braithwaite, *Crime, Shame, and Reintegration* (Cambridge University Press, 1989), 55

68 Dougie Brimson and Eddie Brimson, *Everywhere We Go: Behind the Matchday Madness* (Headline, 1996), 108

69 Charles Lloyd, George Mair, and Mike Hough, *Explaining Reconviction Rates: A Critical Analysis* (Home Office Research and Statistics Department, Research Findings 12, 1994), 4–5; Probation Service, *Three Year Plan for the Probation Service 1996–99* (Home Office, 1996), 10; *idem, Three Year Plan for the Probation Service 1997–2000* (Home Office, 1997), 26; Anthony E. Bottoms, *Intensive Community Supervision for Young Offenders: Outcomes, Process, and Cost* (University of Cambridge Institute of Criminology, 1995), 15

70 Steven D. Levitt, 'The effect of prison population size on crime rates: evidence from prison overcrowding litigation', *Quarterly Journal of Economics*, May 1996, 319–51, esp. 345

71 David Smith and Stephen Grey, 'Cost of crime exceeds £30 bn.', *Sunday Times*, 23 March 1997, 4

72 Association of London Authorities, *Making London Safer: Young People and Crime* (Association of London Authorities, 1995), 4

73 In 2003 the Home Office told me the current cost of a prison place, which includes depreciation of prison assets, and the cost of the capital investment tied up in those assets. I used government inflation records to adjust this sum to 2004 costs.

74 William Spelman, *Criminal Incapacitation* (Plenum, 1994), 51–2, 74–6; Anne Morrison Piehl and John J. DiIulio Jr., '"Does prison pay?" Revisited', *Brookings Review*, Winter 1995, 21–5, esp. 25; Hagell and Newburn, *Young Offenders*, 69; Bottoms, *Intensive Community Supervision*, 9; Department of Health, *NTORS: The National Treatment Outcome Research Study: Summary of the Project, the Clients, and Preliminary Findings* (Department of Health, 1996), 3rd page

75 Mark A. Cohen, 'Pain, suffering, and jury awards: a study of the cost of crime to victims', *Law and Society Review* 22, 1988, 537–55, esp. 540–7; Hagell and Newburn, *Young Offenders*, 69

76 Alfred Blumstein, David P. Farrington, and Soumyo Moitra, 'Delinquent careers: innocents, desisters, and persisters', in Michael Tonry and Norval Morris (eds.), *Crime and Justice: An Annual Review of Research*, vol. 6 (University of Chicago Press, 1985), 187–219, esp. 194; Gibbs, 'Criminal Element', 78; Roger Tarling, *Analysing Offending: Data, Models, and Interpretations* (HMSO, 1993), 55–6; Spelman, *Incapacitation*, 147; Blumstein, Cohen, Roth and Visher, *Criminal Careers*, 5

77 Tarling, *Analysing Offending*, 49; Spelman, *Incapacitation*, 163

78 *Ibid.*, 167

79 Benyon, *Law and Order*, 102; David J. Smith, 'Youth crime and conduct disorders: trends, patterns, and causal explanations', in Michael Rutter and David J. Smith, *Psychosocial Disorders in Young People: Time Trends and Their Causes* (Wiley, 1995), 389–489, esp. 469

80 Thomas B. Marvell and Carlisle E. Moody, 'The lethal effects of three-strikes laws', *Journal of Legal Studies* 30, 2001, 89–106, esp. 96, 98, 99

81 Hagell and Newburn, *Young Offenders*, 69; Home Office, *Protecting the Public: The Government's Strategy on Crime in England and Wales* (Command No. 3190, HMSO, 1996), 52

82 *Ibid.*, 47; *Guardian Education*, 21 January 1997, 11; Tarling, *Analysing Offending*, 44; Blumstein, Cohen, Roth and Visher, *Criminal Careers*, 5

83 BBC Radio 4, 25 July 1996

84 Penal Affairs Consortium, 'Reducing Reoffending' (Penal Affairs Consortium, draft Briefing Paper, April 1997), 7. (This was kindly given to me by Paul Cavadino.)

CHAPTER 6

1 Hans-Dieter Klingemann, Richard I. Hofferbert, and Ian Budge, *Parties, Policies and Democracy* (Westview Press, 1994), 2, 13, 16, 64, 68, 71, 78, 239, 240 249, 255, 256, 259, 262, 268, 269; Herbert Kitschelt, 'Citizens, politicians, and party cartellization: political representation and state failure in post-industrial democracies', *European Journal of Political Research* 37, 2000, 149 –79, esp.164, 173

2   Geoffrey Garrett, 'The politics of structural change: Swedish social democracy and Thatcherism in comparative perspective', *Comparative Political Studies* 4, 1993, 521–47, esp. 524, 525, 529, 530, 538, 542

3   Greg Philo, 'Introduction: a critical media studies', in Greg Philo (ed.), *Message Received: Glasgow Media Group Research 1993–1998* (Longman, 1999), ix–xvii, esp. xi; Jenny Kitzinger, 'A sociology of media power: key issues in audience reception research', in *ibid.*, 3–20, esp. 8, 13–15; David Miller and Greg Philo, 'The effective media', in *ibid.*, 21–32, esp. 29; Thomas R. Dye, *Top-down Policy Making* (Chatham House, 2001), 109, 111, 114; Patrick Rossler and Michael Schenk, 'Cognitive bonding and the German reunification: agenda-setting and persuasion effects of mass media', *International Journal of Public Opinion Research* 12, 2000, 29–47, esp. 33, 36, 37, 39, 43; Michael Ryan, 'Framing the War against Terrorism: US Newspaper Editorials and Military Action in Afghanistan', *Gazette: The International Journal for Communication Studies* 66, 2004, 363–82; Robert M. Entman, 'Cascading Activation: Contesting the White House's Frame after 9/11', *Political Communication* 20, 2003, 415–31

4   *Gallup Poll Monthly* 1998, 1999, searched under 'inequality' at www. gallup.com; Roger Jowell, John Curtice, Alison Park, Lindsay Brook, and Katarina Thompson (eds.), *British Social Attitudes: the 13th Report* (Dartmouth, 1996), 277

5   Peter Hetherington, 'The jobs are out there, but not the right sort of worker', *Guardian*, 1 October 1998, 25; Commission on Social Justice, *Social Justice: Strategies for National Renewal* (Vintage, 1994), 390

6   Cynthia Kite, 'The Globalized, Generous Welfare State: Possibility or Oxymoron', *European Journal of Political Research* 41, 2002, 307–43, esp. 330, 332, 337; Stein Kuhnle, 'The Scandinavian welfare state in the 1990s: challenged but viable', *West European Politics* 23, 2000, 209–28, esp. 211, 213, 218, 220, 224–7; Stephen Nickell, Luca Nunziata, Wolfgang Ochel, and Glenda Quintini, 'Why do jobless rates differ?', *Centrepiece (Journal of the London School of Economics Centre for Economic Performance)*, Autumn 2001, 7–16, esp. 7–8

7   Kite, 'Globalized Welfare State', 332, 337; Thomas R. Cusack, 'Partisanship in the the Setting and Coordination of Fiscal and Monetary Policies', *European Journal of Political Research* 40, 2001, 93–115, esp. 101, 103; Philippe Legrain, *Open World: The Truth about Globalization* (Abacus, 2002), 148–9; Peter Birch Sorensen, 'The case for international tax co-ordination reconsidered', *Economic Policy,* 2000, 429–72, esp. 447; Larry Elliott and Dan Atkinson, *The Age of Insecurity* (Verso, 1999), 98, 311; John Vidal, *McLibel: Burger Culture on Trial* (Macmillan, 1997), extract in *Guardian (Society)*, 30 April 1997, 5

8   David E. Wildasin, 'Factor mobility and fiscal policy in the EU: policy issues and analytical approaches', *Economic Policy,* 2000, 337–78, esp. 370; Dick Taverne, 'Europe and the tax question', *Prospect*, July 2000, 54–7, esp. 55; John Callaghan, *The Retreat of Social Democracy* (Manchester University Press, 2000), 175, 222; Elliott and Atkinson, *Age of Insecurity*, 268; John Pilger, *The New Rulers of the World* (booklet to accompany the TV programme of the same name, Carlton Television, 2001), 6; Andreas Haufler and Ian Wooton, *Tax Competition for Foreign Direct Investment* (Centre for Economic Policy Research, Discussion Paper 1583, 1997), 11,

17, 18

9 Nick Cohen, 'The taxpayer always foots the bill', *New Statesman*, 9 July 2001, 13–5; Angela Jameson, 'Billion-pound rail warning', *The Times (Business)*, 7 March 2002, 1

10 Larry Elliott, 'Quid pro quo', *Earth Matters*, Spring 1997, 16–17; *see also* Friends of the Earth, *Working Future? Jobs and the Environment* (Friends of the Earth, 1994), 21, 57, 63, 66, 67

11 Walter H. Corson, 'Recognising hidden environmental and social costs and reducing ecological and societal damage through tax, price, and subsidy reform', *The Environmentalist* 22, 2002, 67–82, esp. 75

12 Sarah Boseley, 'Parties' problem in making the polluter pay', *Guardian*, 25 April 1997, 13; Charles Secrett, 'Seeing red over Brown's green stance', *Guardian*, 23 March 1998, 19; Larry Elliott, 'Going from red to green with a pollution solution', *Guardian*, 19 May 1997, 18

13 Pilger, *New Rulers of the World*, 9; Daniel C. Esty, *Greening the GATT: Trade, Environment, and the Future* (Institute for International Economics, Washington DC, 1994), 102–03; Larry Elliott, 'Free trade, no choice', in Barbara Gunnell and David Timms (eds.), *After Seattle: Globalisation and its Discontents* (Catalyst, 2000), 7–12, esp. 11; World Development Movement, *Wake up to Seattle: Report on WTO Negotiations* (press briefing, 4 December 1999); George Monbiot, 'US trade threat is hard to stomach', *Guardian*, 13 May 1999, 20; *idem*, 'Lies, trade, and democracy', in Gunnell and Timms, *After Seattle*, 13–18, esp.17

14 Edward Chancellor, 'Millennial market', *Prospect*, November 2001, 28–33; 'This third way had better work', *New Statesman* (editorial), 12 November 2001, 6–7; Philippe Legrain, 'The not so global economy', *Prospect*, November 2001, 44–7; Barbara Gunnell, 'Trade', *New Statesman*, 22 October 2001, 23–4

15 George Monbiot, *The Age of Consent: A Manifesto for a New World Order* (Flamingo, 2003); 'A Cotton-picking Victory', *New Statesman*, 3 May 2004, 7. For information about fair trade products in various countries, visit www.fairtrade.net/sites/contact/ni.html or www.transfairusa.org

16 Elliott and Atkinson, *Age of Insecurity*, 268; 'The global economy: the facts', *New Internationalist*, January/February 2000, 24–5; John Grieve Smith, *Closing the Casino: Reform of the Global Financial System* (Fabian Society, 2000), 5; Joseph E. Stiglitz, *Globalization and its Discontents* (Allen Lane, 2002), 123–5

17 John Plender, *Going off the Rails: Global Capital and the Crisis of Legitimacy* (Wiley, 2003), 6–79; Stiglitz, *Globalization*, 106–08, 110, 111, 119, 121,198–209, 231; Michael Jacobs, Adam Lent, and Kevin Watkins, *Progressive Globalisation: Towards an International Social Democracy* (Fabian Society, 2003), 45–6; John Grahl and Photis Lysandrou, 'Sand in the wheels or spanner in the works? The Tobin tax and global finance', *Cambridge Journal of Economics*, 27, 2003, 597–621

18 Jamie Peck, 'Getting real with welfare-to-work: hard lessons from America', *Renewal* 7, 1999, 39–49, esp. 42; Nickell, Nunziata, Ochel, and Quintini, 'Jobless rates', 10; Charlotte Denny, 'New deal for young enjoys biggest success', *Guardian*, 31 December 1999; Robert Reich, 'We must still tax and spend', *New Statesman*, 3 May 1999, 20

19 Arend Lijphart, *Patterns of Democracy: Government Forms and*

Performance in Thirty-six countries (Yale University Press, 1999), 286; Dye, *Policy Making*, 12, 83, 120, 162; Jonathan Freedland, *Bring Home the Revolution: How Britain Can Live the American Dream* (Fourth Estate, 1998), 180; 'Public opinion in the EU', *Standard Eurobarometer 57*, 2002, section 1.4, at http://europa/eu.int/comm/public_opinion/archives/eb/eb57/eb57_en.pdf; Kitschelt, 'Citizens, Politicians', 158, 167

20 David Niven, 'The mobilization calendar: the time-dependent effects of personal contact on turnout', *American Politics Research* 30, 2002, 307–22, esp. 307–08; Russell J. Dalton, 'Citizen attitudes and political behavior', *Comparative Political Studies* 33, 2000, 912–40, esp. 928; Vox Populi, *Expecting More Say: A Study of American Public Attitudes on the Role of the Public in Government Decisions* (at www.vox-populi.org/digest/ems/ems_part1.html); Jim Shultz, *The Democracy Owner's Manual: A Practical Guide to Changing the World* (Rutgers University Press, 2002), 17

21 Peter Mair and Ingrid Van Biezen, 'Party membership in twenty European democracies, 1980–2000', *Party Politics* 7, 2001, 5–21, esp. 8, 11; Dalton, 'Citizen Attitudes', 929; Peter A. Hall, 'Social capital in Britain', *British Journal of Politics* 29, 1999, 417–61, esp. 451–3

22 'Millions join peace marches', *Guardian Weekly,* 20 February 2003, 4, Elizabeth S. Smith, 'The effects of investments in the social capital of youth on political and civic behaviour in young adulthood: a longitudinal analysis', *Political Psychology* 20, 1999, 553–80, esp. 554; Justin Davis Smith, *1997 National Survey of Volunteering* (National Centre for Volunteering, 1998), 27

23 Kitschelt, 'Citizens, Politicians', 157, 158, 165; Alan S. Gerber and Donald P. Green, 'The effects of canvassing, telephone calls and direct mail on voter turnout: a field experiment', *American Political Science Review* 94, 2000, 653–63, esp. 653, 654, 658, 660; Niven, 'Mobilization Calendar', 309, 317

24 Dye, *Policy Making*, 6, 67, 68, 70, 74, 77, 84, 87, 88–90, 92, 96, 133, 168; Opensecrets.org, '04 elections expected to cost nearly $4 billion: Presidential Race to top $1.2 billion', 21 October 2004,www.opensecrets.org/pressreleases/2004/04spending.asp; Lydia Saad, 'Americans speak out on state of the union', Gallup Poll Analyses, 23 January 2003, at www.gallup.com/poll/releases/pr030123.asp?Version=p; Callaghan, *Social Democracy*, 198, 217; Will Hutton, *The World We're In*, (Little, Brown, 2002), 30; Frank Newport, *What if Government Really Listened to the People?* (at www.gallup.com/poll/fromtheed/ed9710.asp, October 1997); Martin Kettle, 'Bush's allies bury campaign finance reform', *Guardian*, 14 July 2001, 13; Kitschelt, 'Citizens, politicians', 170

25 Helmut Anheier and Lester Salaman, *Volunteering in Cross-national Perspective* (Centre for Civil Society, London School of Economics, 2001), 4; Davis Smith, *1997 National Survey*, 157; Nathan Teske, *Political Activists in America: The Identity Construction Model of Political Participation* (Cambridge University Press, 1997), 28–9

26 Davis Smith, *1997 National Survey of Volunteering*, 22; European Commission, Directorate-General for Employment and Social Affairs, Unit E1, *The Social Situation in the EU, 2000,* Section 2.4.5, accessed at http://europa.eu.int/comm/dgs/employment_social/news/2000social_

report_en.pdf; Saul Rosenthal, Candice Feiring, and Michael Lewis, 'Political volunteering from late adolescence to young adulthood: patterns and predictors', *Journal of Social Issues* 54, 1998, 477–93, esp. 479

27 Peter Lynn and Justin Davis Smith, *The 1991 National Survey of Voluntary Activity* (Volunteer Centre UK, 1991), 31; David Gerard, 'Values and voluntary work', in Mark Abrams, David Gerard, and Noel Timms (eds.), *Values and Social Change in Britain* (Macmillan, 1985), 204; Jil Matheson, *Voluntary Work: Supplement to General Household Survey 1987* (Office of Population Censuses and Surveys, 1990), 9, 11; James N. Morgan, Richard F. Dye, and Judith H. Hybels, 'Results from two national surveys of philanthropic activity', in *Research Papers Sponsored by the Commission on Private Philanthropy and Public Need: Vol. 1, History, Trends, and Current Magnitudes* (U. S Department of the Treasury, 1977), 166–7

28 Davis Smith, *1997 National Survey*, 33; Robert D. Putnam, *Bowling Alone: The Collapse and Revival of American Community* (Simon and Schuster, 2000), 196–200, 238, 278; David Gerard, 'Values and voluntary work', in Abrams, Gerard, and Timms (eds.), *Values and Social Change*, 203; Matheson, *Voluntary Work*, 7; *General Household Survey 1981* (Office of Population Censuses and Surveys, 1983), 167; Morgan, Dye, and Hybels, 'Two national surveys', 209–10

29 Ronald Inglehart, 'Political action: the impact of values, cognitive level, and social background', in Samuel H. Barnes and Max Kaase, *Political Action: Mass Participation in Five Western Democracies* (Sage, 1979), 343–80, esp. 357–9; Paul R. Abramson and Ronald Inglehart, 'Generational replacement and value change in eight West European societies', *British Journal of Political Science* 22, 1992, 183–228, esp. 184; Michelle Benson and Thomas R. Rochon, 'Interpersonal Trust and the Magnitude of Protest: a Micro and Macro Level Approach', *Comparative Political Studies* 37, 2004, 435–57, esp. 446, 453; Gerard, 'Values', 208, 231. These correlations remained significant when controlled for social class.

30 Ronald Inglehart, 'Intergenerational changes in politics and culture: the shift from materialist to postmaterialist value priorities', *Research in Political Sociology* 2, 1986, 81–105, esp. 91

31 Putnam, *Bowling Alone*, 308, 358–9

32 Edward J. Walsh and Rex Warland, 'Social movement involvement in the wake of a nuclear accident: activists and free riders in the Three Mile Island area', *American Sociological Review* 48, 1983, 764–80, esp. 772; John P. Robinson, Jerrold G. Rusk, and Kendon B. Head, *Measures of Political Attitudes* (Survey Research Centre, Institute for Social Research, University of Michigan, 1968), 459

33 Karl-Dieter Opp, 'Community integration and incentives for political protest', *International Social Movement Research* 1, 1988, 83–101, esp. 90–6; Abraham Wandersman, Paul Florin, Robert Friedmann, and Ron Meier, 'Who participates, who does not, and why? An analysis of voluntary neighbourhood organizations in the United States and Israel', *Sociological Forum* 2, 1987, 534–55, esp. 543; Richard Sennett and Jonathan Cobb, *The Hidden Injuries of Class* (Cambridge University Press, 1972), 122, 164, 270

34 Natalie J. Allen and J, Philippe Rushton, 'Personality characteristics of

community mental health volunteers: a review', *Journal of Voluntary Action Research* 12, 1983, 36–49, esp. 46; Putnam. *Bowling Alone*, 291; Robert D. Putnam, with Robert Leonardi and Raffaella Y. Nanetti, *Making Democracy Work: Civic Traditions in Modern Italy* (Princeton University Press, 1993), 167; J. L. Sullivan and J. E. Transue, 'The psychological underpinnings of democracy: a selective review of research on political tolerance, interpersonal trust, and social capital', *Annual Review of Psychology* 50, 1999, 625–50; Alberto F. Alesina and Eliana La Ferrara, 'Who trusts others?', *Journal of Public Economics* 85, 2002, 207–34, esp. 208; Benson and Rochon, 'Interpersonal Trust', esp. 446, 453; David Gerard, 'Values and Voluntary Work', in Abrams, Gerard, and Timms (eds), *Values and Social Change*, 208–11

35 Everett Waters, Nancy S. Weinfield, and Claire E. Hamilton, 'The stability of attachment security from infancy to adolescence and early adulthood: general discussion', *Child Development* 71, 2000, 703–06, esp. 703–04; Everett Waters, Susan Merrick, Dominique Treboux, Judith Crowell, and Leah Albersheim, 'Attachment security in infancy and early adulthood: A twenty year longitudinal study', *Child Development* 71, 2000, 684–9, 686–8; Hall, 'Social Capital', 447; Rosenthal, Feiring, and Lewis, 'Political volunteering', 481, 490

36 Ronald P. Rohner, *They Love Me, They Love Me Not: a Worldwide Study of the Effects of Parental Acceptance and Rejection* (Human Relations Area Files, 1975), 103; Richard Koestner, Carol Franz, and Joel Weinberger, 'The family origins of empathic concern: a 26 year longitudinal study', *Journal of Personality and Social Psychology* 58, 1990, 709–17, esp. 712

37 David Rosenhan, 'Prosocial behavior of children', in William W. Hartup (ed.), *The Young Child: Reviews of Research*, vol. 2 (National Association for the Education of Young Children (USA), 1972), 340–59, esp. 342–5; Kenneth Keniston, *Young Radicals: Notes on Committed Youth* (Harcourt Brace Jovanovitch, 1968), 113; Samuel P. Oliner and Pearl M. Oliner, *The Altruistic Personality: Rescuers of Jews in Nazi Europe* (Free Press, 1988), 297–8; John Snarey, Linda Son, Valerie Shahariw Kuehne, Stuart Hauser, and George E. Vaillant, 'The role of parenting in men's psychosocial development: a longitudinal study of early adulthood infertility and midlife generativity', *Developmental Psychology*, 1987, 593–603, esp. 598–9; Tim Root, 'The motivation of volunteers in charitable, political, and recreational organisations, with reference to dogmatism' (unpubl. MPhil thesis, University of East London, 1994), Chap. 4; Mario Mikulincer, Omri Gilath, Vered Halevy, Neta Avihou, Shelly Avidan, and Nitzan Eshkoli, 'Attachment theory and reactions to others' needs: evidence that activation of the sense of attachment security promotes empathic responses', *Journal of Personality and Social Psychology* 81, 2001, 1205–24, esp. 1209, 1215, 1218, 1220–2

38 Robert Wuthnow, *Acts of Compassion: Caring for Others and Helping Ourselves* (Princeton University Press, 1991), 212–13; Allen and Rushton, 'Personality Characteristics', 46; Peter L. Benson, John Dehority, Lynn Garman, Elizabeth Hanson, Martha Hochschwender, Carol Lebold, Roberta Rohr, and Jane Sullivan, 'Intrapersonal correlates of non-spontaneous helping behavior', *Journal of Social Psychology* 110, 1980, 87–95, esp. 91; Stephen D. Harding, David R. Phillips, and Michael Fogarty, *Contrasting*

Values in Western Europe: Unity, Diversity and Change (Macmillan, 1986), 190; Gerard, 'Values and voluntary work', 214. This correlation remained significant with social class controlled.

39 Mikulincer et al., 'Attachment theory', 1205–06

40 Greta Salem, 'Maintaining participation in community organisations', *Journal of Voluntary Action Research* 7, 1978, 18–27, esp. 25; Root, 'Motivation of volunteers', chap. 4, pt. 4; Robert R. Friedmann, Paul Florin, Abraham Wandersman, and Ron Meier, 'Local action on behalf of local collectives in the US and Israel: how different are leaders from members in voluntary associations?', *Journal of Voluntary Action Research* 17, 1988, 36–54, esp. 43

41 David Mark Mantell, *True Americanism: Green Berets and War Resisters: A Study of Commitment* (Teachers' College Press, 1974), 201; Mary-Beth Rogers, *Cold Anger: a Story of Faith and Power Politics* (University of North Texas Press, 1990), 30

42 R. Rogers Kobak and Amy Sceery, 'Attachment in late adolescence: working models, affect regulation, and representations of self and others', *Child Development* 59, 1988, 135–46, esp. 140; Marc B. Levy and Keith E. Davis, 'Love styles and attachment styles compared: their relations to each other and to various relationship characteristics', *Journal of Social and Personal Relationships* 5, 1988, 439–71, esp. 457; M. Carole Pistole, 'Attachment in adult romantic relationships: style of conflict resolution and relationship satisfaction', *Journal of Social and Personal Relationships* 6, 1989, 505–10, esp. 508; Nancy L. Collins and Stephen J. Read, 'Adult attachment, working models, and relationship quality in dating couples', *Journal of Personality and Social Psychology* 58, 1990, 644–63, esp. 652–3

43 Mikulincer et al., 'Attachment theory', 1207, 1209, 1215, 1218, 1220–2

44 Arthur Koestler, chapter in Richard Crossman (ed.), *The God that Failed: Six Studies in Communism* (Hamish Hamilton, 1950), 32, 43, 59; Lewis Fischer, chapter in Crossman (ed.), *God that Failed*, 213

45 Joan Smith, 'Men and women at play: gender, life cycle, and leisure', in John Horne, David Jary, and Alan Tomlinson (eds.), *Sport, Leisure, and Social Relations: the Changing Work–Leisure Balance in Britain 1961–1984* (Routledge, 1987), 51–85, esp. 64

46 Putnam, *Bowling Alone*, 228, 231, 234, 235, 238–41

47 John R. Kelly, *Leisure* (Prentice Hall, 1990, 2nd edition), 60, 246; Lois M. Haggard and Daniel R. Williams, 'Identity affirmation through leisure activities: leisure symbols of the self', *Journal of Leisure Research* 24, 1992, 1–18, esp. 3

48 Luo Lu and Michael Argyle, 'Happiness and cooperation', *Personality and Individual Differences* 12, 1991, 1019–30, esp. 1023

49 Wandersman, Florin, Friedmann, and Meier, 'Who participates, who does not', 534–55, esp. 547

50 Stacy G. Ulbig and Carolyn L. Funk, 'Conflict avoidance and political participation', *Political Behavior* 21, 1999, 265–82, esp. 275–6

51 Putnam, *Bowling Alone*, 253, 255, 256, 268–75; Alsesina and La Ferrara, 'Who trusts others?', 219

52 Putnam, *Bowling Alone*, 291

53 *Ibid.*, 213, 215, 261–4, 283–4
54 Putnam, Leonardi and Nanetti, *Making Democracy Work*, 96, 100, 113–14, 226
55 Putnam, *Bowling Alone*, 204
56 *Attitudes Towards Minority Groups in the EU: A Special Analysis of the Eurobarometer Survey* (European Monitoring Centre on Racism and Xenophobia, 2000: accessed via http://europa.eu.int/comm/public_opinion); Lauren McLaren, 'Immigration and the new politics of inclusion and exclusion in the EU', *European Journal of Political Research* 39, 2001, 81–108, esp. 86
57 Yueh-Ting Lee, Victor Ottati and Imtiez Hussain, 'Attitudes toward "illegal" immigration into the United States: California Proposition 187', *Hispanic Journal of Behavioral Sciences* 23, 2001, 430–43, esp. 436–9; Charles R. Chandler and Yung-mei Tsai, 'Social factors influencing immigration attitudes: an analysis of data from the general social survey', *Social Science Journal* 38, 2001, 177–88, esp. 180–5
58 Joseph D. Hovey et al., 'Proposition 187 reexamined: attitudes toward immigration among California voters', *Current Psychology* 19, 2000, 159–74; Edward J. Rickert, 'Authoritarianism and economic threat: implications for political behavior', *Political Psychology* 19, 1998, 707–20, esp. 708; 'Attitudes to race and immigration', *British Public Opinion*, Nov.–Dec. 2000, 14
59 Marcel Lubbers and Peer Scheepers, 'Explaining the trend in extreme right-wing voting: Germany 1989–1998', *European Sociological Review* 17, 2001, 431–49, esp. 440
60 Peter Fysh and Jim Wolfreys, *The Politics of Racism in France* (Macmillan 1998), 69, 71; Frank Adler, 'Immigration, insecurity, and the French Far Right', *Telos* 120, 2001, 31–48, esp. 31; *Attitudes Towards Minority Groups in the EU* (see note 56 above)
61 Marcel Lubbers, Morove Gijsberts, and Peer Scheepers, 'Extreme right-wing voting in Western Europe', *European Journal of Political Research* 41, 2002, 345–78, esp. 362–4; Pia Knigge, 'The ecological correlates of right-wing extremism in Western Europe', *European Journal of Political Research* 34, 1998, 249–79, esp. 266; Lubbers and Scheepers, 'Explaining the Trend', 440; *idem*, 'French *Front National* voting: a micro and macro perspective', *Ethnic and Racial Studies* 25, 2002, 120–49, esp. 130; Silvia Kobi, 'Immigrants and the changing relations of trust between governments and electorates', in Andrew Geddes and Adrian Favell, *The Politics of Belonging: Migrants and Minorities in Contemporary Europe* (Ashgate, 1999), 125–38, esp. 130
62 Chandler and Tsai, 'Social Factors', 181; Lee et al., 'Attitudes toward "illegal" immigration', 139; *Attitudes Towards Minority Groups in the EU* (see note 56, above), 20
63 *Ibid.*, 32–3; *The Mail on Sunday*, asylum poll, 2001, at www.mori.com/polls/2001/ms010106.shtml; *Public Opinion in the EU*, Spring 2002, Standard Eurobarometer 57, at http://europa/eu.int/comm/public_opinion/archives/eb/eb57/eb57_en.pdf
64 *Attitudes Towards Minority Groups in the EU* (see note 56 above), 48; Chandler and Tsai, 'Social Factors', 184
65 Florence Haegel, 'Xenophobia on a suburban Paris housing estate',

Patterns of Prejudice 34, 2000, 29–38

66 Michael O. Emerson, Rachel Tolbert Kimbro, and George Yancey, 'Contact theory extended:the effects of prior racial contact on current social ties', *Social Science Quarterly* 83, 2002, 745–61; Margo J. Monteith and C. Vincent Spicer, 'Contents and correlates of whites' and blacks' racial attitudes', *Journal of Experimental Social Psychology* 36, 2000, 125–54, esp. 147; Stephen M. Saideman, David J. Lanoue, Michael Campenni, and Samuel Stanton, 'Democratization, political institutions, and ethnic conflict: a pooled cross-sectional time-series analysis from 1985–1998', *Comparative Political Studies* 35, 2002, 103–29, esp. 120; Roger Karapin, 'Major anti-minority riots and national legislative campaigns against immigrants in Britain and Germany', in Ruud Koopmans and Paul Statham (eds.), *Challenging Immigration and Ethnic Relations Politics: Comparative European Perspectives* (Oxford University Press, 2000), 312–47, esp. 338–40; Thomas F. Pettigrew and Linda R. Troop, 'Does Intergroup Contact Reduce Prejudice? Recent Meta-analytic Findings', in Stuart Oskamp (ed), *Reducing Prejudice and Discrimination* (Lawrence Erlbaum, 2000), 93–114; David W. Johnson and Roger T. Johnson, 'The Three C's of Reducing Prejudice and Discrimination', in Oskamp (ed), *Reducing Prejudice*, 239–68

67 John Bell, *Community Development Teamwork: Measuring the Impact – Wrexham Maelor Community Agency 1984–1990* (Community Development Foundation, 1992), 37; *see also* Hall, 'Social capital', 443

68 Roberta Woods, *Pennywell Neighbourhood Centre: Evaluation Report* (Save the Children Fund, 1993), 75; *see also* Barbara Bryant and Richard Bryant, *Change and Conflict: a Study of Community Work in Glasgow* (Aberdeen University Press, 1982), 147

69 Rogers, *Cold Anger*, 50, 51, 59, 60, 95, 97, 101, 108, 121, 134, 150, 195; *see also* Charles H. Kieffer, 'Citizen empowerment: a developmental perspective', *Prevention in Human Services* 3, 1984, 9–36, esp. 20, 21, 28

70 Paul Whiteley, Patrick Seyd, and Jeremy J. Richardson, *True Blues: The Politics of Conservative Party Membership* (Clarendon, 1994), 191; Pamela Brown, 'Beyond the ballot box: reviving local democracy', *SCCD News* 12, 1995, 7–8, esp. 7 (SCCD is the Standing Conference on Community Development); Andrew Stephen, 'America', *New Statesman*, 11 November 2002, 12–3

71 David M. Farrell, *Comparing Electoral Systems* (Prentice Hall/Harvester Wheatsheaf, 1997), 159; Martin Kettle, 'Rupert or Paddy: who's it to be?', *Guardian*, 29 March 1997, 23

72 Lijphart, *Patterns of Democracy*, 260, 264, 268, 283, 294–9

73 Markus M. L. Crepaz, 'Constitutional structures and regime performance in 18 industrialized democracies: a test of Olson's corporatist system', *European Journal of Political Research* 29, 1996, 87–104, esp. 95

74 Elizabeth L. Carter, 'Proportional representation and the fortunes of right-wing extremist parties', *West European Politics* 25, 2002, 125–46, 134, 137; Saideman, Langue, Campenni, and Standon, 'Democratization', 118, 122

75 Rebecca Smithers, 'PR "only way to put more women in Parliament" ' *Guardian*, 6 February 1997, 8

76   Ian McAllister, 'Leaders', in Lawrence LeDuc, Richard G. Niemi, and Pippa Norris, *Comparing Democracies: Elections and Voting in Global Perspective* (Sage, 1996), 280–98, esp. 281, 290, 291, 293, 296–8; Ian McAllister, 'Prime Ministers, Opposition Leaders and Government Popularity in Australia', *Australian Journal of Political Science* 38, 2003, 259–77, esp. 273; Peter Kellner, 'Why Ideology is Not the Answer', *Fabian Review*, Winter 2003, 10, 11. A Canadian study suggests that party leaders have a strong influence there: Andre Blais, Richard Nadeau, Elisabeth Gidengil, and Neil Nevitte, 'The formation of party preferences: testing the proximity and directional models', *European Journal of Political Research* 40, 2001, 81–91, esp. 88

77   Kellner, 'Ideology is Not the Answer', 10,11; Robert Worcester, 'Follow the polls, go for EMU', *New Statesman*, 7 November 1997, 21; Andrew Adonis and Geoff Mulgan, 'Back to Greece: the scope for direct democracy', *Demos Quarterly*, No. 3, 1994, 2–9, esp. 5, 8. Tony Blair has suggested that local councils could regularly hold referendums: Tony Blair, *Leading the Way: A New Vision for Local Government* (Institute for Public Policy Research, 1998), 15; David B. Magleby, 'Direct legislation in the United States', in Butler and Ranney (eds.), *Referendums*, 218–57, esp. 254

78   David Butler and Austin Ranney, 'Theory', in David Butler and Austin Ranney (eds), *Referendums Around the World: the Growing Use of Direct Democracy* (Macmillan, 1994), 11–23, esp. 19; Kris W. Kobach, 'Switzerland', in *ibid.*, 98–153, 109; Kris W. Kobach, *The Referendum: Direct Democracy in Switzerland* (Dartmouth, 1993), 5; Magleby, 'Direct legislation', 246; *see also* Des McNulty, *Referenda and Citizens' Ballots: The Scope and Limitations of Direct Democracy at Local Level* (Commission for Local Democracy, Report 15, 1995), 11; Wolf Linder, *Swiss Democracy: Possible Solutions to Conflict in Multicultural Societies* (Macmillan, 1994), 143

79   McNulty, *Referenda*, 5; *see also* Association of District Councils, *Voter Behaviour in Local Tax Referendums* (Association of District Councils, 1997), 3–6

80   Magleby, 'Direct legislation', 242; Iris Bohnet and Bruno S. Frey, 'Direct-democratic rules: the role of discussion', *Kyklos* 47, 1994, 341–54, esp. 347

81   Kobach, 'The Referendum', 136; Linder, *Swiss Democracy*, 126

82   Bohnet and Frey, 'Direct-democratic rules', 350

83   Magleby, 'Direct legislation', 226, 229; Kobach, 'The Referendum', 246

84   David Prior, John Stewart, and Kieron Walsh, *Citizenship: Rights, Community, and Participation* (Pitman, 1995), 87–8; Rainald Borck, 'Jurisdictional size, political participation, and the allocation of resources', *Public Choice* 113, 2002, 251–63, esp. 260; Angelika Vetter, 'Local political competence in Europe: a resource of legitimacy for higher levels of government?', *International Journal of Public Opinion Research* 14, 2002, 3–18, esp. 8; Danny Burns, Robin Hambleton, and Paul Hoggett, *The Politics of Decentralization: Revitalizing Local Democracy* (Macmillan, 1994), 184, 185, 199, 200, 272; Jeffrey M. Berry, Kent E. Portney, and Ken Thomson, *The Rebirth of Urban Democracy* (Brookings Institution, 1993), 120, 126

85 Borck, 'Jurisdictional size', 260
86 Vetter, 'Political competence', 12–13
87 William Julius Wilson, 'Rising inequality and the case for coalition politics', *Annals of the American Academy of Political and Social Science* 568, 2000, 78–99, esp. 90; 'Three in four defy Child Agency', *Guardian*, 28 August 1996, 7
88 Jon Henley, 'Downturn Forces Jospin to Retreat on 35 Hour Week', *Guardian*, 29 August 2001, 3
89 Stuart Holland (ed.), *Towards a New Bretton Woods: Alternatives for the Global Economy* (Spokesman, with Associate Research in Economy and Society, 1994), 116
90 Rogers, *Cold Anger*, 28–30, 192, 186
91 David W. Johnson and Roger T. Johnson, 'Constructive conflict in the schools', *Journal of Social Issues* 50, 1994, 117–37, esp. 119
92 Interview with Dave Lehman, principal of the Ithaca Aternative Public High School, Ithaca, New York (Centre for Living Democracy, RR1 Black Fox Road, Brattleboro, VT 05301, USA, n.d., c. 1994); Teske, *Political Activists*, 140
93 Grace Feuerverger, *Oasis of Dreams: Teaching and Learning Peace in a Jewish–Palestinian Village in Israel* (RoutledgeFalmer, 2001), 110, 153

Acknowledgements

Many people have helped me by reading drafts of chapters of this book. For this, I appreciate very much the help of Tirrill Harris, Andra St. Quintin, Viv Williamson, Michael Jones, Trevor Blackwell, Sheila Nicholson, Yvette Walczak, Maria Foster, Natasha Foster, Sarah Braybrooke, Michelle Friend, Susanna Schwarz, Lucy Craig, Mario Marrone, Isidoros Diakides, Narendra Makanji, Marcel Lubbers, Nigel Willmott, Michael Watson, Mary Southcott, Felicity De Zelueta, Carles Muntaner, Helen Carr, Tim Jordan, Alan Richardson, Jane Pimlott, Roger Warren Evans, James Park, Pat Johnsen, Penny Vinson and friends, Alan Stewart, Pat Byrne, Jo Moller, Peter Hanson, Joanne O'Brien, and Mike Rodney.

I am very grateful to Margaret O'Brien who supervised me in undertaking the research for my M. Phil at the University of East London. Professor Michael Rustin encouraged me from the beginning. Many thanks also to Carole Satyamurti, Barry Richards, Kate Bloor, and the computing and audio-visual technicians.

Other people helped me by giving feedback on, or asking others to complete, certain questionnaires, or be interviewed, for which I am grateful to my mother Eileen Root, my late father Bob Root, Milly Fionda, Sybil Ashton, Pat Palmer, Matthew Appleton, Andrea Hall, David and Judith Robinson, and Elspeth Campbell. I am also very grateful to all my interviewees, and those who completed questionnaires.

I was also supported and encouraged in the process of seeking a publisher by Jeremy Seabrook, Jonothan Porritt, Sheila Kitzinger, Michael Jacobs, John O'Loughlin, Paul Hoggett, Phil Cohen, Bob Holman, Deborah Jackson, Amitai Etzioni, Watson Little, Jeffrey Simmonds, and Justin Vaughan.

I wrote seeking information to a large number of organisations and academics to whom I am grateful.

Many thanks to librarians everywhere, and to ingentaconnect. com.

Miguel Ortiz helped kindly and patiently with various computer problems.

I undertook a vast amount of research with insufficient time, and no doubt in the process I have overlooked someone. Please forgive me.

Jeannie Cohen of Open Gate Press responded to my queries and suggestions thoughtfully and patiently.

I am especially grateful to my close friends Hilary Alton, Geoff Buckingham, and Jos Hincks, who were helpful and supportive in many ways.

Above all lots of love and thanks to my dear wife Ines, who has been so patient, supportive and rigorous in helping me in a vast number of ways.

Index